D1726186

European Yearbook of International Economic Law

EYIEL Monographs - Studies in European and International Economic Law

Volume 39

Series Editor

Marc Bungenberg, Saarbrücken, Germany

Christoph Herrmann, Passau, Germany

Markus Krajewski, Erlangen, Germany

Jörg Philipp Terhechte, Lüneburg, Germany

Andreas R. Ziegler, Lausanne, Switzerland

EYIEL Monographs is a subseries of the European Yearbook of International Economic Law (EYIEL). It contains scholarly works in the fields of European and international economic law, in particular WTO law, international investment law, international monetary law, law of regional economic integration, external trade law of the EU and EU internal market law. The series does not include edited volumes. EYIEL Monographs are peer-reviewed by the series editors and external reviewers.

Afolabi Oluwatomiwa Adekemi

Attracting African States Participation in a Multilateral Investment Court

Reforming Substantive and Procedural Law through an MIC

 Springer

Afolabi Oluwatomiwa Adekemi
Chair of Public Law, Public International Law, and European Law
Saarland University
Saarbrücken, Saarland, Germany

ISSN 2364-8392 ISSN 2364-8406 (electronic)
European Yearbook of International Economic Law
ISSN 2524-6658 ISSN 2524-6666 (electronic)
EYIEL Monographs - Studies in European and International Economic Law
ISBN 978-3-031-73860-9 ISBN 978-3-031-73861-6 (eBook)
https://doi.org/10.1007/978-3-031-73861-6

This Springer imprint is published by the registered company Springer Nature Switzerland AG
The registered company address is: Gewerbestrasse 11, 6330 Cham, Switzerland

If disposing of this product, please recycle the paper.

Dedication
This work is dedicated to the glory of the Lord Almighty! *(1 Corinthians 3:6-7).*

Preface

This book is the culmination of my doctoral thesis, which I successfully defended at the Faculty of Law of Saarland University, Germany, in the winter semester of 2023/2024. The journey to this point has been both challenging and rewarding, and I owe a great debt of gratitude to many exceptional individuals who have supported and guided me along the way.

First and foremost, I extend my heartfelt gratitude to my doctoral thesis supervisor, Professor Dr. Marc Bungenberg, at Saarland University. His excellent mentorship and unwavering support not only provided the foundation upon which this work stands, but also offered me the opportunity to grow professionally by working as a research associate under his tutelage at the Chair of Public International Law, Saarland University. His intellectual insights, support, and dedication to my career development have been invaluable throughout this journey.

I also wish to express my deep gratitude to Professor Dr. Torsten Stein of blessed memory. Before his glorious exit from this world, Professor Stein generously undertook the second evaluation of my thesis, despite his failing health. His thorough evaluation and contribution to the successful completion of my doctoral program will never be forgotten. Furthermore, my appreciation extends to the doctoral defence committee comprising Professor Dr. Thomas Geigerich (chair), the late Professor Stein, Professor Dr. Helmut Rüßmann, and Professor Bungenberg. The highly engaging and intellectually stimulating discussions during my thesis defence remain indelible in my memory and in my understanding of the underlying issues surrounding my topic.

Also, I would like to say a special thanks to Prof. Dr. Hélène Ruiz Fabri for hosting me as a visiting scholar at the Max Planck Institute (MPI) for Procedural Law, Luxembourg, along with providing funding that significantly contributed to the successful completion of this thesis. The time spent at the MPI was enriching and crucial for my research. I also wish to acknowledge my former colleagues at the Chair of Public International Law, at Saarland University. A special mention goes to Andrés Alvarado-Garzón, who reviewed the thesis and offered thought-provoking feedback that optimised the final outcome.

Additionally, I am profoundly grateful to the editors of the EYIEL series—Professor Dr. Marc Bungenberg, Professor Dr. Christoph Hermann, Professor Dr. Markus Krajewski, Professor Dr. Jörg Philipp Terhechte, and Professor Dr. Andreas R. Ziegler—for accepting my thesis into the EYIEL monographs—*Studies in European and International Economic Law*. Their support has been instrumental in bringing this work to a broader audience.

Furthermore, I extend my sincere gratitude to Professor Dr. Georg Borges, head of the Chair of Business Law and Legal Informatics at Saarland University, who warmly welcomed me into his team after my doctoral program. This opportunity allowed me to meet and work with amazing new colleagues, further broadening my professional horizons. The same goes for Mr. Marc Montalbine, head of the law firm deKieffer & Horgan European Office, whose offer to join the firm has opened new pathways for my professional career development.

Finally, the story behind the successful completion of my PhD program would be incomplete without recognising the indispensable role of my family, who undertook this journey with me. While I undertook the research and writing part, the time, prayers, emotional, and psychological cost invested in this doctoral journey was shared with my amazing family. At the frontline of this support is Aderiike mi, my lovely wife and the beautiful woman with whom I have found love. She is the pinnacle of my success. Then, my father, Oladosu Adekemi, who though has passed on to glory; his work ethic and values continue to inspire me and guide my daily pursuits without regret. To my mother, Modupe, the angel who gave me her wings to fly, and to my siblings, Tejumade, Adedapo, and Adedoyin, your sacrifices and support remain the bedrock of my success.

This work is as much theirs as it is mine, and I so declare with all my love and gratitude.

Saarbrücken, Germany   Afolabi Oluwatomiwa Adekemi

Contents

Abbreviations

ADP	Articles on Diplomatic Protection
ADR	Alternative Dispute Resolution
AfCFTA	African Continental Free Trade Area
AJT	Administrative and Judicial Treatment
BEE	Black Economic Empowerment
BIT(s)	Bilateral Investment Treaties
BLEU	Belgium-Luxembourg Economic Union
CETA	Comprehensive and Economic Trade Agreement
CIL	Customary international law
CJEU	Court of Justice of the European Union
ECOWAS	Economic Community of West African States
ELR	Exhaustion of Local Remedies
EU	European Union
f/ff	Following (page or paragraph)/Following (pages or paragraphs)
FDI	Foreign Direct Investment
FET	Fair and Equitable Treatment
FMV	Fair Market Value
Fn.	Foot Note
FPS	Full Protection and Security
FTC	Free Trade Commission (NAFTA)
GNTI	Guiding Note on Treaty Interpretation
HDSAs	Historically Disadvantaged South Africans
IA*Reporter*	Investment Arbitration Reporter
ICS	Investment Court System
ICSID	International Centre on the Settlement of Investment Dispute
IIA(s)	International Investment Agreement(s)
IIL	International Investment Law

ILC Draft Articles	International Law Commission's Draft Articles on Responsibility of States for Internationally Wrongful Acts
ISDS	Investor-State Dispute Settlement
MFN	Most Favoured Nation
MIC	Multilateral Investment Court
MN (mn)	Marginal Note
MST	Minimum Standard of Treatment
NAFTA	North-American Free Trade Agreement
NDP	Non-Disputing Parties
OECD	Organisation for Economic Cooperation and Development
p/pp	Page/Following Pages
PAIC	Pan-African Investment Code
para(s)	Paragraph/Following Paragraphs
PCA	Permanent Court of Arbitration
R2R	Right to Regulate
SCC	Stockholm Chamber of Commerce
SD	Sustainable Development
SIAC	Singapore International Arbitration Centre
SIDS	State-Investor Dispute Settlement
SSDS	State-to-State Dispute Settlement
TFEU	Treaty on the Functioning of the European Union
TTIP	Transatlantic Trade and Investment Partnership
UN	United Nations
UNCITRAL	United Nations Commission On International Trade Law
UNCTAD	United Nations Conference on Trade and Development
WLC	War Loss Clause
WWII	World War Two

Chapter 1
General Introduction: African States' Introduction to the International Investment Law System

Upon the emergence from colonial rule that began in the second half of the twentieth century, newly independent African states inherited one common goal, that is, the driving of economic growth and development within their respective borders. The race towards economic development had begun with each state setting its deadline towards economic emergence.[1] The abundance of human and natural resources offered great hope to the new sovereigns that with the right economic and investment policies—African states would, in time, equal the imbalance in economic relations between the developed industrialised nations of the West[2] and the developing post-colonial states of Africa.

Certainly, one important factor for economic advancement in any given state is the availability of capital needed to finance projects that can stimulate economic growth and development. In this regard, Foreign Direct Investments ('FDI') become a must-have to fulfil the African states' developmental agenda. According to the United Nations Conference on Trade and Development ('UNCTAD'), FDI is 'an investment reflecting a lasting interest and control by a foreign direct investor, resident in one economy, in an enterprise resident in another economy (foreign affiliate)'.[3] The Organisation for Economic Cooperation and Development ('OECD') defines FDI as:

> [A] category of cross-border investment in which an investor resident in one economy establishes a lasting interest in and a significant degree of influence over an enterprise resident in another economy. Ownership of 10 percent or more of the voting power in an

---

[1] Kamto (2020), p. 7.

[2] The West (western states), in this context and for the purpose of this thesis, primarily refers to developed capital-exporting nations of Europe and North America, e.g., the United Kingdom, France, Germany, the United States of America, Canada, etc.

[3] UNCTAD (2023).

enterprise in one economy by an investor in another economy is evidence of such a relationship.[4]

Given its commercial attributes, FDI can catalyse economic growth and development in any given state because it *inter alia* provides the 'needed capital for investment, increases competition in the host country industries, and aids local firms to become more productive by adopting more efficient technology or by investing in human and/or physical capital'.[5]

To attract the needed FDI to complement domestic investment activities, African nations primarily sought private investors from Western states capable of financing capital-intensive projects that stimulate economic growth. This moment in African history, beginning in the 1960s, marked the continent's first contact with the international investment protection regime and its dispute settlement system.

Pre-decolonisation, a foreign investment protection regime had been in existence providing a set of rules for the protection of investment in host economies abroad. In seeking FDI, a state cannot welcome foreigners into its territory to trap them.[6] Once accepted, a state is expected to protect foreign nationals as if they were its citizens and offer them full security to the greatest extent possible.[7] It is on these basic principles, informed by European neo-liberal ideas, that certain legal norms were developed for the protection of foreign investors and their investments in host territories abroad.[8]

Although international investment law has evolved in many different ways in the past three centuries,[9] its primary focus largely remains unchanged—that is, the imposition of certain legal obligations on host states aimed at protecting foreign investors and their investments in the host's territory. Today, those legal obligations are extensively codified in International Investment Agreements ('IIAs'). These IIAs are investment treaties contracted at various levels of state-to-state relations, mostly bilaterally,[10] but now also included in regional and plurilateral agreements.[11] Also, states now unilaterally take on investment protection obligations parallel to those typically found in IIAs, by enacting them under domestic legislation.[12]

Despite the divergent background of the IIAs in existence, the substantive guarantees contained therein are quite often similar, if not identical, in language.[13]

---

[4] OECD iLibrary, FDI, https://www.oecd-ilibrary.org/finance-and-investment

[5] Ajayi (2006) p. 11 f.

[6] de Nanteuil (2020), p. 2.

[7] *Ibid.*

[8] See further on this, Miles (2010), p. 1.

[9] See on evolution of IIL, Subedi (2020), p. 28 ff; Cameron (2014), p. 1355 ff.

[10] See, UNCTAD IIA Database, https://investmentpolicy.unctad.org/international-investment-agreements

[11] Schefer (2020), p. 33 ff.

[12] Born (2021), p. 497.

[13] UNCITRAL, *Report of Working Group III (Investor-State Dispute Settlement Reform)* of 26/2/2018, A/CN.9/930/Add.1/Rev.1, para. 27.

The similarity in substantive obligations contained in today's multiple networks of IIAs can be attributed to the fact that a vast majority of them were inspired by common sources.[14] For example, a notable source are the legal norms on the protection of foreign investments developed in the late eighteenth century through the commerce and navigation treaties entered into by the United States and some European governments.[15] Also, the 1959 *Hermann Abs* and *Lord Shawcross* draft on the protection of foreign investment proposed certain rules that later became a blueprint for negotiating European BITs post-1959.[16] Likewise in 1967, the OECD published a Draft Convention on the Protection of Foreign Property.

All these models went on to inspire the drafting of IIAs post-1960s, mostly finalised in the form of Bilateral Investment Treaties ('BITs'). The most common substantive obligations derived from these models include the duty to afford the foreign investor and its investment: full protection and security ('FPS'); fair and equitable treatment ('FET'); guarantees against expropriation; non-discriminatory treatment, including the most favoured nations ('MFN') and national treatment guarantee.

Significantly, the BITs that evolved post-decolonisation did not just offer substantive guarantees on the protection of foreign investment. They included a procedural mechanism for the enforcement of these guarantees, known as the investor-state dispute settlement ('ISDS') system. Customarily, investor-state disputes were settled through the process of diplomatic protection[17] or were brought before the local courts of the host state by the affected investor.[18] Even the first generation of BITs involving African states did not integrate ISDS but adopted a state-to-state dispute settlement ('SSDS') mechanism.[19] However, as more BITs came into force, given the upsurge in independent states seeking to attract FDI, investors began to lobby their home states to contract BITs, which gave private parties more control over the dispute settlement process.[20] By 1968, the first BIT with an ISDS provision came into light in Article 11 of the Indonesia-Netherlands BIT (1968).[21] The following year, the ISDS clause was found in Article 7 of the Chad-Italy BIT (1969),[22] marking its earliest incorporation into a BIT involving an African state.

---

[14] Subedi (2020), p. 34.

[15] See, Treaty of Amity and Commerce between the United States and Kingdom of Prussia, 10 September 1785; Treaty of Amity, Commerce and Navigation between His Britannic Majesty and the United States of America, 19 November 1794.

[16] Abs, Herman and Hartley Shawcross, Draft Convention on Investments Abroad (1959).

[17] Choudhury (2013), p. 486; Bishop et al. (2014), p. 998.

[18] See Bray (2018), p. 102.

[19] Article 11, Germany-Togo BIT (1961), signed 16 May 1961; Article 8, Niger-Switzerland BIT (1962), signed 28 March 1962.

[20] Schefer (2020), p. 475.

[21] Article 11, Indonesia-Netherlands BIT (1968), signed 7 July 1968.

[22] Article 7, Chad-Italy BIT (1969), signed 11 June 1969.

By design, the ISDS system differed from SSDS as it offered private investors direct recourse against a host state before an **investment arbitration tribunal**—to enforce the guaranteed rights and protections afforded under the relevant BIT.[23] Today, investment arbitration is the most common ISDS procedure, with a majority of the cases administered by the International Centre on the Settlement of Investment Dispute ('ICSID').[24] Like the substantive guarantees in BITs, consent to the jurisdiction of ICSID by post-colonial African states was motivated by the same need. As argued by *Kidane*:

> [t]he historical record clearly indicates that the only reason that the African states accepted ICSID is because they thought that they had to do so in order to attract private foreign investment to develop their ailing post-colonial economies.[25]

Ultimately, the desire to attract FDI for economic development impelled post-colonial African states to consent to substantive and procedural guarantees in numerous IIAs. Between January 1960 and December 2000, three hundred and twenty-four (324) extra-African IIAs had been in force.[26] The first of this kind was the France-Chad BIT of 1960.[27] This was followed by the Germany-Togo BIT of 1961 and the Niger-Switzerland BIT of 1962.[28] By December 2023, this number had risen to four hundred and ninety-nine (499).[29] In terms of the geographical distribution of extra-African BITs, the majority in force as of December 2023 are with European countries, totaling three hundred and seven (307).[30] This is followed by Asia with one hundred and sixty-one (161),[31] North America with eighteen (18),[32] Latin America and the Caribbean with twelve (12), and lastly Oceania with one (1).[33] Also, as of the aforementioned date, forty-nine (49) intra-African BITs were in force.[34]

Significantly, a vast majority of these IIAs, especially those preceding the year 2000, were based on pre-drafted models from developed western states, inherently not tailored to meet the socio-economic and developmental needs of the contracting African states. They were merely a conduit to increase FDI flows into Africa,[35] with

---

[23] Born (2021), p. 491.

[24] ICSID, Caseload – Statistics, https://icsid.worldbank.org/resources/publications/icsid-caseload-statistics

[25] Kidane (2014), p. 585 f.

[26] See, UNCTAD IIA Database, https://investmentpolicy.unctad.org/international-investment-agreements/advanced-search

[27] *Ibid.*

[28] *Ibid.*

[29] *Ibid.*

[30] *Ibid.*

[31] *Ibid.*

[32] *Ibid.*

[33] *Ibid*

[34] *Ibid.*

[35] Mbengue (2019), p. 458.

less thought put in by earlier African governments on the effects of the Western-modelled IIAs they contracted to their peculiar developmental needs. For the purpose of the foregoing analysis, IIAs preceding the year 2010 contracted by African states predominantly on Old-European and North American models are characterised as old-generation IIAs.

Unlike the African governments in the early years of decolonisation, the twenty-first-century African states have evolved from being just rule-takers to rule-makers, charting a new course on the protection of foreign investment.[36] Fundamentally, for FDI to promote meaningful development, the economic activity the investor fuels must be sustainable. On this basis, Africa's investment protection policy, as observed in some recent bilateral and regional investment treaties now demands the core objective of IIAs to be on the protection of FDIs that foster sustainable development ('SD').[37] While there is no universal definition for the term 'sustainable development', for the purpose of this thesis, the United Nations ('UN') delineation of its core components is employed.

Specifically, the UN recognises three **interdependent pillars** upon which the notion of sustainable development must stand in any given society, i.e. environmental protection, economic development, and social development.[38] Hence, in the context of recent investment protection policies originating from Africa, any investment activity that strengthens one of these pillars at the expense of the others is not sustainable and unworthy of protection.

The new African approach to investment protection is a significant departure from the old Western-styled IIAs that maintained a structure of dominance by investors.[39] The old-generation IIAs predominantly impose substantive obligations on states towards the protection of foreign investments, without a countervailing investor obligation to engage in economic activities that promote sustainable development, nor offer certainty regarding the regulatory space afforded to states to protect such interests without breaching their IIA commitments, even when there is harm to a covered investor.

As demonstrated by the case examples later analysed in this thesis, attempts to safeguard SD interests through domestic regulations have encountered fierce resistance from foreign investors against such government regulations that conflict with their IIA guarantees. This, in turn, has exposed multiple African states to significant financial damages in ISDS proceedings (→ Sect. 3.1.1). As argued by *El-Kady* and *De Gama*, African countries had *'built a wall of legally binding international*

---

[36] El-Kady and De Gama (2019), p. 483; Akinkugbe (2021), p. 26.

[37] See for examples, Article 1 (definition of investment), Draft Pan-African Investment Code ('PAIC') (2016); Article 1(3) Nigeria-Morocco BIT (2016), signed 3 December 2016; Article 1 (definition of investment), Protocol to the Agreement Establishing the African Continental Free Trade Area on Investment (2023).

[38] UN Documents, *Johannesburg Declaration on Sustainable Development* of 4/9/2002, UN DOC A/CONF.199/20, para. 5.

[39] Akinkugbe (2021), p. 18.

commitments without having sufficiently analysed the implications of these treaties on their right to regulate'.[40]

Admittedly, the shortcomings and adverse effects of the 'substantive' and 'procedural' guarantees in old-generation IIAs are not unique to Africa. This is a global challenge that ultimately triggered the beginning of ISDS reform discussions at UNCITRAL Working Group III in late 2017. This working group was mandated to identify the concerns and challenges associated with the current ISDS system and explore potential reforms to ensure a more balanced and transparent framework for resolving investment disputes.[41] It is against this background that a plethora of procedural reform options are currently under consideration in UNCITRAL Working Group III, and African states have contributed their distinctive perspectives to these discussions.[42] However, it is not within the scope of this thesis to delve into the multiple reform proposals under consideration. Rather, this thesis is focused on the Multilateral Investment Court ('MIC') proposal—chiefly put forward by the European Union ('EU') as a suitable alternative to traditional ISDS.[43]

Unlike the traditional ISDS system rooted in multiple arbitration forums set up under different institutional and non-institutional (*ad-hoc*) bodies that are independent of one another,[44] the MIC is contemplated as a centralised investment dispute resolution body, comprised of full-time judges (both in the first and second instance court), divided into several chambers in the court, and with long term appointments.[45]

While recognising that the backlash against traditional ISDS and attempts to address the challenge is a global concern, this thesis specifically addresses the African disenchantment with the traditional ISDS system and the propriety of an MIC as a suitable alternative. To become an acceptable alternative, an MIC must necessarily be free from the negative vices that plague the traditional ISDS system. However, there is currently no guarantee that this will be the case.

As critiqued by the South African government in its submission to the UNCITRAL Working Group III, the establishment of an MIC does not address the concerns against traditional ISDS because the problem does not lie in the procedure itself but rather originates from the substantive guarantees underlying ISDS claims

---

[40]El-Kady and De Gama (2019), p. 486 f.

[41]UNCITRAL, *Report of Working Group III (Investor-State Dispute Settlement Reform)* of 19/12/2017, A/CN.9/930/Rev.1, para. 6.

[42]See generally, UNCITRAL, ISDS Reform Elements, https://uncitral.un.org/en/working_groups/3/investor-state

[43]See in general, UNCITRAL, *Submission from the European Union and its Member States* of 24/1/2019, A/CN.9/WG.III/WP.159/Add.1.

[44]Schefer (2020), p. 371 ff, (detailing the ICSID and Non-ICSID forums available for investor-state arbitration).

[45]EI – IILCC Study Group on ISDS Reform (2022), p. 27; for further discussions on the MIC, see *infra* (Sect. 4.1).

widely adopted in old-generation IIAs.[46] As valid as the South African criticism is, the current UNCITRAL Working Group III mandate is exclusively limited to addressing procedural concerns.[47] This raises a legitimate scepticism that an MIC will still not protect its members from the undesirable effects of the old-generation IIAs any better than the traditional ISDS system, where the substantive inequities in old-generation IIAs remain unaddressed.

The central question then is, how can an MIC be designed to attract African states' participation, in light of the exclusion of substantive law reform from the ongoing UNCITRAL Working Group III reform debates? To answer this question, this thesis argues that there is a viable pathway to address the substantive and procedural law concerns of African states, even within the limited procedural reform discussions regarding an MIC.

To establish this conclusion, this thesis will proceed by introducing the substantive standards of treatment commonly invoked against African states in ISDS (Chap. 2). Subsequently, it will delve into the dilemma faced by African states within the existing ISDS system, focusing on the adverse effects of both the substantive standards of treatment and the ISDS clauses in old-generation IIAs as applied by arbitral tribunals (Chap. 3). These preceding chapters would provide the historical context necessary to understand the pitfalls that triggered the backlash against traditional ISDS and the call for reform from an African perspective. The following chapter, which is the core of this thesis, introduces the MIC and outlines crucial considerations for its attractiveness as a suitable alternative to traditional ISDS for African states. Subsequently, this chapter provides recommendations on how those crucial considerations may be addressed within the constitutional framework of an MIC to attract African states' participation (Chap. 4). Finally, this thesis concludes with an overview of the recommendations developed within its pages. While it acknowledges that the final decision to join an MIC rests with the individual African nations, nonetheless, the recommendations put forward offer a promising path towards attracting African states' participation in a future MIC (Chap. 5).

Other Documents

UN Documents, Johannesburg Declaration on Sustainable Development of 4/9/2002, UN DOC A/CONF.199/20

UNCITRAL, Report of Working Group III (Investor-State Dispute Settlement Reform) of 26/2/2018, A/CN.9/930/Add.1/Rev.1

---

[46] UNCITRAL, *Submission from the Government of South Africa* of 17/7/2019, A/CN.9/WG.III/WP.176, para. 19 ff.

[47] UNCITRAL, *Report of Working Group III (Investor-State Dispute Settlement Reform)* of 19/12/2017, A/CN.9/930/Rev.1, para. 20.

UNCITRAL, Report of Working Group III (Investor-State Dispute Settlement Reform) of 19/12/2017, A/CN.9/930/Rev.1

UNCITRAL, Submission from the European Union and its Member States of 24/1/2019, A/CN.9/WG.III/WP.159/Add.1

UNCITRAL, Submission from the Government of South Africa of 17/7/2019, A/CN.9/WG.III/WP.176

References

Ajayi SI (2006) The determinants of foreign direct investment in Africa: A survey of the evidence. In: Ajayi SI (ed) Foreign direct investment in Sub-Saharan Africa: origins, targets, impact and potential. African Economic Research Consortium, Nairobi, pp 11–32

Akinkugbe OD (2021) Africanization and the reform of international investment law. CWRJIL 53: 7–34

Bishop RD, Crawford J, Reisman WM (2014) Foreign investment disputes: cases, materials and commentary, 2nd edn. Kluwer Law International, Hague

Born G (2021) International arbitration: law and practice, 3rd edn. Kluwer Law International, Alphen aan den Rijn

Bray HL (2018) Understanding change: evolution from international claims commissions to investment treaty arbitration. In: Schill S, Tams C, Hofmann R (eds) International investment law and history. Elgar, Cheltenham, pp 102–135

Cameron AM (2014) The origins of international investment law: empire, environment and the safeguarding of capital. CJICL 3(4):1355–1360

Choudhury B (2013) International investment law as a global public good. LCLR 17(2):481–520

de Nanteuil A (2020) International investment law. Elgar, Cheltenham

EI – IILCC Study Group on ISDS Reform (2022) Reform of investor-state dispute settlement – current state of play at UNCITRAL. ZEuS 01:15–74

El-Kady H, De Gama M (2019) The reform of the international investment regime: an African perspective. ICSID Rev FILJ 34(2):482–495

Kamto M (2020) The development of international investment law in Africa. In: Hodu YN, Mbengue MM (eds) African perspectives in international investment law. Manchester University Press, Manchester, pp 7–17

Kidane W (2014) The China-Africa factor in the contemporary ICSID legitimacy debate. UPJIL 35(3):559–674

Mbengue MM (2019) Africa's voice in the formation, shaping and redesign of international investment law. ICSID Rev FILJ 34(2):455–481

Miles K (2010) International investment law: origins, imperialism and conceptualizing the environment. CJIELP 21(1):1–48

Schefer KN (2020) International investment law: text, cases and materials, 3rd edn. Elgar, Cheltenham

Subedi SP (2020) International investment law: reconciling policy and principle, 4th edn. Hart, Oxford

UNCTAD (2023) FDI – handbook of statistics 2023. https://hbs.unctad.org/foreign-direct-investment/

Chapter 2
The Substantive Standards of Treatment Commonly Invoked Against African States in ISDS

While a range of substantive standards commonly exists in IIAs across the globe today, this chapter is not aimed at reviewing all the various standards. Although not peculiar to Africa,[1] the focus is centered on three of the most commonly invoked standards against African states before ISDS tribunals. These are the FET standard (2.1), the guarantees against expropriation (2.2), and the FPS standard (2.3).

2.1 The Guarantee of Fair and Equitable Treatment (FET)

Although the exact meaning, content, and level of obligation required under the FET standard remains unsettled,[2] arbitral jurisprudence evince that the standard includes the obligation of states to: protect the legitimate expectation of an investor; compliance with contractual obligations; provide procedural propriety and due process; offer transparency; act in good faith; protect investors from coercion and harassment.[3]

Historically, the FET obligation predates the BITs which emerged post-1960s. It emanated from a number of post-second World War ('WWII') economic recovery treaties that never came into force. For example, the Havana Charter. This was an international instrument meant to establish the International Trade Organization to aid the recovery of the global economy post WWII. Although the charter never came

---

[1] UNCTAD (2017), p. 5.

[2] *Oxus Gold plc v. Republic of Uzbekistan*, UNCITRAL, Final Award (17 December 2015), para. 313; *Joseph Charles Lemire v. Ukraine II*, ICSID Case No. ARB/06/18, Decision on Jurisdiction and Liability (14 January 2010), para. 247 f; *Invesmart, B.V. v. Czech Republic*, UNCITRAL, Award (26 June 2009), para. 200; *Consortium R.F.C.C. v. Kingdom of Morocco*, ICSID Case No. ARB/00/6, Final Award (22 December 2003), para. 51.5.

[3] See, Dolzer et al. (2022), p. 205 ff.

© The Author(s), under exclusive license to Springer Nature Switzerland AG 2024
A. O. Adekemi, *Attracting African States Participation in a Multilateral Investment Court*, EYIEL Monographs - Studies in European and International Economic Law 39, https://doi.org/10.1007/978-3-031-73861-6_2

into force, it required that 'just and equitable treatment' be provided to foreign investments. This standard was later incorporated in diverse terms in other international instruments on the protection of investment between the 1950s–1960s,[4] including the earlier mentioned 1959 *Hermann Abs* and *Lord Shawcross* draft,[5] and the 1967 OECD Draft Convention on the Protection of Foreign Property.[6]

Since the mid-1960s, the FET obligation has become a common BIT standard. While the majority of treaties maintain the common expression 'fair and equitable', some treaties retain the Havana charter expression—'just and equitable',[7] or 'equitable and reasonable treatment'.[8] Regardless of the variation in treaty expression, investment tribunals generally regard the difference between the terms 'fair', 'just', or 'reasonable' treatment as immaterial, and treat the terms as identical.[9]

Several extra Africa and intra-Africa BITs incorporate the FET standard, the majority of which adopts the textually broad and vague approach of the old European or North American models. In practical terms, there are a number of Western models adopted in IIAs with African states' signatories.[10] First, is the model where the FET clause is incorporated as a stand-alone clause without any specific reference to another treaty standard. For example, Article 3(1) of the BLEU ('Belgium-Luxembourg Economic Union')—Ethiopia BIT of 2006 is worded:

> All investments made by investors of one Contracting Party shall enjoy a fair and equitable treatment in the territory of the other Contracting Party.

This FET formulation is quite common with treaties signed between BLEU and African states,[11] but not limited to that.[12] Due to their stand-alone character, tribunals often interpret them broadly.[13] Particularly, their autonomous nature allows for their ordinary meaning not to be limited to the minimum standard of treatment ('MST') under international law.[14]

---

[4] Sabahi et al. (2019), p. 632; Reinisch and Schreuer (2020), p. 255.

[5] *See*, Abs, Herman and Hartley Shawcross, Draft Convention on Investments Abroad (1959).

[6] OECD, Draft Convention on the Protection of Foreign Property (1967).

[7] Article IV(1), Spain-Mexico BIT (2006), signed 10 October 2006; Article 2(2), German Model BIT (2005); Article 4(2), Switzerland-Chile BIT (1999), signed 24 September 1999; Article 2(2), Italy-Argentina BIT (1990), signed 22 May 1990.

[8] Article III, Norway-Lithuania BIT (1992), signed 16 June 1992.

[9] *Luigiterzo Bosca v. Lithuania*, UNCITRAL, Award (17 May 2013), para. 196 *OKO Pankki Oyj and others v. Republic of Estonia*, ICSID Case No. ARB/04/6, Award (19 November 2007), para. 214f; *Parkerings-Compagniet AS v. Rep. of Lithuania*, ICSID Case No. ARB/05/8, Award (11 September 2007), para. 277 f; see further, *Reinisch/Schreuer*, p. 262 f.

[10] De Brabandere (2017), p. 534.

[11] Article 3(1), BLEU-Uganda BIT (2005), signed 1 February 2005; Article 3(1), BLEU-Tunisia BIT (1997), signed 8 January 1997; Article 3(1), BLEU-Egypt BIT (1999), signed 28 February 1999.

[12] Article 4(1), Germany-Kenya BIT (1996), signed 3 May 1996.

[13] De Brabandere (2017), p. 534.

[14] Sabahi et al. (2019), p. 634 f.

The second common model is the incorporation of the FET standard together with the FPS standard. A majority of IIAs incorporate the FET and FPS standards closely together,[15] separated by a comma, or the word 'and'.[16] This FET formulation is commonly found in African states' IIAs with the United Kingdom. An example is found in Article 2(2) Nigeria-United Kingdom BIT, which provides:

> Investments of nationals or companies of each Contracting Party shall at all times be **accorded fair and equitable treatment and shall enjoy full protection and security** in territory of the other Contracting Party.[17]

Identical FET formulations can be found in several other BITs between African states and the United Kingdom.[18]

The third FET formulation, unlike the "autonomous" or "FPS" connected model, is the FET connection to 'international law'. This approach ensures that tribunals interpret the content of FET guided by the 'principles of international law, including, but not limited to, customary international law'[19] ('CIL'). An example of this approach is found in Article II(2) of the South Africa-Canada BIT (1995) provides:

> Each Contracting Party shall accord investments or returns of investors of the other Contracting Party; (a) fair and equitable treatment in accordance with principles of international law.

Fourth, is the model where FET is expressly qualified with customary international law minimum standard. This is the classic North American Free Trade Agreement ('NAFTA') approach.[20] Which has been exported by NAFTA states (particularly the USA and Canada) into treaties with third countries, including African states. For example, Article 10.5 of the Morocco-United States of America ('USA') FTA (2004) provides:

> 1. Each Party shall accord to covered investments treatment in accordance with customary international law, including fair and equitable treatment [. . .].
> 2. For greater certainty, paragraph 1 prescribes the customary international law minimum standard of treatment of aliens as the minimum standard of treatment to be afforded to covered investments. The concepts of "fair and equitable treatment" [. . .] do not require

---

[15] Reinisch and Schreuer (2020), p. 550, para. 48.

[16] *Ibid.*, para. 52.

[17] Article 2(2), Nigeria-United Kingdom BIT (1990), signed 11 December 1990.

[18] See for examples, Article 2(2), Congo-United Kingdom BIT (1989), signed 25 May 1989; Article 2(2), Morocco-United Kingdom BIT (1990), signed 30 October 1990; Article 2(2), Tanzania-United Kingdom BIT (1994), signed 7 January 1994; Article 2(2), Côte d'Ivoire-United Kingdom BIT (1995), signed 8 June 1995.

[19] UNCTAD (2012), p. 22.

[20] See, NAFTA Free Trade Commission: Notes of interpretation of certain Chap. 11 provisions, 31 July 2001: ('Article 1105(1) prescribes the customary international law minimum standard of treatment of aliens as the minimum standard of treatment to be afforded to investments of investors of another Party. The concepts of "fair and equitable treatment" [. . .] do not require treatment in addition to or beyond that which is required by the customary international law minimum standard of treatment of aliens').

treatment in addition to or beyond that which is required by that standard, and do not create additional substantive rights.

Article 6 of the Nigeria-Canada BIT (2014) is worded:

1. Each Party shall accord to a covered investment treatment in accordance with the customary international law minimum standard of treatment of aliens, including fair and equitable treatment [...]
2. The concepts of "fair and equitable treatment" [...] in paragraph 1 do not require treatment in addition to or beyond that which is required by the customary international law minimum standard of treatment of aliens.

The fifth approach is the least common FET formulation among the prior. It involves incorporating the FET alongside specific substantive content such as unreasonable or discriminatory measures. For example, Article 3(1) BLEU-Morocco BIT (1999) provides:

Each Contracting Party undertakes to provide in its territory for investments by investors of the other contracting party fair and equitable treatment excluding any unjustified or discriminatory measure which could adversely affect in any way the management, maintenance, use, enjoyment or liquidation.

A similar provision also exists in Article 4(1) Egypt-Switzerland BIT (2010) provides:

Investments and returns of investors of each Contracting Party shall at all times be accorded fair and equitable treatment [...]. Neither Contracting Party shall in any way impair by unreasonable or discriminatory measures the management, maintenance, use, enjoyment, extension or disposal of such investments.

Also, Article 4(1) Tunisia-Switzerland BIT (2012) provides:

The investments and incomes of the investors of each Contracting Party shall be accorded fair and equitable treatment on a continuous basis [...]. Neither Contracting Party shall in any manner hinder, through unjustified or discriminatory measures, the management, maintenance, use, enjoyment, increase or sale of such investments.

Overall, the FET standard in extra and intra-African BITs largely mirrors in one form or another the above models from developed capital-exporting countries. This rule-taking approach has two notable challenges. First, it creates an unequal advantage by focusing on the fair treatment of investors, without a corresponding investor obligation to treat the host state fairly with investment activities that address their specific developmental needs. Second, the Western nature of these models excuses investment tribunals to interpret the FET standard strictly guided by the treaty formulation and Western jurisprudence on the meaning of the standard, regardless of the developing or least developed status of the respondent states.[21]

Based on available UNCTAD data as of December 2023, out of one hundred and seventy-one (171) publicly known ISDS claims brought against African states',[22]

---

[21] Ofodile (2019), p. 297.
[22] UNCTAD ISDS Database, https://investmentpolicy.unctad.org/

the FET standard has been invoked sixty-six (66) times.[23] The first was *Wena Hotels v. Egypt*,[24] initiated under the Egypt-United Kingdom BIT. Twenty-six (26) of these cases have resulted in a finding of liability, while thirty (30) have been successfully defended by the respondent host state, with eleven (11) dismissed for lack of jurisdiction and nineteen (19) cases dismissed on the merits. One (1) case has been discontinued, three (3) settled, and six cases (6) remain pending.[25]

2.2 The Guarantees Against Expropriation

Next to FET, the substantive guarantees against expropriation are the most invoked IIA standards by claimants in African ISDS history.[26] Although there is no universally recognised definition for the term, as defined by *Subedi*, '[i]n simple terms, "expropriation" means the taking of the assets of foreign companies or investors by a host state against the wishes or without the consent of the company or investor concerned'.[27]

Primarily, there are two forms of expropriation recognised in ISDS, i.e. direct and indirect expropriation.[28] A direct expropriation occurs when an investor is deprived of the enjoyment and benefits of its investment as a result of the host state's non-consensual **appropriation of title** to the investor's tangible or intangible assets.[29] It could also occur through outright seizure of investor's property by the host state.[30] In contrast, an indirect expropriation takes place when an investor is substantially deprived of the enjoyment and benefits of its private property, due to

---

[23] *Ibid.*

[24] *Wena Hotels Limited v. Arab Republic of Egypt*, ICSID Case No. ARB/98/4, Award (8 December 2000).

[25] UNCTAD ISDS Database, https://investmentpolicy.unctad.org/

[26] A total number of 62 direct and indirect expropriation claims are recorded on UNCTAD ISDS Database as of 31 December 2023, https://investmentpolicy.unctad.org/investment-dispute-settlement/advanced-search

[27] Subedi (2020), p. 159.

[28] See in this regard, Kriebaum (2015), p. 970 ff.

[29] BG Group Plc v. Argentina, UNCITRAL, Final Award (24 December 2007), para. 259; *Waguih Elie George Siag and Clorinda Vecchi v. The Arab Republic of Egypt*, ICSID Case No. ARB/05/15, Award (1 June 2009), para. 427; *Suez, Sociedad General de Aguas de Barcelona S.A. and Vivendi Universal S.A v. Argentine Republic*, ICSID Case No. ARB/03/19, Decision on Liability (30 July 2010), para. 132.

[30] *Caratube International Oil Company LLP and Devincci Salah Hourani* v. Republic of Kazakhstan, ICSID Case No. ARB/13/13, Award (27 September 2017), para. 822; *JSC Tashkent Mechanical Plant and others v. Kyrgyz Republic*, ICSID Case No. ARB(AF)/16/4, Award (17 May 20239), para. 546.

certain measures of the host state, even though the property title remains with the investor.[31]

Significantly, under international law, the non-consensual taking of an investor's property (direct or indirect) by the host state is not prohibited.[32] This right is borne out of the sovereign authority of all states to govern over their territories as they deem fit without any external interference. However, international law likewise recognises the duty of a host state to protect aliens and their properties, and a failure to do so may attract international responsibility. As a result, while the right to expropriate may be a lawful exercise of sovereign power, it becomes questionable when it is done in violation of certain norms to which all states are obliged under international law, in order to exercise a lawful expropriation.

The proviso for a lawful expropriation implemented in most IIAs across the globe has its origin in CIL, with some of the earliest treaty codifications found in the FCN treaties signed by the USA with foreign governments.[33] Today, most IIAs now recognise that for an expropriation to be deemed as internationally lawful, it must be done for—'public purpose' (2.2.1), 'non-discriminatory' (2.2.2), follow the 'due process of law' (2.2.3) and accompanied with 'prompt, adequate and effective compensation' (2.2.4).

2.2.1   Must Be for Public Purpose (Interest)

The first consideration for a lawful expropriation under international law is that it must serve a **'public purpose'** also identified as public interest. Public interest entails acts in the general interest of the populace, and only the concerned state can define what is in the general interest of its populace.[34] As a result, there is no universal definition of what constitutes public interest under international law.

---

[31] *Middle East Cement Shipping and Handling Co. S.A. v. Arab Republic of Egypt*, ICSID Case No. ARB/99/6, Award (12 April 2002), para. 107; BG Group Plc. v. Republic of Argentina, (fn. 29), para. 260 ff; *Suez, Sociedad General de Aguas de Barcelona S.A. and Vivendi Universal S.A v. Argentine Republic*, ICSID Case No. ARB/03/19, Decision on Liability (30 July 2010), para. 132; *PL Holdings S.A.R.L. v. Republic of Poland*, SCC Case No V2014/163, Partial Award (28 June 2017), para. 320.

[32] Dolzer and Schreuer (2008), p. 89.

[33] See, Article I Treaty of Friendship, Commerce and Consular Rights between Republic of Latvia and the United States, 20 April 1928, ('The nationals of each High Contracting Party shall receive within the territories of the other [. . .]. Their property shall not be taken without due process of law and without payment of just compensation'); See also, Article I Treaty of Friendship, Commerce and Consular Rights between Austria and the United States, 19 June 1928.

[34] de Nanteuil (2020), p. 312; See also *Guaracachi America, Inc. and Rurelec PLC v. Plurinational State of Bolivia*, PCA Case No. 2011–17, Award, 31 January 2014, para 437, (as affirmed by the tribunal 'the precise contours of public purpose and social benefit lie with the internal constitutional and legal order of the State in question [. . .]').

The requirement that an expropriatory act must serve public interest is incorporated in the vast majority of African IIAs post-1960, albeit in diverse formulations. For example, Article 3(2) of the Togo-Germany BIT (1961) provides *inter alia*:

> Investments of nationals and companies of a Contracting Party may **only be expropriated** in the territory of the other Contracting Parties **for the general good** [. . .].[35]

Similarly, according to Article 3(2) of the Liberia-Germany BIT (1961):

> Investments of nationals or companies of either contracting party in the territory of the other contracting party **shall not be expropriated except for the public benefit** [. . .].[36]

Article 6 of the Liberia-Switzerland BIT (1963) provides:

> The High Contracting Parties **shall not expropriate or nationalize property, rights or interests** belonging to the nationals [. . .] of the Other nor directly or indirectly dispossess them, **except when such measures are taken in the public interest** [. . .]

While the term 'public interest' is the most common expression in IIAs across the globe, the above examples show that there are other expressions used in treaty practice.[37] Whether expressed as 'public interest', 'public benefit', or the 'general good' etc., these are simply interchangeable terms with equivalent meanings.

Albeit it is within a state's sovereign power to implement measures it considers is in the general interest of its populace, arbitral tribunals are yet empowered to scrutinize whether such powers have been misused or abused.[38] However, to what extent this power of scrutiny can be used (scope of review) has been a topic of divergent views in arbitral practice. On one hand, some arbitral tribunals favour allowing a state, wide discretion, in determining what is in its public interest. For example, as opined in *LIAMCO* v. *Libya*:[39]

> [m]otives are indifferent to international law, each State being free to judge for itself what it considers useful or necessary for the public good... The object pursued by it is of no concern to third parties.[40]

Further, in *Goetz v. Burundi*,[41] the tribunal held that:

> [i]n the absence of an error of law or fact, manifest error of assessment or misuse of powers, it is not for the Tribunal to substitute its own judgment for the assessment made at the discretion of the Government of Burundi of the imperatives of public utility... or of national interest.[42]

---

[35] Article 3(2), Togo-Germany BIT (1961), signed 16 May 1961.

[36] Article 3(2), Liberia-Germany BIT (1961), signed 12 December 1961.

[37] See further on this Reinisch and Schreuer (2020), p. 190, para. 907.

[38] de Nanteuil (2020), p. 312.

[39] *Libyan American Oil Company (LIAMCO) v. The Government of the Libyan Arab Republic*, Arbitral Award (12 April 1977).

[40] *Ibid.*, para. 241.

[41] *Antoine Goetz et consorts v. République du Burundi [I]*, ICSID Case No. ARB/95/3, Award—Embodying the Parties' Settlement Agreement (10 February 1999).

[42] *Ibid.*, para. 126.

The above decisions show that these tribunals accorded significant deference to the Respondent states challenged measures, thereby refraining from second-guessing what the states consider to be in their public interest, save for finding an obvious case of abuse. Notably, both cases after applying this wide margin of discretion to the states concluded that the impugned state measures satisfied the public interest test for its international lawfulness.[43]

On the other hand, there are tribunals that favour a much more substantive (critical) evaluation of a state's expropriatory measure to determine whether it indeed passed the public interest test. In *Siag v. Egypt*,[44] the dispute revolved around the claimant's touristic investment (an oceanfront property) in Egypt, which it later claimed was unlawfully expropriated. In its defence, Egypt argued that the ocean-front property in issue was to be used for a pipeline construction having a public purpose. While the tribunal acknowledged that this defence might indeed satisfy the public purpose requirement, it refused to defer to Egypt's justification of the expropriatory act. Rather, the tribunal provided its own detailed reasoning as to why it is convinced that Egypt unlawfully expropriated the claimant's investment for other reasons unrelated to public interest.[45]

Another notable investment dispute related to Africa where the tribunal refused deference to the state's public purpose argument is in von *Pezold v. Zimbabwe*.[46] This dispute arose in the context of a land reform program introduced by the respondent state to reclaim and redistribute the nation's farmlands, which pre-reform was majority-owned by white farmers, whose ownership was rooted in Zimbabwe's colonial history. Due to the slow progress of the reform, public unrest ensued as the disadvantaged indigenous population began to invade and occupy white farmlands, including that of the claimant. In the aftermath of the public unrest, the state amended its constitution and thereafter implemented a number of measures that effectively expropriated part of the claimant's land title without compensation. In its defence, the state argued that the expropriation was lawful given its legitimate public purpose aimed at righting historical wrongs against its indigenous people. The tribunal disagreed, holding *inter alia* that it cannot:

> [...] accept these arguments as support for the expropriation of the Zimbabwean Properties having been carried out for a 'public purpose'. Once taken, large parts of the properties have not actually been re-distributed to a historically disadvantaged or otherwise landless population, but remain in the *de facto* possession of the Claimants. With regard to the land that has been re-distributed, there appears to be a clear trend towards politically-motivated

---

[43] *Libyan American Oil Company (LIAMCO) v. The Government of the Libyan Arab Republic*, Arbitral Award (12 April 1977), paras. 241–253; *Goetz v. Burundi [I], Ibid.*

[44] *Waguih Elie George Siag and Clorinda Vecchi v. The Arab Republic of Egypt*, ICSID Case No. ARB/05/15, Award (1 June 2009).

[45] *Ibid.*, para. 431.

[46] *Bernhard von Pezold and others v. Republic of Zimbabwe*, ICSID Case No. ARB/10/15, Award (28 July 2015).

allocations of land. Therefore, there is no evidence that the expropriation of the Zimbabwean Properties was in the public interest or served a genuine public purpose.[47]

One pivotal reason why the tribunal arrived at this conclusion, refusing deference to the Respondent's public interest argument, is the finding that the repossessed lands largely remained in control of Zimbabwe's political elite, rather than the historically disadvantaged indigenes the land taking was purposed to benefit. In its defence to this, the Respondent had argued that:

> Given the overwhelming Public Interest, elite, having land, which is normal in any society, does not negate Public Purpose. One of the worst legacies of machine gun proclaimed "white superiority" was to crush African Zimbabweans' self confidence. Certain men rose above this handicap, [. . .]. Senior officials holding land is not "corruption". Many of those officials risked their lives to liberate their country from the yoke of the foreign oppressor. "Zimbabwe Takes back its Land" concludes "Many Zimbabweans think fairness requires preference for war veterans and that occupiers should receive priority." [. . .].[48]

Essentially, the important context the respondent attempted to offer the tribunal here is that Africans do not forget the freedom fight of their heroes, i.e. those who liberated them from the yoke of colonial rule. To an average Zimbabwean, these freedom heroes have priority status in the society. Therefore, allocation of expropriated farmlands to the political elite, many of whom were freedom fighters (including then President Robert Mugabe) does not negate Zimbabwe's public interest. Despite this specific societal context offered by the respondent, the *von Pezold* tribunal refused the respondent such a wide margin of discretion that the redistribution of expropriated lands to political elites serves the public interest of the state.

Further, in *Lahoud v. DR Congo*,[49] where the state was silent on the public interest nature of its actions against the claimant, the tribunal found that this sufficed that the impugned state action lacked public purpose.[50]

In summary, the above cases suggest that whether a state's action satisfies the public interest requirement for a lawful expropriation largely depends on the scope of review the tribunal chooses to apply. The wider the discretion afforded to states, the likelier the state measure is deemed to satisfy public interest, save where an obvious (manifest) abuse is found. The opposite is the case where a tribunal chose to conduct a closer scrutiny of the states' conduct. In this case, a tribunal may find a lack of public purpose even though this lack is not *prima facie* obvious.

---

[47] *Ibid.*, para. 502.

[48] *Ibid.*, para. 483.

[49] *Antoine Abou Lahoud and Leila Bounafeh-Abou Lahoud v. Democratic Republic of the Congo*, ICSID Case No. ARB/10/4, Award (7 Feb 2014).

[50] *Ibid*, para. 514.

2.2.2   Must Be Non-Discriminatory

Non-discrimination is the second essential requirement for an internationally lawful expropriation. By ordinary definition, discrimination is 'the practice of treating somebody or a particular group in society less fairly than others'.[51] Discrimination may occur in different ways,[52] based on race, sex, gender, religious beliefs etc. Notably, when it comes to the field of investment law, discrimination has been mainly challenged on the basis of nationality, however, this does not mean it is limited to that. As held by the tribunal in *National Grid v. Argentina*,[53] the applicable treaty 'does not limit discrimination to discrimination on the basis of nationality and may cover measures based on other grounds'.[54]

The requirement that an expropriatory act be non-discriminatory is commonly formulated in African IIAs with words such as **expropriation—'in a non-discriminatory manner'** or **'on a non-discriminatory basis'**. Some relevant examples include Article III(1) of the DR Congo-USA BIT (1990) which provides that:

> Investments shall not be expropriated or nationalized [...] except [...]; **in a non-discriminatory manner** [...].[55]

Article 5(1) of the Burundi-United Kingdom BIT (1990):

> Investments of nationals or companies of either Contracting Party shall not be nationalised, expropriated [...] except [...]; **on a non-discriminatory basis** [...].[56]

Notwithstanding the different linguistic expressions, the above provisions render an expropriation unlawful, if it is targeted at a particular foreign investor to the exclusion of others in a similar circumstance, without a reasonable justification.[57]

In essence, for a conduct to be discriminatory, there needs to be an identified comparator, the comparator must have been treated more favourably, and there is no reasonable justification by the state for the unequal treatment between the comparator and the claimant investor.[58] Besides being a requirement for a lawful

---

[51] Oxford Advance Learners Dictionary Online, https://www.oxfordlearnersdictionaries.com

[52] Newcombe and Paradell (2009), p. 304 ff; Reinisch and Schreuer (2020), p. 835.

[53] *National Grid P.L.C. v. Argentina Republic*, UNCITRAL, Award (3 November 2008).

[54] *Ibid.*, para. 198.

[55] Article III(1), DR Congo-USA BIT (1990) signed 12 February 1990; see also Article 10(1), Cameroon-Canada BIT (2014), signed 3 March 2014.

[56] Article 5(1), Burundi-United Kingdom BIT (1990), signed 13 September 1990.

[57] *Bernhard von Pezold and others v. Republic of Zimbabwe*, ICSID Case No. ARB/10/15, Award (28 July 2015), para. 501; *Crystallex International Corporation v. Bolivarian Republic of Venezuela*, ICSID Case No. ARB(AF)/11/2, Award (4 April 2016), para. 715.

[58] *Olin Holdings Ltd v. Libya*, ICC Case No. 20355/MCP, Final Award (25 May 2018), para. 204.

expropriation, non-discriminatory treatment is a stand-alone treaty obligation in many IIAs that can be invoked independently by a covered investor.[59]

2.2.3 Must be in Accordance with Due Process of Law

The requirement for 'due process of law' contemplates the compliance of an expropriation with the rule of law. The rule of law notion in the context of a lawful expropriation entails that—*first*, the expropriation follows proper procedure; and *second*, that the investor has the possibility to challenge the expropriation before an independent and impartial body.[60] The absence of any of these two factors will render a state expropriation of a foreign investment unlawful.

Conformity with the due process of law is a common feature for a lawful expropriation in many IIAs. As typical, its textual formulation is not uniform across IIAs, but this bears no significance on its general understanding as a guarantee of the procedural fairness required for an internationally lawful expropriation. Some African IIA examples of this provision include, Article III of the Tunisia-USA BIT (1990) provides:[61]

(1) Investments shall not be expropriated [. . .] except [. . .] **in accordance with due process of law** [. . .].

(2) A national or company of either Party that asserts that all or part of its investment has been expropriated shall have a right to prompt review by the appropriate judicial or administrative authorities of the other Party to determine whether any such expropriation has occurred and, if so, whether such expropriation, and any compensation therefor, conforms to the principles of international law.

Article 7 of the Ghana-Switzerland BIT (1991) provides that:[62]

---

[59] See for examples, Article 2(2), Italy-United Republic of Tanzania BIT (2001), entered into force 25 April 2003; Article 2(3), Nigeria-China BIT (2001), entered into force 18 February 2010; see also Article 3(2), Libya-Austria BIT (2002), entered into force 1 January 2004; Article 2(2), Libya-Cyprus BIT (2004), entered into force 12 February 2005; Article 2(3), Egypt-Germany BIT (2005), entered into force 22 November 2009; see also Article 2(2), Ghana-Germany BIT (1995), entered into force 23 November 1998; Article 2(3), Gabon-Korea BIT (2007), entered into force 9 August 2009; Article 2(2), Zimbabwe-Germany BIT (1995), entered into force 14 April 2000; Article 3, Morocco-Spain BIT (1997), entered into force 13 April 2005; Article 3(2), BLEU-Madagascar BIT (2005), entered into force 29 November 2008; also see Article 2(3), Italy-Mozambique BIT (1998), entered into force 17 November 2003; Article 3(1), Egypt-Spain BIT (1992), entered into force 26 April 1994.

[60] *Rusoro Mining Ltd. v. Bolivarian Republic of Venezuela*, ICSID Case No. ARB(AF)/12/5, Award (22 August 2016), para. 389.

[61] Article III, Tunisia-USA BIT (1990), entered into force 7 February 1993.

[62] Article 7, Ghana-Switzerland BIT (1991), entered into force 16 June 1993.

(1) Investments of investors of either Contracting Party shall not be nationalised, expropriated [...] unless [...]: (a) the measures are taken [...] **under due process of law.**

(2) The investor affected shall have a right, under the law of the Contracting Party making the expropriation, [...] to prompt review, by a judicial or other independent authority of that Party [...].

Article 5 of the Libya-Singapore BIT (2009) provides that:[63]

(1) Neither Contracting Party shall take any measure of expropriation, [...] unless the measures are taken [...], **in accordance with its laws** [...].

(2) Any measure of expropriation or valuation may, at the request of the investors affected, be reviewed by a judicial or other independent authority of the Contracting Party taking the measures in the manner prescribed by its laws.

Goetz v. Burundi (1)[64] is the first publicly known investment dispute involving an African state where a tribunal had to determine whether Burundi's expropriation of Goetz investment followed the due process of law. The IIA provision in consideration was Article 4 of the Burundi-BLEU BIT (1989) which provides that:

> Each Contracting Party undertakes to refrain from any expropriatory or restrictive measure in respect of property [...], unless [...] (a) [t]he measures shall be taken **in accordance with a legal procedure** [...].[65]

According to the *Goetz* tribunal, the above provision necessitates that the international lawfulness of the impugned measure 'must not only be based on valid reasons, it must also have been taken according to a legal procedure'.[66] For the tribunal, this legal procedure includes following the laid down procedure under national law.[67] The tribunal found this requirement as satisfied in this case.[68]

In *Middle East Cement v. Egypt,*[69] while ruling on the lawfulness of Egypt's expropriatory actions against the claimant's investment, the tribunal found that the seizure and auctioning of the claimant's ship without proper notice to the claimant breached the due process requirement under the national law, rendering the expropriation unlawful under the applicable BIT.[70]

---

[63] Article 5, Libya-Singapore BIT (2009), entered into force 8 April 2009.

[64] *Antoine Goetz et consorts v. République du Burundi [I]*, ICSID Case No. ARB/95/3.

[65] Article 4(1)(a), Burundi-BLEU BIT (1989), entered into force 12 September 1993.

[66] *Antoine Goetz et consorts v. République du Burundi [I]*, ICSID Case No. ARB/95/3, Award—Embodying the Parties' Settlement Agreement (10 Feb 1999), para. 127.

[67] *Ibid.*

[68] *Ibid.*

[69] *Middle East Cement Shipping and Handling Co. S.A. v. Arab Republic of Egypt*, ICSID Case No. ARB/99/6, Award (12 April 2002).

[70] *Ibid.*, para. 143.

Notably, the tribunal in *Siag v. Egypt*[71] expanded further on the requirement of due process for a lawful expropriation by categorising it into substantive and procedural due process. In terms of substantive due process, after finding that claimant had 7 months to complete phase one of the contractual project, which was prematurely cancelled by Egypt.[72] The tribunal concluded that this premature cancellation constitutes a denial of substantive due process.[73] On procedural due process, as in the *Middle East Cement* case, the *Siag* tribunal also found that Egypt expropriated the claimant's investment without affording the claimant the proper notice to be heard, until after the fact. Hence, the failure to provide proper notice to the claimant to contend against Egypt's expropriatory actions in time amounts to a denial of procedural due process under the BIT.[74]

The investors' ability to seek judicial review of an expropriatory act in time before an independent and impartial local court is the hallmark of the due process guarantee that cannot be circumvented even by the dictate of national law. In *Border Timbers v. Zimbabwe*,[75] although earlier guaranteed under national law, the respondent's constitutional amendment had expunged the investors' right to challenge Zimbabwe's expropriatory measures.[76] The tribunal concluded that this constitutional amendment did not just constrain but eliminated access to due process, which cannot be lawful under international law.[77]

In summary, the requirement to expropriate an investment in accordance with due process of the law may be expressed in varying texts across IIAs, but what is expected does not necessarily differ in meaning. What is generally expected is that the substantive rights of an investor in the process leading to the expropriation are respected, and most importantly, the procedural rights of the affected investor in challenging the legality of the expropriation before an independent and unbiased domestic forum is guaranteed.

2.2.4 With Prompt, Adequate and Effective Compensation

Under CIL, a state's sovereign right to expropriate an investment within its territory is conditioned upon payment of compensation to the affected investor, albeit the

---

[71] *Waguih Elie George Siag and Clorinda Vecchi v. The Arab Republic of Egypt*, ICSID Case No. ARB/05/15, Award (1 June 2009).

[72] *Ibid.*, para. 441.

[73] *Ibid.*

[74] *Ibid.*, para. 442.

[75] *Border Timbers Limited, Border Timbers International (Private) Limited and Hangani Development Co. (Private) Limited v. Republic of Zimbabwe*, ICSID Case No. ARB/10/25, Award, 28 July 2015.

[76] *Ibid.*, 499.

[77] *Ibid.*, 500.

criteria for determining the exact amount due remains unsettled.[78] Today, virtually all IIAs recognises the CIL guarantee that a lawful expropriation must be accompanied by compensation. Further, they mostly clarify the criterion for deciding the actual amount of compensation due,[79] thereby avoiding the uncertainty in CIL. For expropriation, most IIAs adopt the compensation formula commonly referred to as the *Hull Formula*, i.e. 'prompt, adequate and effective compensation'.[80] One of the earliest examples of this *Hull* approach in an African IIA includes Article 5(1) of the Egypt-Kingdom BIT (1975) which provides:[81]

> Investments of nationals or companies of either Contracting Party shall not be nationalised, [...] except [...] against prompt, adequate and effective compensation.

Several other African IIAs mirror the *Hull* compensation formula, most prevalent in IIAs signed with the United Kingdom, USA, and Canada.[82] Other IIAs simply refer to the term *'compensation'*, especially those modelled after the German model BIT,[83] including African IIAs.[84] The terms 'just compensation', 'appropriate compensation', or 'full compensation' are other terms that are used in treaty practice.[85]

Further, most IIAs clarify that what constitutes 'just' or 'adequate' compensation is the 'fair market value' ('FMV') of the expropriated investments,[86] with the valuation date being 'immediately before the expropriation or before the impending expropriation became public knowledge, whichever is the earlier'.[87] However, arbitral tribunals do not always consider this treaty valuation date as appropriate in all circumstances, especially in cases where the tribunal finds an unlawful expropriation. For example, in *Siag v. Egypt*,[88] the tribunal majority held that the valuation date for FMV provided in Article 5 of the Egypt-Italy BIT only applies to a lawful expropriation, hence inapplicable since it found an unlawful expropriation.[89] The

---

[78] Reinisch and Schreuer (2020), p.226, para. 1090 ff.

[79] *Ibid.*, p. 229, para. 1111.

[80] *Ibid.*, p.224, para. 1078.

[81] Article 5(1), Egypt-United Kingdom BIT (1975), entered into force 24 February 1976.

[82] Article 5(1), Congo-United Kingdom BIT (1989), entered into force 9 November 1990; Article III (1), Cameroon-United States of America BIT (1986), entered into force 6 April 1989; Article VIII (1), Egypt-Canada BIT (1996), entered into force 3 November 1997.

[83] Article 4(2), German Model BIT (2004).

[84] Article 4(2), Egypt-Germany BIT (2005), entered into force 22 November 2009; Article 4(2), Madagascar-Germany (2006), entered into force 17 October 2015; Article 5(2), Guinea-Germany BIT (2006), entered into force 14 August 2014.

[85] Reinisch and Schreuer (2020), p. 224, para. 1079.

[86] *Ibid.*, p. 230, para. 1117.

[87] Article 5(1), Nigeria-United Kingdom BIT (1990), entered into force December 1990; Article 7(1)(b), Ghana-Switzerland BIT (1991), entered into force 16 June 1993; Article 4(c), Egypt-Greece BIT (1993), entered into force 6 April 1995; Article 4(1), Côte d'Ivoire-United Kingdom BIT (1995), entered into force 9 October 1997.

[88] *Waguih Elie George Siag and Clorinda Vecchi v. The Arab Republic of Egypt*, ICSID Case No. ARB/05/15, Award (1 June 2009).

[89] *Ibid.*, para. 539.

dissenting arbitrator however found his colleagues in error for refusing to base the investment's FMV at the time of the expropriation as required under the BIT.[90]

Notably, the dissent only found the departure unjustified because *'the project had not actually began to operate, generate profits or provide any other element'* to allow the tribunal to factor in any long-term effect of the expropriation on the claimant.[91] Otherwise, the dissenter would have agreed with the majority decision. A similar reasoning to the majority view in *Siag* was followed by the tribunal in *von Pezold v. Zimbabwe*, where the investment's FMV on the date of the award was deemed as the appropriate time for determining the value of compensation due to the claimant on the basis that this was an unlawful expropriation.[92]

Overall, according to UNCTAD's data as of December 2023, out of the 62 cases in which the treaty expropriation guarantee has been invoked against an African state, twenty-three (23) of these cases have resulted in a finding of liability, while twenty-six (26) have been successfully defended by the respondent host state, with twelve (12) dismissed for lack of jurisdiction and fourteen (14) cases dismissed on the merits.[93] Three (3) cases have been discontinued, five (5) settled, and five cases (5) remain pending.[94]

2.3   The Guarantee of Full Protection and Security (FPS) Standard

As a substantive standard of treatment regularly provided in IIAs,[95] the FPS standard is another often invoked standard against African states in ISDS proceedings. Once provided in a treaty, the standard guarantees the host state's police protection, through the physical protection of foreign investors and their assets,[96] from unlawful third-party interference.[97] Essentially, the duty traditionally obliges a host state to

---

[90] *Ibid*, Dissenting Opinion of Professor Francisco Orrego Vicuña (of the Award), p. 5.

[91] *Ibid.*

[92] *Bernhard von Pezold and others v. Republic of Zimbabwe*, ICSID Case No. ARB/10/15, Award (28 July 2015), para. 755–763 ff.

[93] UNCTAD ISDS Database, https://investmentpolicy.unctad.org/investment-dispute-settlement/advanced-search

[94] *Ibid.*

[95] Reinisch and Schreuer (2020), p. 540, para. 1.

[96] *Ibid.*, p. 558; *Saluka Investments BV (The Netherlands) v. Czech Republic*, PCA Case No. 2001–04, Partial Award (17 March 2006), para. 483; *OI European Group B.V. v. Venezuela*, ICSID Case No. ARB/11/25, Award (10 March 2015), para. 580.

[97] Schefer (2020), p. 384.

prevent third parties from causing physical damage to an investor or its investments.[98]

Like the FET, the origin of the FPS standard pre-dates the decolonisation of Africa. It is rooted in the rules governing the treatment of aliens under customary international law.[99] Under the international minimum standard (IMS) on the treatment of aliens, it is behoved upon states to ensure the protection and security of foreign nationals.[100] Over time, this IMS duty attained treaty status in the late eighteenth century through the commerce and navigation treaties entered into by the United States with foreign governments.[101] This treaty recognition continued into the nineteenth and twentieth centuries.[102] In Europe, the 1959 *Hermann Abs* and *Lord Shawcross* draft convention on investments abroad contained a provision on 'constant protection and security' to foreign property.[103] Similarly, the 1967 OECD Draft Convention on the Protection of Foreign Property contained an FPS provision, with the similar formulation 'constant protection and security'.[104] Hence, it is not surprising that this substantive standard rooted in IMS and several IIAs pre-dating the decolonisation of Africa found its way into the numerous BITs signed by African states on Western templates post-1960.

The Togo-Germany BIT (1961) represents one of the earliest examples of the FPS standard in African IIA history. According to Article 3(1):

'[i]nvestments by nationals and companies of a Contracting Party shall enjoy **full protection and full security** in the territory of the other Contracting Parties'.[105]

A similar provision is contained in Article 3(1) of the Liberia-Germany BIT (1961) providing that:

"[i]nvestments by nationals or companies of either contracting party shall enjoy **full protection and security of the law** in the territory of the other contracting party.[106]

---

[98] *Cengiz İnşaat Sanayi ve Ticaret A.S v. Libya*, ICC Case No.21537/ZF/AYZ, Award (07 November 2018), para. 403; *Frontier Petroleum Services v. Czech Republic*, UNCITRAL, PCA Case No. 2008–09, Final Award (12 November 2010), para. 261; Zeitler (2005), p. 2.

[99] See in general, Borchard (1934), p. 360 ff; Lorz (2015), p. 766.

[100] *Noble Ventures, Inc. v. Romania*, ICSID Case No. ARB/01/11, Award (12 October 2005), para. 164.

[101] See, Article XVIII, Treaty of Amity and Commerce between the United States and Kingdom of Prussia, 10 September 1785; Article II and XIV, Treaty of Amity, Commerce and Navigation between His Britannic Majesty and the United States of America, 19 November 1794.

[102] *Suez, Sociedad General de Aguas de Barcelona S.A. and Vivendi Universal S.A v. Argentine Republic*, ICSID Case No. ARB/03/19, Decision on Liability (30 July 2010), para. 155; See also, Vandevelde (1988), p. 204.

[103] Article 1, Abs, Herman and Hartley Shawcross, Draft Convention on Investments Abroad (1959).

[104] Article 1(a), OECD Draft Convention on the Protection of Foreign Property (1967).

[105] Article 3(1), Togo-Germany BIT (1961), entered into force 21 December 1964.

[106] Article 3(1), Liberia-Germany BIT (1961), entered into force 22 October 1967.

The above two examples reveal one of the notable factors for which the FPS standard is well known i.e. the textual divergence. Particularly regarding the qualifying adjectives (2.3.1). In other notable variations, the FPS standard is formulated with reference to customary international law (2.3.2) and/or domestic law (2.3.3). These textual formulations that have an impact on how the FPS standard is interpreted are now considered below with relevant examples from the African experience.

2.3.1   Qualifying Adjectives

The FPS standard is notable for its various qualifying adjectives across treaties,[107] and the African IIAs adopt one of the various textual formulations known in treaty practice. While 'full protection and security' is considered the most common expression,[108] some treaties provide different expressions such as: 'full and constant protection and security',[109] 'full and complete protection',[110] or 'continuous protection and security'.[111] Also, the treaty text can simply state 'protection and security',[112] with no qualifying adjective added.

Regardless of the diversity in treaty expression, investment tribunals largely recognise the textual variation as immaterial, having no effect on the interpretation and application of the standard.[113] Included or not, adjectives such as 'full', 'constant', 'complete', 'continuous' before the term 'protection and security' does not alter the nature of the obligation or the ensuing responsibility of a state under international law. For example, as held by the *AAPL v. Sri Lanka* tribunal—the first to render an investment treaty award on FPS:

> In the opinion of the present Arbitral Tribunal, the addition of words like 'constant' or 'full' to strengthen the required standards of 'protection and security' could justifiably indicate the Parties' intention to require within their treaty relationship a standard of 'due diligence' higher than the 'minimum standard' of general international law. But, the nature of both the obligation and ensuing responsibility remains unchanged, since the added words 'constant' or 'full' are by themselves not sufficient to establish that the Parties intended to transform their mutual obligation into a 'strict liability'.[114]

---

[107] See, Newcombe and Paradell (2009), p. 308; Salacuse (2010), p. 207.

[108] Malik (2011), p. 2.

[109] Article 2(2), Namibia-Finland BIT (2002), entered into force 21 May 2005; Article 2(2) Egypt-Finland BIT (2004), entered into force 5 February 2005.

[110] Article 2(2), China-Uganda BIT (2004), signed 27 May 2004.

[111] Article 3(2), BLEU-Egypt BIT (1999), entered into force 24 May 2002.

[112] Article II(4), DR Congo-USA BIT (1984), entered into force 28 July 1989.

[113] *Frontier Petroleum Services Ltd. v. The Czech Republic*, UNCITRAL, Final Award (12 November 2010), para. 260; *Parking v. Lithuania*, ICSID Case No. ARB/05/8, Award (11 September 2007), para. 354; Junngam (2018), p. 57.

[114] *Asian Agricultural Products Ltd (AAPL) v. Republic of Sri Lanka*, ICSID Case No. ARB/87/3, Final Award (27 June 1990), para. 50.

In another ICSID award, where the tribunal found the FPS provision in the underlying treaty referred only to the word 'protection'.[115]The tribunal nevertheless interpreted the word 'protection' as also meaning 'full protection and security':

> Article III of the Treaty only mentions the term protection. In a number of decisions, Tribunals make reference to the standard of 'full protection and security'. It is generally accepted that the variation of language between the formulation 'protection' and 'full protection and security' does not make a significant difference in the level of protection a host State is to provide. Moreover, *in casu*, the Parties make systematically reference to the standard of 'full protection and security'. Therefore, the Arbitral Tribunal intends to apply the standard of 'full protection and security'.[116]

Similarly, the *MNSS v. Montenegro* tribunal faced with a treaty FPS clause phrased as 'most constant protection and security' held that the expression 'most constant' does not change/increase the level of protection and security as understood under international law.[117]

However, despite the widely adopted view that the textual variation in qualifying adjectives adds no difference to the scope or extent of the FPS standard, some tribunals latch on to the textual variation to deny this popular view. For example, a number of tribunals have relied on the adjective 'full' to extend the scope of the FPS standard to legal security, **going beyond its traditional understanding of protection against physical harm.**[118] A notable example of such an expansive interpretation in an African-related dispute is *Biwater v. Tanzania*.[119]

As later discussed in this thesis, the divergent and imprecisely worded nature of the FPS standard has been a major source of criticism, due to the conflicting outcomes that this standard generates when applied in ISDS ($\rightarrow$ Sect. 3.1.2.1).

2.3.2   Reference to Customary International law (CIL)

Besides the varying qualifying adjectives, another textual variation with a significant impact on how the FPS standard is interpreted regarding its substantive scope—is its reference to CIL. Under CIL, the FPS standard entails the protection of foreign

---

[115] Article III, Lithuania-Norway BIT (1992), entered into force 20 December 1992.

[116] *Parkerings-Compagniet AS v. Republic. of Lithuania*, ICSID Case No. ARB/05/8, Award (11 September 2007), para. 354.

[117] *MNSS B.V. v. Montenegro*, ICSID Case No. ARB(AF)/12/8, Award (4 May 2016), para. 351; See further on the non-significance of textual variation, Reinisch and Schreuer (2020), p. 543 ff.

[118] *CME Czech Republic v. Czech Republic*, UNCITRAL, Partial Award (13 September 2001), para. 613; *Global Telecom Holding v. Canada*, ICSID Case No. ARB/16/16, Award (27 March 2020), para. 664 f; *Anglo American Plc v. Venezuela*, ICSID Case No. ARB(AF)/14/1, Award (18 January 2019), para. 482; *Krederi Ltd. v. Ukraine*, ICSID Case No. ARB/14/17, Award (2 July 2018), para. 652.

[119] *Biwater Gauff (Tanzania) Limited v. United Republic of Tanzania*, ICSID Case No. ARB/05/22, Award (24 July 2008), para. 729.

investors from *physical harm* that does not originate from the acts of the host state itself, but from its *private citizens*.[120] Therefore, arbitral jurisprudence generally recognises that protecting the physical integrity of foreign investors and their investments from adverse third party actions is the primary understanding of the FPS under international law.[121] As held by the *El Paso v. Argentina*:[122]

> The Tribunal considers that the full protection and security standard is no more than the traditional obligation to protect aliens under international customary law and that it is a residual obligation provided for those cases in which the acts challenged may not in themselves be attributed to the Government, but to a third party. The case-law and commentators generally agree that this standard imposes an obligation of vigilance and due diligence upon the government.[123]

When the physical harm suffered by a foreign investor emanates from the host state itself, the *El Paso* tribunal held that the impugned state measure 'should only be assessed in the light of the other BIT standards and cannot be examined from the angle of full protection and security'.[124]

Concurring with the views laid down in *El Paso*, the *Electrabel v. Hungary* tribunal held:

> A well-established aspect of the international standard of treatment is that States must use "due diligence" to prevent wrongful injuries to the person or property of aliens caused by third parties within their territory, and, if they did not succeed, exercise at least "due diligence" to punish such injuries.[125]

Notably, since FPS is an existing international obligation independent of any treaty obligation,[126] it begs the question of whether its explicit incorporation in a treaty should be treated as an autonomous standard—independent of the existing duty under CIL. As a result, some treaties explicitly clarify the relationship between the treaty's FPS standard and the existing duty under CIL. This clarification helps determine whether the contracting parties intend to offer an FPS protection equal (ceiling) to what is expected under CIL (2.3.2.1), or rather whether the standard should be treated as the floor treatment (2.3.2.2), thus may go beyond what is expected under CIL.

---

[120] See further in the regard, Blanco (2019), p. 206 ff.

[121] *Joseph Houben v. Republic of Burundi*, ICSID Case No. ARB/13/7, Award (12 January 2016), para.157; *Border Timbers v. Zimbabwe*, ICSID Case No. ARB/10/25, Award (28 July 2015), para.596; *Saluka v. Czech Republic*, PCA Case No. 2001–04, Partial Award (17 March 2006), para. 483 f.

[122] *El Paso Energy International Company v. Argentine Republic*, ICSID Case No. ARB/03/15, Award (31 October 2011).

[123] *Ibid.*, para. 522.

[124] *Ibid.*

[125] *Electrabel S.A. v. Republic of Hungary*, ICSID Case No. ARB/07/19, Decision on Jurisdiction, Applicable Law and Liability (30 November 2012), para. 7.83.

[126] Reinisch and Schreuer (2020), p. 545, para. 27.

2.3.2.1 CIL as Equivalent or Ceiling to a Treaty's FPS Standard

Several treaties have clarified the relationship between a treaty's FPS standard and CIL in a way that suggests the equalisation of the standard to what exists under CIL.[127] This treaty practice is most common with treaties negotiated under the US Model BITs of 2004 and 2012.[128] A notable example of an African-related IIA is found in Article 5(2) of the Rwanda-USA BIT (2011), stating *inter alia*, the concept:

> [. . .]**"full protection and security" do not require treatment in addition to or beyond that which is required by that standard, and do not create additional substantive rights.** The obligation in paragraph 1 to provide [. . .] b): "full protection and security" requires each Party to provide the level of police protection required under customary international law.

Another African IIA example with a non-USA party is found in Article 6(2) of the Tanzania-Canada BIT (2013), which provides that the concept:

> 'full protection and security' in paragraph 1 do not require treatment in addition to or beyond that which is required by the customary international law minimum standard of treatment of aliens.

Also, an identical provision of this USA Model can be found in Article 7(2) of the Nigeria-Morocco BIT (2016).[129]

When a treaty incorporates an FPS duty with a language such as the examples given above, this has been held as referring to the CIL minimum standard of treatment on the protection of foreign property, and not an autonomous treaty standard.[130] In other words, the provision simply codifies an existing duty under international law, without foreseeing an intention to add to or go beyond the duty that already exists. In *Koch v Venezuela*,[131] the tribunal interpreted Art. 4-(1) Switzerland-Venezuala BIT (1993) which incorporated FPS '[i]n accordance with the rules and principles of international law'. The tribunal concluded that 'these words import the customary international law minimum standards, rather than any autonomous higher standards'.[132]

---

[127] See, Article 12.5(1)(2)(b), China-Korea FTA (2015), entered into force 20 December 2015; Article 10.05(1) and (2)(b), China (Taiwan)-Nicaragua FTA (2006), entered into force 1 January 2008; Article 9.5(1) and 2(b), Korea-Peru FTA (2010), entered into force 1 August 2011.

[128] Blanco (2019), p. 499.

[129] Article 7(2), Nigeria-Morocco BIT (2016), signed 3 December 2016: ('[. . .] "full protection and security" does not require treatment in addition to or beyond that which is required by that standard, and does not create additional substantive rights. [. . .]: (b) "full protection and security" requires each Party to provide the level of police protection required under customary international law').

[130] *Adel A Hamadi Al Tamimi v. Sultanate of Oman*, ICSID Case No. ARB/11/33, Award (3 November 2015), para. 380.

[131] *Koch Minerals Sàrl and Koch Nitrogen International Sàrl v. Bolivarian Republic of Venezuela*, ICSID Case No. ARB/11/19, Award (30 October 2017).

[132] *Ibid.*, para 8.42.

In another case law example, the *Modev v United States*[133] tribunal held that the FPS provision under Article 1105 NAFTA referenced to 'treatment in accordance with international law' incorporates the principles of CIL.[134] Also providing clarity on this point is The NAFTA Free Trade Commission ('FTC') empowered to issue binding interpretation notes on the NAFTA.[135] The FTC interpretative note on Article 1105 states that 'treatment in accordance with international law' means the FPS *'[d]o not require treatment in addition to or beyond that which is required by the customary international law minimum standard of treatment to aliens'.*[136]

Accordingly, when a treaty's FPS standard is equated to CIL as given in the cited examples, the contracting states FPS duty cannot go beyond what is expected under CIL. As already disclosed, the CIL obligation is limited to the host-state's due diligence duty, in the physical protection of aliens against acts of third persons not attributable to the host state.[137]

2.3.2.2   CIL as a Floor

Depending on the treaty language, a state's obligation to protect foreign property may go beyond the expected minimum standard under CIL. This might be the case where the treaty standard and CIL minimum standard are connected with words like *'no less than'*, rather than adopting the much determinative reference that FPS does not add to or go beyond what is expected under CIL. A relevant example of such treaty formulation in an African IIA can be found in Article II(4) DR Congo-USA BIT (1984), which provides that: *'[t]he treatment, **protection and security** of investment [...] **may not be less than** that recognized by **international law**'.*[138] A similar example is contained in Article II(4) Egypt-USA BIT (1986) providing:

> The treatment, **protection and security** of investments **shall never be less than** that required by **international law** and national legislation.[139]

In *AMT v. DR Congo,*[140] the interpretation of Article II(4) Congo-USA BIT (1984) was particularly up for consideration. The tribunal held that the above FPS formulation creates an *'objective obligation which must not be **inferior** to the minimum*

---

[133] *Mondev International Ltd. v. United States of America*, ICSID Case No. ARB(AF)/99/2, Award (11 October 2002).

[134] *Ibid.*, para. 111 f.

[135] See, Article 1131(2), NAFTA.

[136] NAFTA FTC, Notes of Interpretation on Chap. 11, https://www.international.gc.ca/trade-agreements-accord

[137] *Koch Minerals Sàrl and Koch Nitrogen International Sàrl v. Bolivarian Republic of Venezuela*, ICSID Case No. ARB/11/19, Award (30 October 2017), para. 8.46.

[138] Article II(4), Congo-USA BIT (1984), signed 3 August 1984.

[139] Article II(4) Egypt-USA BIT (1986), signed 11 March 1986.

[140] *American Manufacturing & Trading (AMT), Inc. v. Democratic Republic of Congo*, ICSID Case No. ARB/93/1, Award (21 February 1997).

standard of vigilance and of care required by international law'.[141] Another relevant case law example to this point is the decision in *Azurix v. Argentina,*[142] although a non-African related dispute, the similarity in the treaty provision considered by the tribunal—and the aforementioned African IIA examples makes it a relevant precedent.

For consideration by the tribunal was Article II.2(a) US-Argentina BIT (1991) which provides that: *'Investment shall [...] enjoy* **full protection and security** *and shall* **in no case** *be accorded treatment* **less than that required by international law'**. In interpreting this provision, the *Azurix* tribunal concluded that Article II.2 (a) permitted the FPS to be interpreted as a higher standard beyond what is required under international law.[143] In particular, 'the third sentence is to set a floor, not a ceiling, in order to avoid a possible interpretation of the [FPS] below what is required by international law.[144] This conclusion is equally consistent with the decision rendered in *AMT*. This means that qualifying the FPS obligation as 'no less than what is required under CIL' only sets the CIL as a floor below which a state's treatment of an investor must not go.

Therefore, satisfying the MST under CIL may not automatically exclude a state's FPS liability if it is possible to interpret the duty as going beyond.

2.3.3   Reference to Domestic Law

In a much unusual practice, the FPS standard has been textually formulated with reference to domestic law. There are two notable kinds of this uncommon FPS approach in treaty practice:

– FPS with reference to both domestic and international law;
– FPS with reference to only domestic law.

A model example of the first approach in an African-related IIA can be found in Article II(4) of the DR Congo-USA BIT (1984). It provides:

> [...] The treatment, protection and security of investment shall be in accordance with applicable national laws, and may not be less than that recognized by international law.

A similar example is found in Article II(4) of the Egypt-USA BIT (1986) which provides:

> The treatment, protection and security of investments shall never be less than that required by international law and national legislation.

---

[141] *Ibid.*, para. 6.06.

[142] *Azurix Corp. v. The Argentine Republic*, ICSID Case No. ARB/01/12, Award (14 July 2006).

[143] *Ibid.*, para. 361.

[144] *Ibid.*

In *AMT v. DR Congo*,[145] interpreting Article II(4) DR Congo-USA BIT (1984), the tribunal emphasized the need for the host state's FPS conduct not to be less than that recognised under CIL notwithstanding its compliance with national law.[146] In other words, a host state cannot escape its FPS duty under international law on the basis that it has complied with national law.[147]

A more intricate situation is created by the second approach, whereby FPS is formulated by reference to domestic law without any CIL qualification. This approach is common in Russian-modelled BITs.[148] An example of this model with an African signatory is found in Article 4 Zimbabwe-Russia BIT (2012) which provides: *'[e]ach Contracting Party shall **in accordance with its legislation provide full protection and security***'.[149]

From this formulation, unclear is whether the FPS provision expresses the contracting parties' intention to limit their FPS obligation to national law standards, thereby derogating from the CIL standard. Two relevant decisions offer insight into how prior ISDS tribunals have addressed this point. First, in *Bogdanov v. Moldova*,[150] the tribunal was faced with interpreting Article 2(2) of the Russia-Moldova BIT (1998) which provides: *'[e]ach Contracting Party shall guarantee, **in accordance with its law full and unconditional legal protection** for investments of investors of the other Contracting Party'*. The tribunal in its brief three-paragraph decision on FPS affirmed that Article 2(2) of the BIT makes clear that FPS is to be applied in accordance with the host country's laws.[151] Since Moldova's action was found to be consistent with its national law, the claim for FPS was consequently dismissed.[152] Noteworthy that the tribunal's FPS decision was solely based on the assessment of Moldova's conduct under its national law, suggesting a strict adherence to the four corners of the treaty text with no reference to international law.

In another relevant decision, the tribunal in *Tatneft v. Ukraine*[153] had to consider Article 2(2) of the Ukraine-Russia BIT (1998) providing an FPS formulation similar to that in the Russia-Moldova BIT. Like in the *Bogdanov* case, the *Tatneft* tribunal recognised the direct link of Ukraine's FPS duty with its national law as stipulated in the treaty. However, while recognising the contracting parties only guaranteed FPS

---

[145] *American Manufacturing & Trading, Inc. v. Republic of Zaire*, ICSID Case No. ARB/93/1, Award (21 February 1997).

[146] *Ibid.*, para. 606.

[147] *Ibid.*, para. 605.

[148] Article 2(2), Russia-Moldova BIT (1998), entered into force 18 July 2001; Article 2(2), Russia-Ukraine BIT (1998), entered into force 27 January 2000; Article 2(2), Russia-Cyprus BIT (1997), signed 11 April 1997.

[149] Article 4, Zimbabwe-Russia BIT (2012), signed 7 October 2012.

[150] *Iurii Bogdanov, Agurdino-Invest Ltd. and Agurdino-Chimia JSC v. Republic of Moldova*, SCC Case No. 093/2004, Award (22 September 2005).

[151] *Ibid.*, p. 15.

[152] *Ibid.*

[153] *OAO Tatneft v. Ukraine*, PCA Case No. 2008-8, Award (29 July 2014).

in accordance with national law, it held the manner in which the national legislation is implemented or applied may trigger international responsibility.[154]

Overall, the FPS standard has been one of the substantive guarantees whose vague and broadly worded form has contributed to expansive interpretations and conflicting jurisprudence on the meaning of the standard. According to UNCTAD data as of December 2023, the FPS standard has been invoked about thirty-eight (38) times against African states before ISDS tribunals.[155] This positions the standard as the third most frequently invoked among all standards against African states in ISDS. The first recorded dispute was *AMT v. DR Congo*,[156] initiated under United State-DR Congo BIT (1984) and decided in favour of the investor. Overall, eighteen (18) of the FPS claims against African states have resulted in a finding of liability.[157] Sixteen (16) have been successfully defended by the respondent host state, with five (5) dismissed for lack of jurisdiction and eleven (11) claims rejected on the merits. One (1) case has been settled, and three cases (3) remain pending.[158]

2.4   Interim Conclusion

This chapter has specifically examined three key substantive standards that are often invoked against African states in ISDS. It begins with an analysis of the FET guarantee, detailing its definition, origin, and how it has found common expression in IIAs contracted by African states, primarily based on models from developed capital-exporting countries. With a similar origin, this thesis also examines the nuances of expropriation, highlighting the conditions under which a state can lawfully take control of private assets, providing critical insights into the boundaries of state power in this context. Furthermore, the concept of FPS is explored in detail, emphasising its CIL roots and how the textual formulation of this standard, like every other standard discussed, plays a critical role in the interpretation ascribed to it by arbitral tribunals.

By delving into the nuances of the FET, expropriation, and the FPS guarantee, this chapter has laid a vital foundation for comprehending the intricacies of the substantive standards of investment protection often invoked against African states in ISDS. This understanding is crucial, as it provides the necessary context to better appreciate the shortcomings inherent in these standards, thus fuelling the criticism

---

[154] *Ibid.*, para. 425.

[155] UNCTAD ISDS Database https://investmentpolicy.unctad.org/investment-dispute-settlement/advanced-search

[156] *American Manufacturing & Trading (AMT), Inc. v. Democratic Republic of Congo*, ICSID Case No. ARB/93/1, Award (21 February 1997).

[157] UNCTAD ISDS Database https://investmentpolicy.unctad.org/investment-dispute-settlement/advanced-search

[158] *Ibid.*

against the traditional ISDS system. These shortcomings will be elaborated on in the subsequent chapter, particularly from the perspective of African nations.

Finally, it is important to highlight that while this chapter has primarily addressed the three substantive standards frequently invoked against African states in ISDS, there are other standards that, although less commonly invoked, have also stirred controversies regarding their interpretation by ISDS tribunals. These include the War Loss Clause ('WLC'), the Umbrella Clause, the non-discriminatory treatment clause, etc. The next chapter will elaborate on how all of these substantive guarantees contribute to African dissatisfaction with the traditional ISDS system.

Other Documents

NAFTA Free Trade Commission (2001) Notes of interpretation of certain Chapter 11 provisions. https://files.pca-cpa.org/pcadocs/bi-c/2.%20Canad.

References

Blanco SM (2019) Full protection and security in international investment law. Springer, Cham

Borchard EM (1934) The protection of citizens abroad and change of original nationality. Yale Law J 43(3):359–392

De Brabandere E (2017) Fair and equitable treatment and (full) protection and security in african investment treaties between generality and contextual specificity. JWIT 18:530–555

de Nanteuil A (2020) International investment law. Elgar, Cheltenham

Dolzer R, Kriebaum U, Schreuer C (2022) Principles of international investment law, 3rd edn. Oxford University Press, Oxford

Dolzer R, Schreuer C (2008) Principles of international investment law, 1st edn. Oxford University Press, Oxford

Junngam N (2018) The full protection and security standard in international investment law: what and who is investment fully[?] protected and secured from? ABLR 7(1):1–100

Kriebaum U (2015) Expropiation. In: Bungenberg M, Griebel J, Hobe S, Reinisch A (eds) International investment law: a handbook. Nomos, Baden-Baden, pp 959–1030

Lorz RA (2015) Protection and security (including the NAFTA approach). In: Bungenberg M, Griebel J, Hobe S, Reinisch A (eds) International investment law: a handbook. Nomos, Baden-Baden, pp 764–789

Malik M (2011) The full protection and security standard comes of age: yet another challenge for states in investment treaty arbitration? IISD. https://www.iisd.org/system

Newcombe AP, Paradell L (2009) Law and practice of investment treaties: standards of treatment. Kluwer Law International, Alphen aan den Rijn

Ofodile UE (2019) African states, investor–state arbitration and the ICSID dispute resolution system. ICSID Rev FILJ 34(2):296–364

Reinisch A, Schreuer C (2020) International protection of investments: the substantive standards. Cambridge University Press, Cambridge

Sabahi B, Rubins N, Wallace D (2019) Investor-state arbitration, 2nd edn. Oxford University Press, Oxford

Salacuse J (2010) The law of investment treaties, 1st edn. Oxford University Press, Oxford

Schefer KN (2020) International investment law: text, cases and materials, 3rd edn. Elgar, Cheltenham

Subedi SP (2020) International investment law: reconciling policy and principle, 4th edn. Hart, Oxford

UNCTAD (2012) Fair and equitable treatment: UNCTAD series on issues in international investment agreements II. United Nations Publications, United Nations

UNCTAD (2017) Special update on investor-state dispute settlement: facts and figures. https://unctad.org/system/files/official-document/diaepcb2017d7_en.pdf

Vandevelde KJ (1988) The bilateral investment treaty program of the United States. CILJ 21(2): 201–276

Chapter 3
The Existing ISDS System and Its Criticism from an African Perspective

As revealed in the preceding chapter, the substantive standards of investment protection contained in most IIAs today originate from CIL pre-dating the twentieth century. However, the procedural mechanism widely adopted to ensure the enforcement of these substantive guarantees is only a few decades old. This refers to the traditional ISDS system through investment arbitration.

The vast majority of IIAs in existence today contain a clause popularly referred to as the ISDS clause.[1] This clause commonly (albeit not limited) provides the contracting states consent to arbitrate investment disputes between a contracting state and an investor/national of another contracting state.[2] By this clause, IIAs introduced a procedural mechanism for the resolution of investor-state disputes that is otherwise not available under CIL.[3] Its function is to allow private parties' direct recourse against a host state before an international arbitral tribunal to remedy a breach of any substantive right guaranteed under the applicable IIA.[4]

By design, the ISDS clause contained in the thousands of IIAs permits investment arbitration to proceed before different arbitration forums, institutional or non-institutional (*ad-hoc*), that are independent of one another.[5] ICSID is the most popular ISDS forum,[6] the Permanent Court of Arbitration ('PCA') and the

---

[1] Pohl et al. (2012), p. 9.

[2] See *Bureau Veritas v. Paraguay*, ICSID Case No. ARB/07/9, Decision of the Tribunal on Objections to Jurisdiction (29 May 2009), para 65; *Wintershall Aktiengesellschaft v. Argentine Republic*, ICSID Case No. ARB/04/14, Award (8 December 2008), para. 160; *Pan American Energy LLC and BP Argentina Exploration Company v. The Argentine Republic*, ICSID Case No. ARB/03/13, Decision on Preliminary Objections (27 July 2006), para. 33.

[3] Hober (2018), p. 9.

[4] Born (2021), p. 491.

[5] See, Schefer (2020), p. 371 ff.

[6] ICSID, Caseload—Statistics, https://icsid.worldbank.org/resources/publications/icsid-caseload-statistics

---

A. O. Adekemi, *Attracting African States Participation in a Multilateral Investment Court*, EYIEL Monographs - Studies in European and International Economic Law 39, https://doi.org/10.1007/978-3-031-73861-6_3

Stockholm Chamber of Commerce (SCC) follow as the most used arbitral institutions for the administration of investment arbitration.[7] Noteworthy, while IIAs remain the main source of consent to investment arbitration and the designated forum, consent is also derived from investor-state contracts or under the host state's domestic law of investment.[8] For the purpose of this thesis, the ensuing discussions on the backlash against traditional ISDS primarily focus on the disenchantment stemming from treaty-based consent to investment arbitration, considering that this forms the basis for the majority of claims in ISDS proceedings,[9] particularly those initiated under old-generation IIAs.

In Africa, as in the rest of the world, the majority of investment arbitration cases brought against African states have been invoked on the basis of consent derived from BITs.[10] Since the first BIT case against an African state initiated in 1993, i.e. *AMT v. DR Congo*,[11] there has been an exponential increase in the number of investment arbitration cases involving African states. From eight (8) between the year 1993 and 2000, to one hundred and seventy-one (171) as of December 2023.[12] According to the ICSID's all-time caseload statistics, at least 14.3% of the total number of registered cases involved an African state, putting the region in third place on the geographical distribution of ICSID caseload by region.[13] This figure does not account for other non-ICSID-administered disputes involving African states.

According to a 2019 survey, over 50% of African states have been involved in investment arbitration, with the majority of cases originating from North Africa.[14] As of December 2023, Egypt leads as the most sued state in the continent with 46 cases, followed by Libya with 22 cases, and Algeria with 13 cases.[15] The remaining cases are spread across the three geographical zones in the continent: West, East, and Southern Africa.

The above statistics evidently suggest that for the past three decades, investment arbitration has been a welcomed choice for ISDS in Africa. In fact, historical accounts confirm that African states played a decisive role in the establishment of

---

[7] UNCTAD ISDS Database, Administering Institution, https://investmentpolicy.unctad.org/investment-dispute-settlement?status=1000

[8] ICSID, Case Load Statistics (Issue 2024-1), p. 7, https://icsid.worldbank.org/resources/publications/icsid-caseload-statistics

[9] UNCTAD (2017), p. 1.

[10] *See*, UNCTAD ISDS Database, https://investmentpolicy.unctad.org/investment-dispute-settlement/advanced-search

[11] *American Manufacturing & Trading (AMT), Inc. v. Democratic Republic of Congo*, ICSID Case No. ARB/93/1.

[12] UNCTAD ISDS Database, https://investmentpolicy.unctad.org/investment-dispute-settlement/advanced-search

[13] ICSID, Case Load Statistics (Issue 2024-1), p. 10, https://icsid.worldbank.org/resources/publications/icsid-caseload-statistics

[14] Transnational Institute (2019), p. 4.

[15] UNCTAD ISDS Database, https://investmentpolicy.unctad.org/investment-dispute-settlement/advanced-search

the ICSID system, and the development of investment law through the ICSID jurisprudence that has developed overtime.[16] African states were amongst the front-line states that called for the establishment of ICSID.[17] The first of the four meetings to discuss the preliminary draft of the ICSID Convention took place in Africa and had the most attendance with fifty-two state representatives, out of which twenty-nine were from Africa.[18] Further, out of the twenty ratification instruments needed to enter into force, fifteen were from Africa, with Nigeria being the first.[19]

When it comes to the development of ICSID jurisprudence, African states also come first on several fronts. For example, fifteen of the first twenty-five ICSID cases involved African states, with the first ICSID registered case being against the kingdom of Morocco.[20] Being the first in line, the case laid out the *ratione personae* requirement of Article 25(2)(b) of the ICSID convention, later followed by a plethora of ICSID cases involving African states in the early years of ICSID.[21] Also, the classic authority widely referred to in investment arbitration on the definition of an investment under the ICSID convention is derived from the famous *Salini v. Morocco*[22] case. These are only a few of the numerous instances where investment disputes involving African states have set the foundation for the development of ICSID jurisprudence and international investment law altogether.

Although ICSID, and by large the investor-state arbitration system has been widely embraced, African states are now adding their critical voices to the traditional ISDS system due to its inherent weaknesses that have been exposed overtime. Over the last decade, investment arbitration—the traditional ISDS mechanism has been under a strong wave of public criticism. This public criticism however cannot be viewed or effectively addressed in isolation of the legitimacy crisis facing the entire international investment law framework both in substance and procedure. On substance, we have the criticism emanating from the outdated and vaguely drafted substantive guarantees present in the multitudes of old-generation IIAs. While on procedure, we have the fragmented arbitral tribunals who apply the outdated substantive laws as formulated, in a manner revealing their deficiencies.

Although the public criticism against traditional ISDS procedure is not peculiar to Africa, with several commentaries already written on this issue of global concern,[23] this chapter is particularly focused on telling the African experience that has led to

---

[16] See in this regard, Akinkugbe (2019), p. 437 ff; Le Cannu (2018), p. 463 ff.

[17] *Parra* (2017), p. 20 ff.

[18] Le Cannu (2018), p. 461.

[19] *Ibid.*, p. 462.

[20] *Holiday Inns SA and others v Morocco*, ICSID Case No ARB/72/1 (note that: the holiday inns case was a contract based dispute, while the first BIT based dispute involving an African State is *AMT v. DR Congo*).

[21] Le Cannu (2018), p. 463.

[22] *Salini Costruttori SpA and Italstrade SpA v Kingdom of Morocco*, ICSID Case No ARB/00/4, Decision on Jurisdiction (July 16, 2001) para 52.

[23] Polanco (2018), p. 29 ff; Berge (2020), p. 920 ff; Kaushal (2009), p. 491ff; Mavroidis et al. (2011), p. 425 ff.

the disenchantment against the traditional ISDS system. It does so by examining two key aspects, i.e.: the undesirable effect of the substantive standards of treatment as applied by arbitral tribunals (3.1); and the undesirable effect of ISDS clauses as applied by arbitral tribunals (3.2).

3.1   The Undesirable Effect of the Substantive Standards of Treatment as Applied by Arbitral Tribunals

Based on available records from UNCTAD's ISDS database as of December 2023, out of the one hundred and seventy-one (171) cases involving African states, jurisdiction has been denied in twenty-one (21) cases, while decisions on the merits have been rendered in fifty-six (56) cases.[24] This confirms that in at least 56 cases, arbitral tribunals have applied the substantive standards in the relevant IIAs to determine the international lawfulness of African states' conduct concerning foreign investments within their territories. According to UNCTAD's records, African states have been found liable in thirty-two (32) instances and have successfully prevailed on the merits in twenty-four (24) cases.[25]

In summary, the above record demonstrates that African states have indeed fared better in ISDS than the claimant investors, particularly when their success on substantive and procedural (jurisdictional) issues are considered together. However, minus their success in jurisdictional challenges, their relatively limited success on substantive issues is a concern that cannot be overlooked. While a state may have an overall impressive success rate in defending against ISDS claims, the repercussions of a single adverse ISDS award are significant enough to potentially lead that state into economic distress. This vulnerability is especially pronounced for middle and low-income countries, a category to which virtually all African states belong.

Significantly, the African states' disenchantment with the traditional ISDS system does not result from the relatively low success rate in prevailing on substantive issues before arbitral tribunals. Rather, this dissatisfaction principally stems from the formulation of the substantive standards of investment protection in old-generation IIAs in a manner that fails to safeguard a state's right to regulate for sustainable development purposes (3.1.1); fails to ensure consistent interpretation of treaty standards (3.1.2); including the failure to ensure investors accountability (3.1.3).

---

[24] UNCTADS ISDS database, https://investmentpolicy.unctad.org/investment-dispute-settlement/advanced-search

[25] *Ibid.*, (the statistics on African states' liability in ISDS encompass 28 cases decided in favour of investors, and 4 cases where liability was found but no damages awarded).

3.1.1 Failure to Safeguard a State's Right to Regulate ('R2R') for Sustainable Development Purposes

As revealed in Chap. 1, the substantive guarantees provided in old-generation IIAs contracted by African states are based on old Western models. Over the years, hard lessons have been learned from contracting IIAs that offer substantive guarantees for the protection of foreign investment, without any corresponding obligation on the part of investors to foster not just economic, but most importantly, the sustainable development of the host states'. As defined in Chap. 1, sustainable development encompasses three interdependent pillars i.e., economic development, environmental protection, and social development. Hence, the interdependent nature of these pillars necessitates an investment activity to foster economic development concurrently with environmental protection and social development to safeguard sustainable development.

However, the vast majority of IIAs currently in force in Africa, likewise across the globe, do not distinguish between SD-friendly investments that should be protected and non-SD friendly investments that should not be protected. As a result, attempts by African host states to implement SD measures, especially those aimed at environmental protection and social development objectives, have been met with fierce challenges from foreign investors in investment arbitration for conflicting with their capital interests. Significantly, the absent entrenchment of SD safeguards in most IIAs, coupled with the broadly worded nature of the substantive guarantees means that host states remain highly vulnerable to IIA violations when implementing SD measures that are in conflict with investors' substantive IIA guarantees.

Below, we analyse a selection of notable ISDS case examples where African states have encountered treaty-related liabilities while striving to regulate in pursuit of their sustainable development objectives.

3.1.1.1 Biwater v. Tanzania[26] (Bordering on Regulation for Environmental Protection)

3.1.1.1.1 Background to the Dispute

The Claimant in this arbitration, "Biwater Gauff (Tanzania) Limited (**BGT**)" is a water service firm incorporated in the United Kingdom. In 2003, the Respondent (Republic of Tanzania) was awarded 140 million (US dollars) by multiple institutional funders i.e., the World Bank, African Development Bank, and European Investment Bank. This fund was meant to upgrade Tanzania's water and sewerage services system in and around the capital of Dar es Salaam.[27] A condition for

---

[26] *Biwater Gauff (Tanzania) Limited v. United Republic of Tanzania*, ICSID Case No. ARB/05/22, Award (24 July 2008).

[27] *Ibid.*, para. 3.

securing this fund was that the Respondent must appoint a private operator to manage and operate the water and sewerage system. Following a competitive bid process, the Respondent announced BGT as the successful bidder. Subsequently, in compliance with local law requirements, BGT incorporated a local company (**City Water**) as the operating company for the Dar es Salaam Water and Sewerage project.[28] To implement the project, City Water then entered a '**Lease Contract**' with the responsible Tanzanian authority i.e., Dar es Salaam Water and Sewerage Authority (**DAWASA**).

By 1 August 2003, City Water began full operation, providing water and sewerage services to the residents of Dar es Salaam and the surrounding area. However, the existing infrastructure was in such a poor state requiring significant capital for upgrades and repairs to ensure optimal service delivery to the populace. The heavy financial burden required to keep the operations running meant that City Water could not turn profitable in the first 7 years out of the 10-year lifespan of the project.

After the first 11 months of revenue intake below income projections, City Water deemed it necessary to review its lease contract with DAWASA. It based its review request on the unforeseen high cost of operations, and that the volume of water available for distribution in Dar es Salaam is not in line with its Bid expectation. The Tanzanian authorities countered this City Water's demand with a list of defaults in contractual obligations owed to DAWASA, including overdue contractual payments. Eventually, the government minister supervising the project ordered an audit of City Water operations to determine if there was merit in the requested contractual review. The audit report prepared by *Price Water Cooper (PWC)* concluded there is insufficient evidence to proof material change in circumstances to warrant a review of the lease contract. Despite the PWC report, the Respondent later acknowledged City Water's precarious financial condition and agreed to renegotiate the underlying lease contract for the Water and Sewerage Project. Unfortunately, the renegotiation which later commenced failed as the Parties could not reach an agreement.

Ultimately, City Water could no longer meet up with the operational demands of the Dar es Salaam Water and Sewerage project. Considering the environmental impact of such failure on public health and safety, Tanzania through DAWASA terminated the lease contract with City Water and ordered it to transfer operations back to the responsible government agency. City Water refused to comply with this directive. On 1 June 2005, 22 months after the commencement of operations, City Water's senior management staff were arrested by local police and subsequently deported from Tanzania. Simultaneously, the Tanzanian authorities entered and took possession of City Water's offices and assets and installed a new management.

---

[28] *Ibid.*, para. 5.

3.1.1.1.2   The Arbitration

Following the above events, BGT instituted ICSID arbitration against Tanzania, claiming the breach of several substantive guarantees under the Tanzania-UK BIT (1994). This included the breach of 'FET'—Article 2(2); FPS—Article 2(2); protection against 'unreasonable or discriminatory measures'—Article 2(2); and 'unlawful expropriation'—Article 5.

3.1.1.1.3   Tribunal's Decision

Before deciding on the merits, the tribunal acknowledged the SD issues intertwined with BGT's claims under the BIT. These SD issues were well captured in the tribunal's analysis of the *Amici's* submission it had earlier allowed as relevant to the determination of the case.[29] In the *amici*, three general principles were identified as relevant to the merits of BGT's claims against Tanzania, i.e.:[30]

(a) the duty to apply proper business standards to the investment process, including proper due diligence procedures;
(b) the principle of *pacta sunt servanda*; and
(c) the duty to act in good faith both prior to and during the investment period.

According to the *Amici*, BGT's responsibilities under these principles should be assessed in light of the SD goals of the Respondent that irrefutably includes the running of clean water and a good sanitary system, failure of which could have devastating consequence on the entire populace. Consequently, the first principle denotes BGT's duty of due diligence to ascertain the commercial viability and risks associated with its investment project, a responsibility higher in a project of such public significance as the City Water project. However, BGT failed to perform this due diligence duty. It submitted a bid that based on its experience in other similar projects in developing countries should have known was impossible to perform its contractual obligations to Tanzania.[31] Yet it offered this incredulous bid.

The second principle *'pacta sunt sevranda'* signifies that BGT (acting through City Water) became immediately bound by its contractual commitment to DAWASA the moment it signed the Lease Contract. Importantly, the public interest nature of the Dar es Salaam Water and Sewerage project highlights that this is not just a contract between two commercial entities. BGT's contractual obligation is directly owed to the people of Dar es Salaam, who rely exclusively on BGT for their daily water and sanitation service needs. In this context, BGT once again failed to meet public expectations as it had committed to under the Lease Contract.[32]

---

[29] *Ibid.*, para. 35 ff.
[30] *Ibid.*, para. 374.
[31] *Ibid.*, para. 381 f.
[32] *Ibid.*, para. 383.

On the third principle, it was contended that BGT engaged in an abusive 'Renegotiation Strategy'.[33] A strategy whereby a low bid was presented during the public bidding process for the Water and Sewerage project. This was to create an unfair advantage over other higher bids, with the aim of securing the project and then later forcing renegotiations when the state is fully committed. The non-commercially viable bid submitted by BGT and its actions to later force renegotiation suggests that this was indeed BGT's original intention, indicating a lack of good faith prior to and during BGT's investment. Given these self-inflicted failures of BGT and the devastating impact on the environment, which exposed the Tanzanian public to serious public health and safety concerns, the *Amici* concluded that this should vitiate the validity of BGT's claim under the BIT.[34]

3.1.1.1.4   Expropriation Breach

In deciding the treaty claims, the tribunal acknowledged *inter alia* that it was impossible to disregard the circumstances under which the Lease Contract was *'concluded, performed, renegotiated and terminated'*.[35] Having this in view, the tribunal first addressed the expropriation claim and indeed found BGT's performance (through City Water) of the Lease Contract deplorable.[36] Further, the tribunal held that the termination of the Lease Contract following this poor performance was simply a contractual dispute between City Water and DAWASA that did not trigger the responsibility of Tanzania for unlawful expropriation under the BIT.[37] However, according to the tribunal, the Lease Contract provided BGT rights to a *'contractual termination process'* which was unlawfully interfered with by a series of government actions that amounted to expropriation under the BIT i.e.:

- the press conference by a government minister followed by a political rally;[38]
- the occupation and takeover of City Water's facility;[39] and
- the deportation of City Water's Staffs.[40]

Notably, this tribunal's decision is not void of criticism. It is worth noting that in arbitral practice, substantial deprivation of an investor's property rights is the widely established standard for finding expropriation.[41] The decision does not provide

---

[33] *Ibid.*, para. 384 ff.

[34] *Ibid.*, para. 389 ff.

[35] *Ibid.*, para. 470.

[36] *Ibid.*, para. 486.

[37] *Ibid.* para. 491 ff.

[38] *Ibid.* para. 497 ff.

[39] *Ibid.* para. 503 ff.

[40] *Ibid.* para. 511 ff.

[41] *Olympic Entertainment Group AS v. Republic of Ukraine*, PCA Case No. 2019-18, Award (15 April 2021), para. 104; *Charanne B.V. and Construction Investments S.A.R.L. v. Kingdom of*

clarity on how interference with a subset of rights under the Lease Contract i.e. the *contractual termination process*, could constitute a 'substantial deprivation' of BGT's enjoyment of its entire investment. It is important to highlight that at the time of the impugned state measures, BGT's investment was practically non-operational, primarily due to BGT's own faults. Hence, there was practically no enjoyment or benefit being derived from BGT's investment at the time the alleged expropriation occurred. Notably, this factor later became crucial in the decision on damages.[42]

3.1.1.1.5   FET Breach

Although the tribunal had rejected most of BGT's allegations on the FET claim, it nonetheless found Tanzania in breach of the FET standard for failing to meet the legitimate expectation of BGT to properly manage the public perception of the City Water project.[43] This finding was due to the same facts relied upon to find Tanzania in breach of the expropriation standard. According to the tribunal, the public statements by the responsible Tanzanian government minister for the City Water project had further 'inflamed the situation and polarized public opinion' against the underperforming City Water.[44] From that moment, the tribunal concluded that City Water could no longer enjoy the 'unhindered performance of the contractual termination process' as guaranteed under the Lease Contract.[45] Thus, this denial amounted to a violation of FET.

The Tribunal's decision on BGT's FET claim also raises a number of controversial issues. First, this is one rare case where a tribunal had found a state in breach of an investor's legitimate expectation solely based on critical comments made by public officials against an underperforming investor. Secondly, while the tribunal acknowledged that the exact definition or scope of FET is not settled in jurisprudence, it at least recognised that the threshold for breaching the standard is quite high.[46] However, without any other reason given, it is questionable how the critical comments from one government official against an already failed investor's project can suffice to pass the high threshold for violating FET.

Further, despite BGT's abysmal performance of the City Water project, which threatened the environmental safety of the entire Dar es Salaam populace, it is

---

Spain, SCC Case No. 062/2012, Award (21 January 2016), para. 461; *Bosh International, Inc. and B&P, LTD Foreign Investments Enterprise v. Ukraine*, ICSID Case No. ARB/08/11, Award (25 October 2012), para. 218; *CMS Gas Transmission Company v. Republic of Argentina*, ICSID Case No. ARB/01/8, Award (12 May 2005) para. 262.

[42] *Biwater Gauff (Tanzania) Limited v. United Republic of Tanzania,* ICSID Case No. ARB/05/22, Award (24 July 2008), para. 787.

[43] *Ibid.,* para. 624 ff.

[44] *Ibid.,* para. 627.

[45] *Ibid.*

[46] *Ibid.,* para. 597.

questionable how the tribunal found merit in BGT's claim to contractual rights of an 'unhindered termination process' when it has failed to perform its own fundamental duties under the same contract. Moreover, the tribunal failed to describe how: (1) the minister's public comments hindered City Water's performance in the contractual termination process (2) nor indicated any actual loss that City Water suffered due to the purported hindrance to the termination process.

Additionally, the tribunal recognised that prior to the minister's comments, BGT had already lost public confidence due to its poor record.[47] Given this fact, it is valid to question how Tanzania could have undermined BGT's legitimate expectation to properly manage the public perception of the City Water project if the same was already undermined by BGT's own irresponsible conduct.

3.1.1.1.6   Other Treaty Breaches

Again, the public statements by the government minister criticising City Water's underperformance were found to have constituted an 'unreasonable measure' under the BIT, which 'undermined the management authority of City Water—or at least, the performance of the normal contractual termination phase'.[48] As for the breach of FPS, the tribunal first adopted an expansive interpretation of the standard, extending it beyond its traditional conception of physical security to commercial and legal security.[49] Upon this, the tribunal concluded that the seizure of City Water's premises and removal of its staff amounted to a violation of the FPS guarantee under the BIT.

3.1.1.1.7   Damages

Despite the finding of multiple BIT breaches against Tanzania, the tribunal declined to award any financial damages in favour of BGT. Finally, the tribunal had come to the conclusion that any loss suffered by BGT to its investment in Tanzania was caused by its own failures, rooted in the non-performance of the Lease Contract.[50] Although this came as a back-end relief for the respondent, it did not come without a negative cost. One of them is the reputational damage to the state as an unsafe haven for foreign investment, as commercially prudent investors will be weary of investing in a state with a track record of treaty violations. Such a negative public record undermines the inflow of FDI necessary for the sustainable development of any state.

Another damage to Tanzania is the cost of defending against the BIT claims. Although Tanzania's exact cost of defending against BGT's claims was not given in

---

[47] *Ibid.*, para. 627.
[48] *Ibid.*, para. 698.
[49] *Ibid.*, para. 729.
[50] *Ibid.*, paras. 773–808.

the award, it could not have been meagre. According to a 2021 empirical study, the median cost to a respondent state defending an ISDS claim as of May 2020 was 4.7 million U.S. Dollars.[51] Based on this record, one may infer that Tanzania's cost in the *Biwater* case indeed ran into millions of U.S. Dollars. Unfortunately, the state did not recover its cost, as the tribunal decided that each party should bear its own cost.[52]

3.1.1.1.8   Summary Assessment of the Dispute in the Context of the State's R2R for SD

Given the crucial public importance of City Water's contractual obligations to Tanzania, and its eventual failure to sustain operations of the Dar es Salaam Water and Sewerage network system, this exposed the Tanzanian populace to a significant risk of environmental and public health disaster. Averting such risk was the primary reason why a project of such public importance was transferred from public to private hands to enable better service delivery and efficient management. However, this purpose was undermined by BGT's irresponsible conduct.

Where an investor through its own irrational investment undertakings fails to fulfil its commitments to projects of significant public importance, can such an investor meritoriously invoke the shield of a BIT guarantee against the public backlash that ensues. The *Biwater* tribunal confirms that the protection conferred upon investors in old-generation IIAs is quite broad, without qualification based on the investor's conduct. Despite Tanzania's defense that its measures against BGT were necessary due to City Water's underperformance that endangered public safety,[53] coupled with the admitted amici's brief of BGT's abusive investment,[54] the tribunal still resolved that Tanzania's public interest case does not justify its non-compliance with BGT's extensive BIT guarantees.

Notably, the *Biwater* tribunal cannot be faulted for applying the '**law as it is**' to the facts of the case. The old-generation Tanzania-UK BIT (1994) does not foresee any investor obligation to environmental protection, nor is there a treaty requirement that an investment is protected only if it promotes the environmental and welfare needs of the state towards its citizens. Therefore, irrespective of City Water's failure, the treaty has no provision to counterbalance BGT's claims against its level of performance in the host state.

Overall, the *Biwater* decision exemplifies the problem with one-sided and broadly worded IIAs, which leaves room for expansive interpretation by tribunals, even when such does not align with the host state's SD goals to its public.

---

[51] Hodgson et al. (2021), p. 10.

[52] *Biwater Gauff (Tanzania) Limited v. United Republic of Tanzania*, ICSID Case No. ARB/05/22, Award (24 July 2008), para. 813.

[53] *Ibid.*, para. 436.

[54] *Ibid.*, paras. 370–390.

3.1.1.2   Foresti, et al. v. South Africa[55] (Bordering on Regulation for Social Development)

3.1.1.2.1   Background to the Dispute

The Claimants in this arbitration were a group of individuals having Italian nationality and a Luxembourgish corporation with investments in the South African mining industry. In 2002, in a bid to reform the legal landscape of its mining industry, the South African government enacted the Mineral and Petroleum Resources Development Act of 2002 (MPRDA). The MPRDA was combined with a 'Mining Charter', both of which came into effect in 2004. These government legislations *inter alia* enshrined Black Economic Empowerment ('BEE') measures meant to promote socio-economic inclusiveness for Historically Disadvantaged South Africans ('HDSAs'), a socio-economic disadvantage borne out of South Africa's apartheid history.

To achieve its objectives, the MPRDA ceded all mineral and petroleum resources rights to the South African state.[56] While old mining rights in force before the MPRDA took effect would remain in force, mining right holders under the 'old order' must within 5 years convert their mining license to a right under the 'new order'.[57] Further, in line with its BEE objective, the conversion process under the MPRDA required applicants to commit to certain socio-economic and developmental goals to the benefit of HDSAs. According to the claimants, these BEE goals included *inter alia*:

– requiring mining companies to achieve 26% HDSA ownership of mining assets by 2014;[58] and to
– publish employment equity plans directed towards achieving a baseline 40% HDSA participation in management by 2009.[59]

As a result of this new government legislation, the claimants instituted an ICSID arbitration against the South African government, claiming multiple violations of their substantive guarantees under the South Africa-Italy BIT (1997) and the South Africa-Luxembourg BIT (1998) respectively.

---

[55] *Piero Foresti, Laura de Carli & Others v. The Republic of South Africa*, ICSID Case No. ARB(-AF)/07/01, Award (4 August 2010).

[56] Article 3(1), MPRDA 2002. https://www.gov.za/sites/default/files/gcis_document/201409/a28-02ocr.pdf

[57] Article 7(1)(2), *Ibid.*, Schedule II (Transitional Arrangements).

[58] *Piero Foresti, Laura de Carli & Others v. The Republic of South Africa*, ICSID Case No. ARB (AF)/07/01, Award (4 August 2010), para. 56.

[59] *Ibid.*

3.1.1.2.2 The Arbitration

Specifically, the claimants alleged that the MPRDA breached their treaty guarantee against unlawful expropriation.[60] The subject of expropriation is the old-order mining rights associated with forty-four properties, which were effectively and definitively expropriated at the end of the conversion process.[61] Also, it was alleged that the BEE requirement that foreign investors divest 26% of their shares in mining companies to HDSA's amounted to an expropriation of claimants' shares in their operating companies.[62] In addition, the claimants also alleged that the MPRDA and Mining Charter breached South Africa's 'FET' and 'national treatment obligations under its respective BITs' with Italy and Luxembourg.[63]

In response, the South African government denied all allegations of a treaty violation. That assuming *arguendo* there was a claim for expropriation, the claimants' allegations had no merit since both BITs invoked permitted expropriation, provided it was lawful.[64] According to the respondent, the challenged government legislations at the heart of the dispute had an important public purpose amongst which was the need to ameliorate the 'disenfranchisement of HDSAs and other negative social effects caused by apartheid in general'.[65] In particular, the old legal order that regulated the mineral rights sector enacted by the apartheid system had 'entrenched white privilege in the mineral sector', which could not stand in a democratic system.[66] Therefore, any alleged expropriation pursued a lawful public purpose. Secondly, South Africa contended that a compensation procedure was accorded in line with its duty to provide—prompt, adequate, and effective compensation—which was intentionally refused by the claimants.[67] Thirdly the respondent argued there was no discrimination, and any at all in relation to national treatment would have fallen within the respondent's margin of appreciation to implement measures that pursue critical public interest.[68] Lastly, that any alleged expropriation of claimants' investment had followed due process.[69] That these considerations should therefore exonerate South Africa from any treaty liability for unlawful expropriation or any other violation under the invoked BITs'.

---

[60] *Ibid.*, paras. 59–66.

[61] *Ibid.*, para. 60

[62] *Ibid.*, paras. 64–66.

[63] *Ibid.*, para. 78.

[64] *Ibid.*, para. 68.

[65] *Ibid.*, para. 69.

[66] *Ibid.*

[67] *Ibid.*, paras. 70–71.

[68] *Ibid.*, paras. 72.

[69] *Ibid.*, para. 73.

3.1.1.2.3 Tribunal's Decision

The tribunal's award in this case was entered in the form of a default award following a discontinuance request made by the claimants. This request came after a settlement ('offset Agreement') was reached between the disputing parties. According to the claimants, the Offset Agreement had partially ameliorated their concerns for bringing the BIT claim, and the BIT claim was no longer economically prudent.[70] Although South Africa initially objected to such discontinuation, it later consented after the claimants agreed to a discontinuance of the claims with *res judicata* effect.[71]

3.1.1.2.4 Summary Assessment of the Dispute in the Context of the State's R2R for SD

Although the outcome of this arbitration may appear as a victory for South Africa, it is debatable whether this equals to victory in the context of the state's regulatory autonomy to implement measures of significant public interest to its populace. As already mentioned, the claimants' request for discontinuance followed an **'Offset Agreement'** it entered with the South African government. Based on the Offset Agreement as revealed in the tribunal's award, the claimants managed to success-fully pushback on the BEE requirement to sell 26% of their shares to HDSAs.[72] This requirement was replaced by another beneficiating arrangement that does not require a relinquishing of company shares. Also, the BEE requirement for 40% HDSA participation in management by 2009 was substituted for a '5% employee ownership program for employees of the Operating Companies'.[73]

As in the *Biwater* case, the government measures challenged by *Foresti, et al.* are of critical importance to the sustainable development of the respondent state, so much that it attracted *amicus* intervention from multiple NGOs. As rightly captured in one of the *amicus* briefs to the tribunal, the MPRDA was:

> [E]nacted in South Africa for important public policy reasons and in furtherance of consti-tutionally mandated goals. These include: human rights advancement, and in particular the pursuit of substantive equality; sustainable development [. . .]; and the need to proactively redress the apartheid history of exploitative labour practices, forced land deprivations, and discriminatory ownership policies which previously characterised South Africa's mining sector for decades.[74]

As such, domestic law policies that are enacted with purposes as dictated above should be permissible within the ambit of a state's obligation to foreign investors

---

[70] *Ibid.*, para. 79 f.

[71] *Ibid.*, para. 82.

[72] *Ibid.*, para. 79.

[73] *Ibid.*

[74] *Ibid.*, Petition for Limited Participation as non-Disputing Parties (17 July 2009), para. 4.1.

under IIAs. The mere fact that a foreign investor's interest is impaired by a host state's measure meant to advance legitimate public policy objectives, should not amount to a treaty violation. This does not imply that a state can unilaterally enact a local law just to derogate from its IIA obligation. Particularly, the *de facto* implementation of such laws may be a subject of international liability where it is done in a manifestly arbitrary or unjustifiably discriminatory manner.

Although, in the *Foresti, et al.* case, the discontinuance of the dispute prevented the tribunal from reaching a decision on the merits. It is worth noting that if the dispute had been decided on its substantive merits, there is no guarantee that South Africa would have avoided treaty liability based on the public interest nature of the challenged MPDRA. For example, it is noteworthy that ISDS tribunals are divided on whether a state's purpose in implementing an expropriatory measure is relevant in determining whether or not such state measure amounts to a treaty violation and whether compensation is owed.[75] Accordingly, it is uncertain how the tribunal would have decided the expropriation claim against South Africa based on its public interest measures.

Upon being exposed to the BIT claims and knowing its vulnerabilities under the old-generation BIT standards invoked by the claimants, South Africa deemed it prudent to settle with an Offset Agreement. This agreement saw the state substitute its originally intended BEE measures, for other measures, the claimants deemed ameliorating enough to discontinue their BIT claims. However, whether or not the Offset Agreement effectively meets the BEE objectives of the state as contemplated in the MPDRA to remedy the societal injustice against HDSAs remains debatable.

Overall, the *Foresti, et al.* case is another notable example from an African context of how foreign investors can leverage the substantive guarantees in IIAs to deter states from implementing legitimate public policy objectives in furtherance of their sustainable development goals.

3.1.1.3   Pezold v. Zimbabwe[76] (Bordering on Regulation for Social Development)

3.1.1.3.1   Background to the Dispute

The Claimants in this arbitration are a group of individuals from the same family ('von Pezolds') who are of Swiss and German nationality. Between the years 1988 and 2007, the claimants made a series of investments in Zimbabwe.[77] The von Pezolds' investments spanning this period led to the acquisition/ownership of 78,275

---

[75] Leibold (2016), p. 220.

[76] *Bernhard von Pezold and Others v. Republic of Zimbabwe*, ICSID Case No. ARB/10/15, Award (28 July 2015).

[77] *Ibid.*, paras. 118–138.

hectares of Zimbabweans' indigenous farmlands.[78] Being an indigenous land, the historical roots of claimants' farm lands date back to the 1800s when the indigenous inhabitants of Zimbabwe fell under colonial rule. This era in Zimbabwe's history (formerly the 'Rhodesian' era) witnessed the forceful taking of lands from the indigenous people by the foreign colonisers that settled therein which later formed the Rhodesian state. The Rhodesian era ended in 1980, but not before ownership of a vast majority of Zimbabwe's agricultural lands had been vested in the hands of a few commercial white farmers.

Upon the attainment of independence in 1980, the newly formed independent government promised sweeping land reform programs (LRP) to correct the historical wrongs of the colonial era against the indigenous population. At first, the state introduced a 'willing buyer—willing seller system' for land redistribution. However, the voluntary nature of this system ensured that the historical injustice sought to be corrected through the LRP progressed slowly 10 years post-independence.[79] In 1992, the *Land Acquisition Act 1992* was enacted which now empowered the government to *'acquire land and other immovable property compulsorily in certain circumstances'*, and under certain conditions similar to the classic conditions for a lawful expropriation under international law.[80] This reform also did little in accelerating the equitable redistribution of indigenous farmlands been clamoured for by the populace, especially due to the lack of funds to compensate land owners.

Twenty years post-independence, the slow pace of achieving the pressing national goal created a state of socio-political tension in Zimbabwe. This culminated in the invasion of predominantly white-owned farm lands by settlers who now resorted to self-help in repossessing their ancestral lands. To assuage the national tension rapidly escalating into an uprising, the government in July 2000 initiated a new land reform policy called the Fast Track Land Reform Programme (FTLRP). This FTLRP triggered a constitutional amendment that permitted the state acquisition of agricultural lands without compensation, save for 'compensating improvements on the land', itself.[81]

In 2005, another constitutional amendment was enacted. All agricultural lands identified in this amendment had their ownership vested in the state with no compensation payable save for improvements on such lands before it was acquired.[82] Additionally, the right to challenge such acquisition in court was revoked, and possession or occupation of such lands without lawful authority became criminalised.[83] This 2005 constitutional amendment affected most of the Claimants' 78,275 hectares of farmland, identified as indigenous farmland. Also, the

---

[78] TNI (2019), p. 2.

[79] *Bernhard von Pezold and Others v. Republic of Zimbabwe*, ICSID Case No. ARB/10/15, Award (28 July 2015), para. 97.

[80] *Ibid.*, para., 100 f; Jones (2021), p. 23 f.

[81] *Ibid.*, para. 107.

[82] *Ibid.*, para. 116.

[83] *Ibid.*

land invasion which started in early 2000 resulted in the occupation of 22 percent of the Claimants' farmland by settlers. These events informed the Claimants' final decision to institute the ICSID arbitration against Zimbabwe, claiming multiple violations under the Zimbabwe-Germany BIT (1995) and the Zimbabwe-Switzerland BIT (1996).

3.1.1.3.2 The Arbitration

The Claimant alleged that Zimbabwe's measures breached several substantive guaranties under the aforementioned BITs, including 'unlawful expropriation', 'denial of FET', 'unreasonable and discriminatory treatment', and 'denial of FPS'. The following analysis will mainly focus on the expropriation and FET claims.

Regarding the expropriation, the Claimants alleged that several elements of their investment had been unlawfully expropriated, most notably their farmlands by the FTLRP and the 2005 constitutional amendment. It was contended that the expropriation served no public purpose, was discriminatory, lacked due process, and was without a 'prompt, adequate, and effective' compensation.[84] Regarding FET, the claimants alleged that direct assurances received from Zimbabwe's top officials including former President Robert Mugabe about the LRP created a legitimate expectation that their investments will not be expropriated. A breach of this legitimate expectation thus amounts to a denial of FET.[85]

In response, regarding the expropriation, Zimbabwe contended that its challenged measures were effected for a public purpose that prevails over individual interest, particularly to protect the interest of 'indigenous people who were disadvantaged by the colonial land tenure system.[86] The state argued that the issue of discrimination, just like the entire dispute, must be viewed from the lens of history. Particularly, that the land tenure maintained by the colonial system had disproportionately vested 70% of the arable and best lands in Zimbabwe in the hands of the minority white population, leaving the majority black population to compete for reserve native lands that only a few could afford.[87] Consequently, any alleged discrimination *'followed the realities of land ownership'* unjustly perpetuated by the colonial system.[88] Furthermore, the state contended that its 2005 constitutional amendment followed due process. Citing an European Court of Human Rights (ECHR) authority, Zimbabwe argued that the preclusion of judicial review for expropriated farmland in public interest cannot be deemed unlawful.[89] The state further stressed that the protection of public order, threatened by protracted delays in land redistribution,

---

[84] *Ibid.*, para. 69 ff.

[85] *Ibid.*, para. 525 ff.

[86] *Ibid.*, para. 81 ff.

[87] *Ibid.*, paras. 485.

[88] *Ibid.*

[89] *Ibid.*, para. 486 ff.

due to numerous litigations justified the need for a 'constrained due process'.[90] On compensation, the state argued *inter alia* that full compensation was received by the claimants 'in the form of eight years of substantially unencumbered use' of the agricultural lands, enabling claimants to export products at their own independently determined transfer prices.[91]

Regarding the FET violation, Zimbabwe contended that the claimants' legitimate expectations must be weighed against what they could legitimately expect at the time they made their investments. According to the respondent, the claimants were aware that land reform was imminent in Zimbabwe at the time of their investment and it was unrealistic to expect the state to continue with 'Rhodesian business practices'.[92] Accordingly, the claimants 'accepted a high business risk at the time they made their respective investments'.[93] The BIT does not insure from such risk. The Respondent further relied on its lawful expropriation arguments to justify that there has been no breach of the FET owed to the claimants.

3.1.1.3.3   Tribunal's Decision

3.1.1.3.4   Expropriation Breach

In deciding the expropriation claim, first, the tribunal acknowledged an immaterial difference between the criteria for expropriation under Article 4(2) of the Zimbabwe-Germany BIT and Article 6(1) of the Zimbabwe-Switzerland BIT. Therefore, a finding of liability under one will suffice as a finding of liability under the other.[94] Afterward, the tribunal proceeded to address the parties' submissions.

The tribunal agreed with the claimants' submission that even though they had remained in possession of the farm lands in issue (a large part), the transfer of legal title to the state which Zimbabwe had not contested was sufficient to establish expropriation.[95] On whether the expropriation was lawful, the tribunal simply held that as no compensation was paid, an unlawful expropriation was already established without a need to decide whether the government measures fulfilled the other criteria for a lawful expropriation i.e. public purpose, due process, and non-discrimination.[96] Nevertheless, the tribunal briefly addressed these points since the parties had extensively made submissions on it.

---

[90] *Ibid.*, para. 487.

[91] *Ibid.*, para. 480.

[92] *Ibid.*, paras. 535, 537.

[93] *Ibid.*, para. 535.

[94] *Ibid.*, para. 492.

[95] *Ibid.*, para. 494.

[96] *Ibid.*, para. 498.

Starting with due process, the tribunal held that the exclusion of the right of judicial review by the 2005 constitutional amendment amounts to a denial of due process. The tribunal rejected the respondent's attempt to justify the exclusion with the ECHR jurisprudence.[97] Regarding non-discrimination, the tribunal found this requirement for a lawful expropriation unsatisfied because the government's policies were targeted at white farmers excluding black-owned farms, making it racially discriminatory.[98] Finally, it was held that the expropriation lacked public purpose on the basis that a large portion of the lands taken had not been redistributed to the historically disadvantaged but remained in *de facto* possession of claimants, and for those re-distributed, the allocations appear to have been politically motivated.[99] For the foregoing reasons, the tribunal found Zimbabwe liable under the BITs for unlawful expropriation.

3.1.1.3.5   FET Breach

Like the expropriation claim, the tribunal first affirmed that the FET standard under both Article 2(1) of the Zimbabwe-Germany BIT and Article 4(1) of the Zimbabwe-Switzerland BIT are substantively the same.[100] Further, it held that although the FET incorporates the minimum standard of treatment under CIL, the standard has since evolved from the *Neer* case.[101] With this foundation, the tribunal set the legal basis to include the protection of legitimate expectation within the scope of Zimbabwe's FET duty to the claimants.

Following this, the tribunal found that certain assurances from the respondent to the claimants created a legitimate expectation that their investments would not be expropriated.[102] Accordingly, the government's reneging on those assurances amounts to a breach of legitimate expectation in violation of Zimbabwe's FET obligation under the BITs. Although, the respondent had raised the necessity defence provided under Ad Article 3(a) of the Protocol to the Zimbabwe—Germany BIT ('German Protocol'), which provided that 'measures necessary for public security and order [. . .], will not be deemed "treatment less favourable" within the meaning of Article 3'. The tribunal rejected this defense as it found that the FET standard under the BIT is not subject to Article 3(a) of the German Protocol.[103]

Notably, the same facts relied upon to find Zimbabwe in breach of the expropriation and FET standard, were relied upon to find the respondent in breach of the

---

[97] *Ibid.*, para. 499 f.

[98] *Ibid.*, para. 501.

[99] *Ibid.*, para. 502.

[100] *Ibid.*, para. 545.

[101] *Ibid.*, para. 546.

[102] *Ibid.*, para. 547.

[103] *Ibid.*, para. 560.

'unreasonable or discriminatory measures' standard,[104] and in general the remaining treaty obligations to which the state was found wanting under the BITs.

3.1.1.3.6 Summary Assessment of the Dispute in the Context of the State's R2R for SD

One recurring theme in this case that underlies the entire dispute is the lamentable situation of the indigenous people created by the unjust redistribution of land by the colonial regime. Despite recognising that the colonial/Rhodesian land tenure regime was nothing short of devastating to the indigenous people,[105] the tribunal found none of Zimbabwe's public interest defences—to remedy the plight of its indigenous people, justify the breach of the claimants' BIT guarantees.

Noteworthy, the respondent had not introduced an 'expropriation without compensation' policy as challenged by the claimants. Rather, what it did was to introduce the compulsory taking of land with **'compensation limited to improvements on the lands taken'**. There are two rationales that arguably justify this limited form of compensation offered by the state. First, absent the unlawful expropriation by the colonial—Rhodesian regime, the rightful ownership of the contested lands belongs to the indigenous people. Therefore, it is a valid argument that no non-indigene should lawfully claim ownership over indigenous lands rooted in the unlawful expropriations perpetuated by the colonial regime. Such non-indigene claim rooted in the colonial usurpation of land title is a fruit of illegality that arguably remains *void ab initio*. However, improvements on such lands while the unlawful expropriation persists may rightfully belong to the person(s) who made such improvements, which may be subject to compensation when taken.

Second, as provided in the 2005 Constitutional Amendment of Zimbabwe—and argued by the respondent, the former colonial power 'has an obligation to pay compensation for agricultural land compulsorily acquired for resettlement'.[106] This will also be consistent with the CIL requirement for a lawful expropriation subject to compensation. However, the former colonial power never paid such compensation for expropriating indigenous farm lands. Thus, it was Zimbabwe's valid contention that if the colonial power had compulsorily acquired land for resettlement without compensation, the Zimbabwean government is equally justified to compulsorily acquire lands for resettlement without compensation, save for improvements on such lands which it has committed to compensate. This is the case of reversing an unlawful act that is not the state's intention to legitimise or protect when it signed up to its BITs.

However, Zimbabwe's regulatory autonomy as exercised in the 2005 Constitutional Amendment did not stop the Tribunal from ordering the respondent to return

---

[104] *Ibid.*, para. 576 ff.

[105] *Ibid.*, para. 93.

[106] *Ibid.*, para. 107.

the taken lands and pay 65 million (USD) in restitution to the Claimants. Like expected of any other ISDS tribunal, the von *Pezold* tribunal simply interpreted the 'law as it is'. While recognising that the challenged government measures have a historical root of indigenous oppression and deprivation of human rights, the tribunal correctly reiterated that it is a tribunal constituted to adjudicate the dispute in accordance with the ICSID convention and the applicable law, which does not include international human rights law on the rights of the indigenous people.[107] Undoubtedly, the protection of human rights is critical to the sustainable development of any state.

The von *Pezold*, *Foresti*, and *Biwater* cases so far discussed are classic examples of how African states have faced undesirable consequences in ISDS for pursuing SD objectives in conflict with the unqualified IIA guarantees of covered investors. Notably, one cannot fault an ISDS tribunal for merely interpreting the terms of an IIA guarantee as agreed upon by the contracting parties. The fault lies with the states that commit to broad substantive IIA guarantees without the necessary qualifications to safeguard their regulatory interests in pursuit of the state's unique sustainable development objectives.

Without the necessary qualifications to protect their regulatory interests and accommodate their distinctive sustainable development goals in old-generation IIAs, African states find themselves constrained by the very agreements meant to foster economic growth and development, potentially hindering their ability to achieve their unique development objectives.

3.1.2   Failure to Ensure Consistent and Correct Interpretation of Treaty Standards

Amongst the several shortcomings of the traditional ISDS system that have manifested over the years, the lack of consistency in arbitral decision-making is one major displeasure to all stakeholders necessitating a call for reform.[108]

Notably, the desire for consistent treaty interpretation is not intended to disregard the inherent differences in the IIAs being interpreted by arbitral tribunals. The very fact that every IIA independently pursues its own aims and objectives is enough justification for divergent outcomes, notwithstanding similarities with one another.[109] As observed in the UNCITRAL Working Group III reform discussions, divergent interpretations of similar treaty provisions may be justified for being in harmony with Article 31–33 of the VCLT, or justified by the relevant facts and

---

[107] *Ibid.*, para. 2 ff.

[108] See, UNCITRAL, *Possible Reform of Investor-State Dispute Settlement (ISDS): Consistency and Related Matters*: Note by the Secretariat of 28/8/2018, A/CN.9/WG.III/WP.150, para. 4 ff.

[109] Alschner (2022), p. 231.

evidence before a tribunal.[110] Therefore, while consistency is required, correctness (i.e. accuracy) of ISDS decisions to the applicable law and facts to a dispute is the ultimate objective.[111] The lack of consistency in treaty interpretation is only considered problematic when an identical or similar treaty standard or the same rule of customary international law is interpreted differently without a justifiable ground.[112]

Today, several investment cases have generated divergent interpretations of identical or similar treaty standards (substantive and procedural),[113] which consequently questions their accuracy. While recognising that this challenge is not unique to Africa but a global concern. The Afrocentric nature of this thesis warrants considering some specific disputes where inconsistent ISDS decisions have thrived within the African continent.

3.1.2.1   Inconsistent Interpretation of the FPS Standard

As seen in Chap. 2, the FPS standard is one of the most commonly invoked substantive guarantees against African states in ISDS proceedings. Notably, this is also one standard that is infamous for its conflicting jurisprudence. Following its CIL root, the FPS standard obliges a host state to offer police protection, through the

---

[110] UNCITRAL, *Possible Reform of Investor-State Dispute Settlement (ISDS): Consistency and Related Matters*: Note by the Secretariat of 28/8/2018, A/CN.9/WG.III/WP.150, para. 6.

[111] *Ibid.*, para. 8.

[112] *See in this regard,* UNCITRAL, *Report of Working Group III (Investor-State Dispute Settlement Reform)* of 14/5/2018, A/CN.9/935, para. 21.

[113] See, for example, tribunals reaching divergent conclusions on the content of FET, on one hand (interpreting FET broadly): *Metalclad Corporation v. The United Mexican States*, ICSID Case No. ARB(AF)/97/1, Award (30 August 2000); *Técnicas Medioambientales Tecmed, S.A. v. The United Mexican States*, ICSID Case No. ARB (AF)/00/2, Award (29 May 2003); *William Ralph Clayton, William Richard Clayton, Douglas Clayton, Daniel Clayton and Bilcon of Delaware Inc. v. Government of Canada*, UNCITRAL, PCA Case No. 2009-04, Award on Jurisdiction and Liability (17 March 2015); on the other hand, (interpreting FET narrowly), see: *Waste Management Inc. v United States ("Number 2")*, ICSID Case No. ARB(AF)/00/3, Award (30 April 2004); *Saluka Investments B.V. v. Czech Republic*, UNCITRAL, Partial Award (17 March 2006); *Invesmart v. Czech Republic*, UNCITRAL, Award (26 June 2009); or see regarding divergent interpretation on the "Umbrella Clause", on one hand (broad interpretation): *Société Générale de Surveillance S.A. v. The Republic of Paraguay*, ICSID Case No. ARB/07/29, Award (10 February 2012); *EDF International S.A., SAUR International S.A. and León Participaciones Argentinas S.A. v. The Republic of Argentina*, ICSID Case No. ARB/03/23, Award (11 June 2012); on the other hand, (interpreting the umbrella clause narrowly, see: *SGS Societe Generale de Surveillance S.A. v. Islamic Republic of Pakistan*, ICSID Case No. ARB/01/13, Decision of the Tribunal on Objections to Jurisdiction (6 August 2003); *SGS Societe Generale de Surveillance S.A. v. Republic of the Philippines*, ICSID Case No. ARB/02/6, Decision of the Tribunal on Objections to Jurisdiction (29 January 2004); *Bureau Veritas, Inspection, Valuation, Assessment and Control, BIVAC B.V. v. The Republic of Paraguay*, ICSID Case No. ARB/07/9, Decision of the Tribunal on Objections to Jurisdiction (29 May 2009); See further on this, UNCITRAL, *Possible Reform of Investor-State Dispute Settlement (ISDS): Consistency and Related Matters*: Note by the Secretariat of 28/8/2018, A/CN.9/WG.III/WP.150, para. 15 ff; Montineri (2021), p. 165 ff.

physical protection of an investor and its assets against third party interference ($\rightarrow$ Sect. 2.3). This traditional understanding denotes two factors regarding the scope of the FPS standard:

- *First*, it is limited to police protection through the **physical protection** of an investor and/or its assets;
- *Second*, it is limited to state prevention of harmful acts **from third parties** (private citizens) on an investor and/or its assets.

Regarding the first factor established under CIL, arbitral tribunals have held that save a treaty specifies otherwise, the FPS standard does not extend beyond physical protection.[114] Therefore, protecting the physical integrity of an investor and its assets is the sole objective of the FPS standard.[115] On the second factor, arbitral tribunals have also held that the FPS duty does not cover damages directly attributable to state organs, but is limited to damages attributable to third-party interference that the host state failed to diligently prevent.[116]

However, notwithstanding treaty silence, several ISDS tribunals have also held that the FPS duty extends beyond physical security e.g. to legal security.[117] Additionally, that the standard is not limited to failure to prevent unlawful harm attributable to third-parties but extends to state actions and inactions directly attributable to state organs,[118] resulting in unlawful harm to an investor and/or its assets. This

---

[114] *Indian Metals & Ferro Alloys Ltd v. Indonesia*, PCA Case No. 2015-40, Award (29.03.2019), para. 267; *Siemens A.G. v. The Argentine Republic*, ICSID Case No. ARB/02/8, Award (06.01.2007), para. 303.

[115] *Gold Reserve Inc. v. Venezuela*, ICSID Case No. ARB(AF)/09/1, Award (22.09.2014), para. 622 f; *Saluka Investments BV v. Czech Republic*, UNCITRAL, Partial Award (17.03.2006), para. 483 f; *AWG Group Ltd. v. Argentina*, UNCITRAL, Decision on Liability (30.07.2010), paras. 179 f; *BG Group Plc. v. Argentina*, UNCITRAL Case, Final Award (24.12.2007), para. 324.

[116] *El Paso Energy International Company v. Argentina*, ICSID Case No. ARB/03/15, Award (31.10.2011), paras. 521 ff; *Mobil Exploration and Development Inc. Suc. Argentina and Mobil Argentina S.A. v. Argentina*, ICSID Case No. ARB/04/16, Decision on Jurisdiction and Liability (10.04.2013). paras. 999 ff; *Ulysseas, Inc. v. Ecuador*, UNCITRAL Case, Final Award (12.06.2012), paras. 272–274; *Vannessa Ventures Ltd. v. Venezuela*, ICSID Case No. ARB(AF) 04/6, Award (16.01.2013), para. 223; *Jospeh Houben v. Burundi*, ICSID Case No. ARB/13/7, Award (12.01.2016). para. 157; *Mercer International Inc. v. Canada*, ICSID Case No. ARB(AF)/ 12/3, Award (06.03.2018), para. 7.80; *Koch Minerals Sàrl and Koch Nitrogen International Sàrl v. Venezuela*, ICSID Case No. ARB/11/19, Award (30.10.2017), para. 8.46.

[117] *De Sutter and others v. Madagascar (II)*, ICSID Case No. ARB/17/18, Award (17.04.2020), para. 299; *Reinhard Hans Unglaube v. Costa Rica*, ICSID Case No. ARB/09/20, Award (16.05.2012), para. 281; *Levy de Levi v. Peru*, ICSID Case No. ARB/10/17, Award (26.02.2014), para. 406; *National Grid PLC v. Argentina*, UNCITRAL, Award (03.11.2008), para. 189; *Azurix Corp. v. Argentina*, ICSID Case No. ARB/01/12, Award (14 July 2006), para. 408.

[118] *CME Czech Republic B.V. v. Czech Republic*, UNCITRAL, Partial Award (13 September 2001), para. 613; *Peter de Sutter and Kristof De Sutter c. Republic of Madagascar II*, ICSID Case No. ARB/17/18, Award (17 April 2020), para. 303; *Global Telecom Holding S.A.E. v. Canada*, ICSID Case No. ARB/16/16, Award (27 March 2020), para. 664; *Achmea B.V. (formerly Eureko B. V.) v. Slovak Republic I*, PCA Case No. 2008-13, Opinion of the European Court of Justice Advocate General Wathelet (19 September 2017), para. 211; *Frontier Petroleum Services*

conflicting interpretation of the scope of the FPS standard has played out in a number of ISDS awards involving African states. In this regard, a good reference point is the Libyan experience in *Way2B v. Libya*[119] and *Cengiz v. Libya*[120] cases. Both FPS claims arose against the backdrop of the Libyan civil war.

3.1.2.1.1   Way2B ACE v. Libya

In a yet unpublished decision, reported by the Investment Arbitration Reporter ('IA*Reporter*'),[121] this case was brought by a Portuguese claimant (Way2B ACE), a special purpose vehicle created for the purpose of securing and performing construction contracts in Libya. In 2008, Way2B ACE was awarded two construction contracts by Libya's Organization for Development of Administrative Centres (ODAC) to design and construct two university complexes (Al-Khams and Qaryounis project). Out of the two sites allocated for both projects, the claimant only had access to the Al-Khams site, where it had commenced work but discontinued in late 2010 due to unresolved issues with ODAC.[122]

In early 2011, the Libyan civil war broke out forcing the claimant and its personnel to evacuate the Al-Khams site. Afterward, the claimant alleged the Al-Khams site was pillaged leading to the loss of its assets on the site. In February 2011, the claimant sent out an invoice for its work done on the Al-Khams project which Libya failed to honour. This failure eventually triggered the cancellation of the contract by the claimant and the institution of an arbitral claim against Libya before an ICC tribunal. Amongst the several BIT claims of Way2B ACE was the breach of the FPS standard provided in Article 3(2) of the Libya-Portugal BIT (2003):

> **Investments made by investors of one of the Parties** in the territory of the other Party in accordance with its laws and regulations **shall enjoy full protection and security in the territory of the latter**.

To ascertain the scope of Libya's FPS duty under the above provision, first, the tribunal followed the view that FPS clauses are "widely interpreted to extend to **tangible property only**".[123] This narrow interpretation suggests the tribunal understood Libya's FPS guarantee under the BIT as limited to physical protection since it

---

Ltd. v. Czech Republic, UNCITRAL, Final Award (12 November 2010), para. 265; *Compañía de Aguas del Aconquija S.A. and Vivendi Universal S.A. v. Argentine Republic*, ICSID Case No. ARB/97/3, Award (20 August 2007), para. 7.4.16.

[119] *Way2B ACE v. State of Libya*, ICC Case No. 20971/MCP/DDA, Award (24 May 2018).

[120] *Cengiz İnşaat Sanayi ve Ticaret A.S v. Libya*, ICC Case No. 21537/ZF/AYZ, Award (7 November 2018).

[121] IA*Reporter*, *Way2B ACE v. Libya* (8 January 2019), https://www.iareporter.com/arbitration-cases/way2b-ace-v-libya/

[122] *Ibid.*

[123] *Ibid.*

can only be directed toward tangible assets. As a result, the tribunal found the FPS claim by Way2B ACE appeared not actionable because its BIT-protected investments are mainly contractual rights (intangible assets).[124] Notably, in another conclusion that differed significantly from that reached in the *Cengiz* tribunal award discussed below, the *Way2B ACE* tribunal held that Libya's FPS duty is a due diligence obligation to protect investors against physical damage caused by **third parties,** and not acts directly attributable to the state.[125]

While the above conclusions would have sufficed to dismiss the FPS claim on the merits, ultimately, the dismissal of the FPS claim rested on the tribunal's assessment of the due diligence duty owed by Libya. The tribunal adopted a view, consistent with some other tribunals,[126] that the host state's due diligence duty must be measured against the available resources at the state's disposal.[127] This includes the political and economic conditions prevalent in that state.[128] Upon this standard of review, the tribunal concluded that Way2B ACE had not discharged its burden of proof that Libya failed to perform its FPS duty, and thereby dismissed the claim.

In contrast, the tribunal's decision in *Cengiz v. Libya*, which emerged a few months later and shared a similar background to the *Way2B ACE* case, had a different understanding of Libya's FPS duty under the applicable BIT.

3.1.2.1.2 Cengiz v. Libya[129]

Like Way2B ACE, Cengiz is another construction entity—but of Turkish origin,[130] which in 2008 entered into a pair of construction contracts with the Libyan Housing and Infrastructure Board ("HIB"). Cengiz contracted to design and construct housing and related infrastructure e.g. roads, electricity distribution, water supply, etc. in certain remote regions south of Libya i.e. the Wadi Al Hayat (WAH) and Sebha regions.[131] Due to the remote location of the construction sites, the claimant had to

---

[124] *Ibid.*

[125] See, IA*Reporter, Cengiz v. Libya* (9 September 2019), https://www.iareporter.com/articles/revealed-in-cengiz-v-libya (contrasting the tribunals FPS interpretation with the narrow reading adopted in *Way2B v. Libya*).

[126] *Pantechniki S.A. Contractors & Engineers (Greece) v. The Republic of Albania*, ICSID Case No. ARB/07/21, Award (30 July 2009), para. 82; *Ampal-American Israel Corporation and others v. Arab Republic of Egypt*, ICSID Case No. ARB/12/11, Decision on Liability and Heads of Loss (21 February 2017), para. 244; See also, Newcombe and Paradell (2009), p. 310 (commenting on the modified objective standard); Blanco (2019), p. 449.

[127] IA*Reporter, Cengiz v. Libya* (9 September 2019), https://www.iareporter.com/articles/revealed-in-cengiz-v-libya

[128] Reinisch and Schreuer (2020), p. 584, para 188.

[129] *Cengiz İnşaat Sanayi ve Ticaret A.S v. Libya*, ICC Case No. 21537/ZF/AYZ, Award (7 November 2018).

[130] *Ibid.*, para. 105.

[131] *Ibid.*, paras. 122, 124, 136.

first build work camps including, dormitories, offices, and other work facilities, and erected temporary industrial facilities for the production of construction materials.[132]

Subsequently, construction work began in both project regions but was soon halted by the breakout of the Libyan civil war in February 2011. As of March 2011, both the WAH and Shebha projects had reached 9% and 12% project completion respectively.[133] Between mid-March to April 2011, the claimant evacuated its personnel from both the WAH and Shebha project camps due to the deteriorating security situation in the country, leaving behind a skeletal security detail.[134] In August 2011, a group of armed individuals under the command of senior Libyan military/police commanders invaded and looted the claimant's WAH and Sheba project camps.[135] Between October 2011 and early 2012, the security situation in Libya seemed to improve, and new arrangements were reached with HIB to allow the claimant to resume work at the project sites. However, this attempt soon collapsed as Libya descended into a full-blown civil war by March 2012, sparked by the power struggle among various militia groups that had emerged in Libya after the deposition of the former president, Muammar Gadhafi.

Ultimately, the claimant never had the opportunity to return to its work camps to resume work. Both the WAH and Sebha work camps were either totally destroyed and looted or remained outside the control of the claimant.[136] These events eventually informed the claimants BIT claims against Libya. Amongst the multiple BIT claims against Libya was the failure to accord the claimant FPS according to Article 2(2) of the Libya-Turkey BIT (2009) which provides:

> Investments of investors of each Contracting Party [. . .] **shall enjoy full protection in the territory of the other Contracting Party** [. . .].

In contending against its liability under the above provision, Libya argued in line with the CIL roots of the FPS standard that '[a]cts attributable to the state cannot be examined from the angle of FPS'.[137] Thus, since the alleged invasion and looting of the work camps occurred under the command of government forces (not *third-party*—private citizens), this places the claim outside the scope of the FPS standard. In its decision, the tribunal rejected this attempt by Libya to constrain the FPS standard to harmful acts by third-parties. According to the tribunal, the perpetrators of such unlawful interference are irrelevant as— '*it could be the State itself, (including agencies, groups, entities or other organs whose actions can be attributed to the*

---

[132] *Ibid.*, para. 148 ff.

[133] *Ibid.*, paras. 154, 161.

[134] *Ibid.*, paras. 186, 190.

[135] *Ibid.*, para. 192 ff.

[136] *Ibid.*, para. 220.

[137] *Ibid.*, para. 374.

State)'.[138] Precisely, the tribunal held that Libya's FPS duty under the BIT entailed a twofold obligation:[139]

- A negative obligation to refrain from directly harming the investment by acts of violence attributable to the State, plus;
- A positive obligation to prevent that third parties cause physical damage to such investment.

Noteworthy that, the FPS clause in Article 2(2) of the Libya-Turkey BIT (2009) is of no material difference to the FPS clause under Article 3(2) of the Libya-Portugal BIT (2003) applicable in the *Way2B* case. Nevertheless, as opposed to the *Way2B* tribunal, the *Cengiz* tribunal chose to follow a broader interpretation of Libya's FPS duty as extending to protection against harm inflicted by both state and non-state actors. Upon this broad reading, Libya was found in violation of the FPS standard, for actions directly attributable to the state which caused physical harm to the claimant.

The impact of this inconsistent interpretation on Libya is telling in the final outcome of two reported cases above. For instance, the *Way2B* tribunal did not consider the perpetrators of the unlawful interference as irrelevant as the *Cengiz* tribunal did. For the *Way2B ACE* tribunal, failure to ascertain the identity of the third parties responsible for the harm suffered proved fatal to the Claimant's FPS claim.[140] However, the *Cengiz* tribunal's apparent conclusion that the perpetrators of an unlawful interference are irrelevant broadens the state's margin of liability for FPS violation. These conflicting outcomes create an environment of uncertainty for both the state and private investors as to the scope of protection provided by the FPS standard.

Furthermore, although the *Cengiz* tribunal was silent on the point emphasised by the *Way2B ACE* tribunal that the FPS standard applies to 'tangible property only' (→ Sect. 3.1.2.1), the *Biwater v. Tanzania*[141] tribunal's decision is a notable African ISDS award that does not share this view. The FPS claim in that case was brought under Article 2(2) of the Tanzania-UK BIT (1994),[142] which as often the case exhibited no material difference from the FPS formulation under Article 3(2) of the Libya-Portugal BIT (2003). According to the *Biwater* tribunal, *'the content of the standard may extend to matters other than physical security'.*[143] Additionally, the

---

[138] *Ibid.*, para. 403.

[139] *Ibid.*

[140] IA*Reporter*, *Way2B ACE v. Libya* (8 January 2019), https://www.iareporter.com/arbitration-cases/way2b-ace-v-libya/

[141] *Biwater Gauff (Tanzania) Limited v. United Republic of Tanzania*, ICSID Case No. ARB/05/22, Award (24 July 2008).

[142] Article 2(2) of the Tanzania—United Kingdom BIT (1994), entered into force 2 August 1996, ('[i]nvestments of nationals or companies of each Contracting Party [. . .] shall enjoy full protection and security in the territory of the other Contracting Party').

[143] *Biwater Gauff (Tanzania) Limited v. United Republic of Tanzania*, ICSID Case No. ARB/05/22, Award (24 July 2008), para. 729.

tribunal rejected the contention that the FPS standard is limited to a state's failure to prevent harm by third parties, but rather it extends to actions taken by organs and representatives of the state itself.[144]

Overall, it can be said that despite the textual similarity shared across IIAs incorporating the FPS standard, the scope of this standard remains one of the most unsettled in ISDS jurisprudence. However, one area that at least appears settled is the standard of review. Investment tribunals have been unanimous in holding that the FPS standard imposes no strict liability duty. Meaning it is not an absolute duty,[145] but one of **due diligence** in preventing harm, or bringing the perpetrators of harm to justice.[146] However, in contrast to the *Way2B* decision, the degree of due diligence owed is not always linked to the available resources at the disposal of a state. Therefore, not all tribunals agree that the degree of due diligence may vary from state to state.[147]

3.1.2.2 Inconsistent Interpretation of the War Loss Clause

Although the 'war loss clause' ('WLC') is a common provision in IIAs,[148] it is not a commonly invoked standard in ISDS history like the FET, expropriation, or FPS standards. This is quite understandable, since by its very nature, it entails a duty

---

[144] *Ibid.*, 728.

[145] *CME Czech Republic v. Czech Republic*, UNCITRAL, Partial Award (13 September 2001), para. 353*; Saluka Investments BV (The Netherlands) v. Czech Republic*, PCA Case No. 2001-04, Partial Award (17 March 2006), para. 484; *Plama Consortium Limited v. Republic of Bulgaria*, ICSID Case No. ARB/03/24, Award (27 August 2008), para. 181; *Waguih Elie George Siag and Clorinda Vecchi v. The Arab Republic of Egypt*, ICSID Case No. ARB/05/15, Award (1 June 2009), para. 447; *Mohammad Ammar Al-Bahloul v. The Republic of Tajikistan*, SCC Case No. V (064/2008), Partial Award onJurisdiction and Liability (2 September 2009), para. 246; *Suez and Interagua v. The Argentine Republic*, ICSID Case No. ARB/03/17, Decision on Liability (30 July 2010), para. 157 f; *Frontier Petroleum Services Ltd. v. The Czech Republic*, UNCITRAL, Final Award (12 November 2010), para. 269 f; *Spyridon Roussalis v. Romania*, ICSID Case No. ARB/06/1, Award (7 December 2011), para. 322; *Vannessa Ventures Ltd. v. Bolivarian Republic of Venezuela*, ICSID Case No. ARB(AF)04/6, Award (16 January 2013), para. 223; *Tulip Real Estate and Development Netherlands B.V. v. Republic of Turkey*, ICSID Case No. ARB/11/28, Award (10 March 2014), para. 430; *Mobil Exploration and Development Inc. Suc. Argentina and Mobil Argentina S.A. v. Argentine Republic*, ICSID Case No. ARB/04/16, Decision on Jurisdiction and Liability (10 April 2013), para. 1002; *Hesham T. M. Al Warraq v. Republic of Indonesia*, UNCITRAL, Final Award (15 December 2014), para. 625; *Bernhard von Pezold and others v. Republic of Zimbabwe*, ICSID Case No. ARB/10/15, Award (28 July 2015), para. 596; *MNSS v. Montenegro*, ICSID Case No. ARB(AF)/12/8, Award (4 May 2016), para. 351.

[146] *Sergei Paushok, CJSC Golden East Company and CJSC Vostokneftegaz Company v. The Government of Mongolia*, UNCITRAL, Award on Jurisdiction and Liability (28 April 2001), para. 324 f.

[147] *Glamis Gold v. United States of America*, UNCITRAL, Award (June 8, 2009), para. 615; See further, Junngam (2018), p. 56.

[148] Deroche (2020), p. 37; Schreuer (2019) p. 13 f; Spears and Agius (2019), p. 289; UNCTAD (1998), p. 73.

triggered only under exceptional circumstances. Primarily, the WLC is aimed at regulating the treatment of foreign investors in case their investments suffer losses due to war or other civil disturbances in the host state.[149] Given this primary aim, the actual effect of the WLC on other treaty guarantees, especially the FPS clause, has been a subject of controversy and conflicting interpretation by ISDS tribunals.

The point of division lays in whether the WLC is a *lex specialis* treaty clause. Meaning a specialised treaty term that prevails over a general one.[150] If interpreted as *lex specialis*, the WLC then amounts to a specialised compensation regime that displaces compensation for other treaty violations which occurred under the special circumstances stipulated in the WLC—such as: *war, revolution, insurrection, state of national emergency or other civil disturbances*. While some authorities argue that the WLC constitutes a special regime for compensation over any treaty breach once the stipulated situations therein exist,[151] others disagree—holding that the WLC does not function to exculpate a state from the liability or compensation due for violating its treaty obligations.[152] In Africa, these divergent views are particularly evident in ISDS awards that emanated within the context of the Algerian and Libyan civil war.

Starting with the **LESI v. Algeria**[153] (*'LESI'*) case, the claimants, who are of Italian nationality had instituted the claim over a failed contract to construct a water supply dam in the city of Algiers. The dam construction had begun in 1992 but was hampered by several encumbrances which included several attacks on the claimant's facilities and personnel as Algeria descended into a state of civil war at the time.[154] The contract was ultimately terminated by Algeria for *force majeure* after the major project sponsor (African Developmental Bank) demanded that a new bidding process be issued for the dam's construction.[155] Although the claimant was promised compensation for the cancelled contract and invited to participate in the new tender process, it declined participation. Eventually, the claimant initiated the ICSID arbitration against Algeria for the loss of its investment.

---

[149] Pérez-Aznar (2017), p. 697.

[150] *Venezuela Holdings et al. v. Venezuela*, ICSID Case No. ARB/07/27, Award (09.10.2014), para. 243 ff; *ConcoPhillips Petrozuata B.V. & others v. Venezuela*, ICSID Case No. ARB/07/30, Decision on Jurisdiction and Merits (03.09.2013), paras. 309, 315; *Brannigan and McBride v. the United Kingdom*, 26 May 1993, European Court of Human Rights, Series A, No. 258-B, para. 76.

[151] Pérez-Aznar (2017), pp. 705, 713, 715; Hildebrand (2021), p. 1009 f.

[152] *BG Group Plc v. Argentina*, UNCITRAL, Final Award (24.12.2007), para. 381 f; *Sempra Energy International v. Argentina*, ICSID Case No. ARB/02/16, Award (28.09.2007), para. 362 f; *Güris v Syria*, ICC Case No. 21845/ZF/AYZ, Final Award (31.08.2020), para. 230 f; *EDF International S.A and others. v. Argentina*, ICSID Case No. ARB/03/23, Award (11.06.2012), para. 1162.

[153] *L.E.S.I. S.p.A. and ASTALDI S.p.A. v. République Algérienne Démocratique et Populaire*, ICSID Case No. ARB/05/3, Award (12 November 2008).

[154] *Ibid.*, para. 11 ff.

[155] *Ibid.*, para. 35.

Amongst the claimant's BIT claims was the breach of Article 4(1) of the Algeria-Italy BIT (1991) which contained a typical FPS clause. According to the claimant, Algeria's negligence in providing FPS rendered it impossible to perform the contract, which affected the management and enjoyment of its investment.[156] In response to this claim, Algeria contended that the FPS claim is inadmissible by application of the WLC since at the material time the state found itself in one of the situations stipulated under Article 4(5) of the BIT i.e. an 'armed conflict', or in a 'state of national emergency'.[157]

Aligning with the respondent's contention, the tribunal held that Article 4(1) and Article 4(5) of the BIT cannot apply cumulatively when any of the events enumerated in the WLC is at play, otherwise Article 4(5) will be deprived of any meaning.[158] The tribunal reasoned that when the situations stipulated in the WLC exist, like war or other armed conflict, a state's capacity to fulfil its treaty mandate such as FPS becomes weakened. In such exceptional circumstances, Article 4(5) permits a derogation from the general FPS duty by only requiring the state to provide investors who have suffered losses due to such civil disturbances—treatment not less favourable than that accorded to its own nationals or those of most favoured nations who also suffered losses due to a similar circumstance.[159] Applying the facts, the tribunal found that the claimant's losses fell under the stipulated situations in Article 4(5) and there is no evidence that the claimant received treatment less favourable than those the respondent accorded to its nationals or that of a third-state. Accordingly, the FPS claim was dismissed.

About a decade after the *LESI* tribunal's interpretation of the WLC, a series of conflicting interpretations followed within the context of multiple investor claims brought against Libya for investment losses suffered during the Libyan civil war: ***Way2B ACE v. Libya,***[160] ***Öztaş Construction v. Libya,***[161] ***Cengiz v. Libya,***[162] ***Guris v. Libya,***[163] **and** ***Strabag v. Libya.***[164] Noteworthy that, all these cases involved:

– investor claims resulting from losses suffered due to the outbreak of a civil war;
– the invoked BITs contained similarly worded WLC with no material difference to that in *LESI*;
– most importantly, they involved the same respondent-state i.e. Libya.

---

[156] *Ibid.*, paras. 166–168.

[157] *Ibid.*, para. 170.

[158] *Ibid.*, para. 174.

[159] *Ibid.*, para. 174 ff.

[160] *Way2B ACE v. State of Libya*, ICC Case No. 20971/MCP/DDA, Award (24 May 2018).

[161] *Öztaş Construction, Construction Materials Trading Inc. v. Libya*, ICC Arbitration No. 21603/ZF/AYZ, Award (14 June 2018).

[162] *Cengiz İnşaat Sanayi ve* Ticaret A.S v. Libya, ICC Case No. 21537/ZF/AYZ, Award (7 November 2018).

[163] *Güriş İnşaat ve Mühendislik A.Ş. v. Libya*, ICC Case No. 22137/ZF/AYZ, Partial Award on Jurisdiction and Liability (4 Feb 2020).

[164] *Strabag SE v. Libya*, ICSID Case No. ARB(AF)/15/1, Award (29 June 2020).

Despite these factual similarities, the tribunals' disagreed on whether the WLC constitutes a *lex specialis* provision excluding Libya's international liability for investor losses that occurred due to the outbreak of a civil war or other stipulated situations under the applicable WLC.

First off, in contrast to the *LESI* decision, the tribunal in *Way2B ACE v. Libya*[165] (*'WAY2B'*), with facts earlier presented (→ Sect. 3.1.2.1) held that the WLC provided in Article 7 of the Libya-Portugal BIT (2003) do not constitute a *lex specialis* provision that exculpates Libya from liability for failing its treaty duties (including FPS) in times of war.[166] Upon this ruling, the tribunal proceeded to assess the compliance of Libya with its FPS duty. Eventually, on the preponderance of evidence, the tribunal rejected the claimant's FPS claim for failing to establish a breach of the standard against Libya.[167]

However, 3 weeks after the *Way2B* tribunal's award, the tribunal in *Öztaş Construction v. Libya*[168] (*'Öztaş'*) appeared to have adopted a contrary view of the former tribunal's interpretation of the WLC. This dispute had arisen within the context of a failed contract entered between the claimant and the Libyan Investment Development Company (LIDCO). The contract project involved the development of a water supply and transport system which was disrupted by the outbreak of the Libyan civil war in early 2011. In March 2013, the contracting parties reached a mutual termination of the contract, with an agreement obliging Libya to make four tranches of payments to the claimant between May to November 2013.[169] Libya effected none of these payments which ultimately led to the ICC arbitration against the state.

In ruling on Libya's violation of Article 2(2) of the Libya-Turkey BIT (2009) entailing the 'FET, FPS, and Non-Impairment standard', the tribunal's majority opined that the WLC under Article 5 of the BIT is:

> [T]he **proper and only remedy** for Claimant in respect of such losses as it may have suffered as a result of the Libyan Revolution if the conditions of Article 5 are met. **Article 2.2 is not the proper remedy for such losses**.[170]

By this ruling, the tribunal dismissed the applicability of Article 2(2) since the claims for compensation occurred under one of the circumstances stipulated in Article 5 of the BIT:

> Investors of either Contracting Party whose investments suffer losses in the territory of the other Contracting Party owing to war, insurrection, civil disturbance or other similar events shall be accorded by such other Contracting Party treatment no less favourable than that

---

[165] *Way2B ACE v. State of Libya*, ICC Case No. 20971/MCP/DDA, Award (24 May 2018).

[166] See, IA*Reporter*, *Way2B ACE v. Libya* (8 January 2019), https://www.iareporter.com/arbitration-cases/way2b-ace-v-libya/

[167] *Ibid.*

[168] *Öztaş Construction, Construction Materials Trading Inc. v. Libya*, ICC Arbitration No. 21603/ZF/AYZ, Award (14 June 2018).

[169] *Ibid.*, para. 63.

[170] *Ibid.*, para. 167.

accorded to its own investors or to investors of any third country, whichever is the most favourable treatment, as regards any measures it adopts in relation to such losses.

Pursuant to the above provision, the tribunal concluded that the claimant was only entitled to receive compensation for its war losses not less than what Libya accords to its own nationals or those of a third state who suffered losses due to the war. Subsequently, it found that Öztaş had not received any less favourable treatment than what Libya accorded to its own nationals or those of any third state for their war losses.[171]

The *Öztaş* tribunal's reasoning clearly departs from that in the *Way2B* case but aligns with that in *LESI* that the WLC is a *lex specialis* provision intended to govern compensation for investment losses that occur in a state of war or other civil unrest. For losses under such exceptional circumstances, the state is only expected not to discriminate in the treatment or relief it offers to foreign investors vis-à-vis its own nationals or those of a third state.

About 5 months post *Öztaş* award, the interplay between Article 2(2) and Article 5 of the Libya-Turkey BIT (2009) was again up for interpretation in *Cengiz v. Libya*[172] (*'Cengiz'*). Given the facts of the case earlier summarised (→ Sect. 3.1.2.1), Libya had argued that Cengiz was '*precluded from invoking Article 2 in respect of losses allegedly caused by war, insurrection or other similar events*', otherwise Article 5 will be meaningless.[173] The claimant objected to this view, asserting that Article 5 does not constitute a *lex specialis* provision that displaces Libya's Article 2 obligations.[174]

In contrast to the *Öztaş* tribunal's decision on **the same legal question** and the **same treaty provisions** up for interpretation, the *Cengiz* tribunal decided that Article 2(2) and Article 5 of the BIT are different in scope making the application of the *lex specialis* principle unwarranted.[175] The tribunal read the contended treaty provisions as dealing with different subject matters creating independent obligations. Consequently, the application of one cannot amount to a derogation from another.[176]

Besides the *Cengiz* decision, the tribunals in subsequent awards against Libya, such as **Güris v. Libya**[177] (*'Güris'*) **and Strabag v. Libya**[178] (*'Strabag'*) also disagreed with the *Öztaş* decision that the WLC is *lex specialis*. In the unpublished

---

[171] *Ibid.*, para. 167.

[172] *Cengiz İnşaat Sanayi ve Ticaret A.S v. Libya*, ICC Case No. 21537/ZF/AYZ, Award (7 November 2018).

[173] *Ibid.*, para. 351.

[174] *Ibid.*, para. 352.

[175] *Ibid.*, para. 354.

[176] *Ibid.*, para. 357 f.

[177] *Güriş İnşaat ve Mühendislik A.Ş. v. Libya*, ICC Case No. 22137/ZF/AYZ, Partial Award on Jurisdiction and Liability (4 Feb 2020).

[178] *Strabag SE v. Libya*, ICSID Case No. ARB(AF)/15/1, Award (29 June 2020).

but reported *Guris* award,[179] the tribunal rejected Libya's attempt to frame same Article 5 of the Libya-Turkey BIT (2009) as *lex specialis*. According to that tribunal, nothing in the Libya-Turkey BIT suggests the parties' intention to have Article 5 prevail over other treaty standards in difficult times.[180] In *Strabag*, ruling on a similarly worded WLC in Article 5 of the Libya-Austria BIT (2002), the tribunal found that the WLC does not have a preclusive effect as contended by Libya.[181] According to the tribunal, had the contracting parties intended such a result, they would have made this clear in the treaty.[182]

The cases explored above illustrate the challenges a state may encounter when faced with varying interpretations of its treaty obligations. While the analysis has primarily centered on Libya's struggles with the interpretation of the WLC by ISDS tribunals, it is crucial to understand that the uncertainty arising from the conflicting outcomes experienced by Libya is not unique to the North African state. All African states, as well as states across the globe, are potentially subject to this same uncertainty. The lack of clarity regarding the interaction between the WLC and other treaty guarantees permeates the majority of IIAs that incorporate the WLC, leaving them susceptible to conflicting interpretations.

3.1.2.3 Inconsistent Interpretation of the Umbrella Clause

The umbrella clause is primarily a treaty guarantee that requires each contracting party to respect the contractual undertakings it has entered with the nationals of the other contracting party.[183] Thus, once included in a treaty, the umbrella clause becomes a catch-all phrase that elevates non-treaty commitments (e.g. contractual) that the state has entered with an investor into treaty commitments that must be performed.[184]

Although not one of the most common treaty guarantees as those discussed in Chap. 2, the umbrella clause is yet a treaty guarantee that has found expression in numerous IIAs since the Abs-Shawcross Draft Convention on Investments Abroad of 1959. According to Article II of the 'Abs-Shawcross Draft', *'[e]ach Party shall at all times ensure the observance of any undertakings which it may have given in relation to investments made by nationals of any other Party'*.[185] In the same year,

---

[179] See, IA*Reporter, Güris v. Libya* (5 March 2020), https://www.iareporter.com/articles/analysis-tribunal-in-guris-v-libya

[180] *Ibid.*

[181] *Strabag SE v. Libya*, ICSID Case No. ARB(AF)/15/1, Award (29 June 2020), para. 224.

[182] *Ibid.*, para. 227.

[183] *Eureko B.V. v. Republic of Poland*, UNCITRAL, Partial Award and Dissenting Opinion (19 August 2005), para. 251.

[184] Cf. Reinisch and Schreuer (2020), p. 857, para. 2 (not limited to contractual obligations, may also be derived from unilateral acts and national legislation).

[185] See further on this, Sinclair (2004), p. 421.

the Germany–Pakistan BIT (1959) became the first BIT to include an umbrella clause that provided that: *'[e]ither Party shall observe any other obligation it may have entered into with regard to investments by nationals or companies of the other Party'*.[186] Since then, the umbrella clause has featured in several IIAs, including those contracted by African states post-independence.[187]

Like other treaty standards, the textual formulation of the umbrella clause is not uniform across treaties. While the variance has been used to justify divergent outcomes as to its effect,[188] some tribunals consider the different wordings as immaterial to justify divergent outcomes as to their meaning.[189] Additionally, whether the umbrella clause is treated as a substantive obligation or otherwise has been determined by where it is placed in the treaty.[190] However, regardless of the textual formulation and different interpretations that have emerged from this, the exact scope and effect of the umbrella clause remain widely debated, generating both a narrow and broad interpretation of the clause in arbitral practice.[191]

Given the above introduction, the following discussion is not meant to focus on the unsettled scope and effect of the umbrella clause,[192] but rather to show how this clause has been inconsistently applied in African-related disputes. For this, the *Strabag,*[193] *Güris,*[194] *and Way2B*[195] cases also serve as a good reference point, including *Consutel v. Algeria.*[196]

In *Strabag*, the dispute arose from several construction contracts signed by the claimant's local subsidiary (Al Hani) with three Libyan SOEs (i.e., Housing and Infrastructure Board (HIB), the Roads and Bridges Authority (RBA), and the

---

[186] Article 7 Germany-Pakistan BIT (1959), entered into force 28 April 1962; Reinisch and Schreuer (2020), p. 866, para. 34.

[187] See for examples: Article 3(4), Zimbabwe-Netherlands BIT (1996), entered into force 1 May 1998; Article 11 Libya-Switzerland BIT (2003), entered into force 28 April 2004; Article 2(2), Tanzania-United Kingdom BIT (1994), entered into force 2 August 1996; Article 12(2), Egypt-Finland BIT (2004), entered into force 5 February 2005; Article 2(4), Mozambique-Italy BIT (1998), entered into force 17 November 2003.

[188] See *Bureau Veritas* v. *Paraguay*, Decision of the Tribunal on Objections to Jurisdiction, 29 May 2009, para. 141; *Noble Ventures, Inc. v. Romania*, ICSID Case No. ARB/01/11, Award (12 October 2005), para. 56 ff.

[189] See, *El Paso* v. *Argentina*, Decision on Jurisdiction (27 April 2006), para. 70; *Pan American Energy* v. *Argentina* and *BP America Production Company* v. *Argentina*, Decision on Preliminary Objections (27 July 2006), para. 99.

[190] Yannaca-Small (2006), p. 9.

[191] See, UNCITRAL, *Possible Reform of Investor-State Dispute Settlement (ISDS): Consistency and Related Matters*: Note by the Secretariat of 28/8/2018, A/CN.9/WG.III/WP.150, paras. 16.

[192] See in this regard, Reinisch and Schreuer (2020), p. 928 ff.

[193] *Strabag SE v. Libya*, ICSID Case No. ARB(AF)/15/1, Award (29 June 2020).

[194] *Güriş İnşaat ve Mühendislik A.Ş. v. Libya*, ICC Case No. 22137/ZF/AYZ, Partial Award on Jurisdiction and Liability (4 Feb 2020).

[195] *Way2B ACE v. State of Libya*, ICC Case No. 20971/MCP/DDA, Award (24 May 2018).

[196] *Consutel Group S.p.A. in liquidazione v. People's Democratic Republic of Algeria*, PCA No. 2017-33, Final Award (3 Febraury 2020).

Transportation Projects Board (TPB)).[197] These contracts varied in particular but included obligations of payments and approval mechanisms for several road construction projects in Libya.[198] In 2011, as the contracts were in progress, with one in Benghazi completed, the Libyan civil war broke out causing a halt to construction works under other contracts. After the war, Al Hani signed certain agreements with TPB to resume works on three of its uncompleted contracts (i.e. Misurata, TIAR, and Garaboulli road contracts). Pursuant to this, TPB agreed to pay 50% of the amounts due for previously completed works and pay the balance within 6 months.[199] However, this agreement was never fully implemented putting Al Hani in a precarious financial situation that remained until the claim was submitted to arbitration.

Given the contractual origin of the dispute, a significant portion of the claimant's contention was based on Libya's breach of the umbrella clause under Article 8(1) of the Libya-Austria BIT (2002) which provided that:

> Each Contracting Party shall observe any obligation it may have entered into with regard to specific investments by investors of the other Contracting Party.

Relying on *Burlington Resources v. Ecuador*,[200] Libya contended *inter alia* that the umbrella clause cannot apply since the state was not privy to the contracts that were allegedly breached.[201] According to Libya, these contracts were entered *'with RBA, TPB or HIB all of which have their own legal personality, separate from the State'*, and carrying out commercial activities independently under Libyan law.[202] Objecting to this narrow interpretation, the claimant contended that Libya's privity argument has no basis under Article 8 of the BIT.[203] Moreover, that contracts entered into by Libyan public authorities are attributable to the state.[204]

In deciding the issue of whether the undertakings of RBA, TPB, and HIB can be attributed to Libya, the tribunal relied on Article 5 of the International Law Commission's Draft Articles on Responsibility of States for Internationally Wrongful Acts ("ILC Articles") and concluded that *'States may operate through parastatal entities, which exercise elements of governmental authority in place of State organs'.*[205] Applying this rule, the tribunal found that RBA, TPB, and HIB were mandated to carry out functions of important state interest normally exercised by state organs.[206] Additionally, the tribunal found that the SOEs where under the

---

[197] *Strabag SE v. Libya*, ICSID Case No. ARB(AF)/15/1, Award (29 June 2020), para. 56 ff.

[198] *Ibid.*, para. 61 ff.

[199] *Ibid.*, para. 89.

[200] *Burlington Resources Inc. v. Republic of Ecuador*, ICSID Case No. ARB/08/5, Decision on Liability (14 December 2012), para. 212 ff.

[201] *Strabag SE v. Libya*, ICSID Case No. ARB(AF)/15/1, Award (29 June 2020), para. 142.

[202] *Ibid.*, para. 143.

[203] *Ibid.*, para. 151.

[204] *Ibid.*, para. 152.

[205] *Ibid.*, para. 170.

[206] *Ibid.*, para. 173.

direction and control of the Libyan state, fulfilling the requirement of Article 8 ILC Articles for attributing their conduct (including the contracts) to Libya.[207] On this premise, the tribunal assumed jurisdiction over the umbrella clause claims and found Libya liable for a series of contractual defaults by its SOEs in violation of Article 8(1) of the BIT. In contrast, this decision conflicts with two earlier decisions on a similar issue involving Libya, i.e. *Güris v. Lybia,*[208] and *Way2B v. Lybia.*[209]

In *Guris*, the claimant, a construction company of Turkish origin had entered a series of construction contracts with the state-owned Organisation for the Development of Administrative Centres (ODAC).[210] The contracts covered three different projects related to the construction of a university, hospital, and public parks in Tripoli. Due to the outbreak of the Libyan civil war in 2011, construction works were halted. Between 2012 and 2014, work resumed on some projects after ODAC agreed to extensions of the contracts' original terms and effected some progress payments.[211] However, in 2014, work was again suspended after the resumption of armed hostilities in Libya. The construction projects never resumed afterward. Although the contracts were not terminated, all negotiation attempts to agree on work resumption and recoupment of rights due under the existing contracts failed.

In 2016, Guris initiated an ICC arbitration against Libya under the Libya-Turkey BIT (2009). In an attempt to hold Libya responsible for the contractual breaches of ODAC, the claimant invoked the BIT's most favoured nations (MFN) clause to import the umbrella clause under the Libya-Switzerland BIT (2003). Ultimately, the tribunal rejected the umbrella clause claim based on the determination that under Libyan law, ODAC is not a state organ but an entity independent of the Libyan government.[212] As such, Libya is not privy to the contracts with Guris. In contrast, however, the *Strabag* tribunal had held that questions as to who are the formal parties to a contract require a search beyond the local law.[213]

Conceivably, the factual nuances in the *Strabag* and *Guris* cases might have justified the divergent outcomes on the privity of Libya to the contracts at issue. However, as reported, the *Guris* tribunal's further clarification[214] that Libya will not become privy to the contracts even if ODAC's actions were attributable to the state is a fundamental departure from the *Strabag* decision, where the tribunal significantly

---

[207] *Ibid.*, para. 176 ff.

[208] *Güriş İnşaat ve Mühendislik A.Ş. v. Libya*, ICC Case No. 22137/ZF/AYZ, Partial Award on Jurisdiction and Liability (4 Feb 2020).

[209] *Way2B ACE v. State of Libya*, ICC Case No. 20971/MCP/DDA, Award (24 May 2018).

[210] See, IA*Reporter, Güris v. Libya* (5 March 2020), https://www.iareporter.com/articles/analysis-tribunal-in-guris-v-libya

[211] *Ibid.*

[212] *Ibid.*

[213] *Strabag SE v. Libya*, ICSID Case No. ARB(AF)/15/1, Award (29 June 2020), para. 168.

[214] See, IA*Reporter, Güris v. Libya* (5 March 2020), https://www.iareporter.com/articles/analysis-tribunal-in-guris-v-libya

relied on the rules of attribution in upholding the umbrella clause claim against Libya.[215]

Similarly, in *Way2B v. Libya* (→ Sect. 3.1.2.1) where the claimant also sought the liability of Libya for the contractual defaults of ODAC, the tribunal held that even if it could exercise jurisdiction over the claimant's umbrella clause claims under the Libya-Portugal BIT (2003), such must fail because the claimant's counterparty was ODAC—an independent legal entity whose undertakings are not attributable to the Libyan state.[216] Again, this tribunal reached the conclusion irrespective of the governmental objectives pursued by ODAC as the Libyan SOEs in the *Strabag* case likewise did.

Another case unrelated to Libya but noteworthy for its similarities to the Libyan cases discussed above is *Consutel v. Algeria*.[217] This dispute arose out of a partnership contract for the design and installation of a telephone network concluded between the claimant's Algerian subsidiary (Spec-Com Algérie) and an Algerian SOE (Algérie Télécom).[218] While the contract execution initially progressed without hindrance, a number of disagreements later arose under the partnership agreement, including Algérie Télécom's failure to honour payment invoices to Spec-Com Algérie.[219] Ultimately, the Spec-Com's project failed leading to the eventual bankruptcy of the claimant due to its huge financial exposure to the failed project. Consequently, the claimant initiated arbitration against Libya under the Algeria-Italy BIT (1991) for its losses.

Given the contractual origin of the dispute, majority of the claimant's contention was based on contractual breaches, as a result, the tribunal had to grapple *inter alia* with the question whether Algeria was privy to the partnership agreement through Algérie Télécom to trigger a possible umbrella clause breach. At first, the tribunal agreed that the claimant—through the BIT's MFN clause could avail itself of the umbrella clause under the Algeria-Switzerland BIT (2004).[220] However, for the tribunal, such efforts will still be futile for several reasons. These includes its finding that Algérie Télécom is an independent entity distinct from the state, whose contractual commitments cannot be deemed as state commitments within the meaning of the umbrella clause.[221] According to the tribunal, even the finding that Algérie Télécom's actions are attributable to Algeria does not change this conclusion:

---

[215] See, IA*Reporter*, *Strabag v. Libya* (23 September 2022), (contrasting the tribunals umbrella clause decision on attribution with that in *Guris v. Libya*). https://www.iareporter.com/arbitration-cases/strabag-v-libya/

[216] IA*Reporter*, *Way2B ACE v. Libya* (8 January 2019), https://www.iareporter.com/arbitration-cases/way2b-ace-v-libya/

[217] *Consutel Group S.p.A. in liquidazione v. People's Democratic Republic of Algeria*, PCA No. 2017-33, Final Award (3 Febraury 2020).

[218] *Ibid*. para. 1.

[219] *Ibid*., para. 108.

[220] *Ibid*., para. 359.

[221] *Ibid*., para. 366.

> The responsibility of a public entity for violation of its contractual obligations can certainly be attributed to the State on the basis of the rules of attribution, but the contractual obligations thus violated remain those of the public entity that underwrote them. The State does not become, through the effect of the allocation rules, the debtor of the obligations contracted by the public company.[222]

As such, this decision is also noteworthy for the fact that it emphasised the attribution of an entity's actions to a state is immaterial in finding such entity's contractual commitments as the state's commitments, for the purposes of invoking the umbrella clause. A position that is not uniformly shared from the cases analysed above.

Concluding this discussion on inconsistent interpretation of treaty standards, it should be emphasised that the cases reviewed above on the interpretation of the FPS clause, the war loss clause, and the umbrella clause, is not intended to assess the quality or correctness of one decision over the other. Rather, they are simply meant to buttress, with certain examples, how inconsistent ISDS outcomes have thrived within the African continent, leaving both the states and investors concerned in a conundrum of uncertainty. As observed in the introduction, this is not a dilemma peculiar to Africa.

As previously stated, the uncertainty created by inconsistent ISDS outcomes also generates doubts about the correctness of ISDS decisions. This undermines states' and investors' confidence in the reliability of the investment protection regime. On one hand, states face difficulties in aligning domestic policies with international obligations due to varying tribunal interpretations. Investors on the other hand are uncertain as to whether certain treatments they have received are in accordance with the host states' treaty obligations.[223] Hence, inconsistency in treaty interpretation by ISDS tribunals is a dilemma for both state and private actors that requires redress for the effective management of investor-state relationships.

3.1.3   Failure to Ensure Investors' Accountability

Over six decades after the inception of the first BIT,[224] the law of international investment protection enshrined in numerous IIAs has remained largely asymmetric in nature. Meaning, that these IIAs expressly impose obligations on contracting states towards covered investors, while the investors have no corresponding obligation in their business dealings within the host states'.

This one-sided nature of IIAs has made it impossible to effectively hold foreign investors accountable for their investment activities, which undermines the sustainable development interest of their host states'. As earlier defined, an investment

---

[222] *Ibid.*, para. 364

[223] UNCITRAL, *Report of Working Group III (Investor-State Dispute Settlement Reform)* of 26/2/2018, A/CN.9/930/Add.1/Rev.1, para. 15.

[224] Germany-Pakistan BIT (1959), entered into force 28 April 1962.

would fall short of a host state's SD interest if it fails to concurrently foster economic development, social development, and environmental protection (→ Chap. 3). A classic example of such detrimental foreign investment, particularly on social development and environmental protection is that of 'Shell Petroleum', a Dutch multinational oil corporation with investment operations in Nigeria.

In 2011, a UN report[225] criticised Shell Petroleum for its failure to address oil spillages from its investment operations in the Niger Delta region of Nigeria.[226] The result of this failure was the destruction of the predominantly aquatic and mangrove environment of the Niger Delta people. According to the UN report, it would cost billions of dollars and between 25 and 30 years to clean up the environmental damage caused by the oil operations in the Niger Delta, which has had a 'disastrous impact' on mangrove vegetation, including *inter alia—'the contamination of wells with potentially cancer-causing chemicals in a region that is home to some 1 million people'.*[227] Despite this damning UN report highlighting Shell Petroleum's shortcomings in Nigeria and the environmental and human rights consequences for the host communities that followed, there has been no means to hold the company internationally accountable for its identified misconduct in the Niger Delta.

In contrast to a host state that can face international accountability for its misconduct against a foreign investor, international law—particularly international investment law, lacks an established framework to hold corporations or other non-state actors internationally accountable for their wrong doings in the host state, especially those that transgress sustainable development norms, encompassing human rights considerations. This is perpetuated by the fact that international treaties on human rights including those on the environment mainly impose obligations on states, neglecting multinational corporations as legal actors equally instrumental to the effective and meaningful implementation of these treaties.[228] Consequently, the only available avenue for redress by aggrieved individuals or host communities are national laws implemented by national authorities, which offer no guarantee of effective redress.

Regarding recourse to national remedy, the Niger Delta communities' experience exemplifies how weak a host state can be in offering adequate protection to its people against the harmful conduct of a foreign investor. As detailed in the UN report on the Niger Delta, the Nigerian Government provided an inadequate regulatory and enforcement regime to protect its communities against harmful investor operations in the oil industry.[229] The UN report *inter alia* criticised the government's regulatory agencies for lacking qualified technical experts and resources, while the main regulatory agency responsible for checking oil spillages wholly relied on the oil

---

[225] UNEP (2011).
[226] Amnesty International (2011).
[227] UN News (2011).
[228] Calatayud et al. (2008), p. 173.
[229] UNEP (2011), p. 140 ff.

industry to carry out its watch-dog duties.[230] In such a paradox, where the state can be characterised as the 'ant' and the investor an 'elephant', it is difficult to foresee how the former can effectively bring the latter to account for its harmful conduct.

Similarly, while local courts remain available as an independent judicial sanctuary that aggrieved individuals/communities can run to for relieve against harmful investor conduct, multinational corporations are still able to push back against domestic court claims both locally and abroad. They can also pursue claims directly against the host state in international arbitration, to challenge local judicial proceedings or outcomes that run contrary to the investor's interests, further delaying the ability of aggrieved locals to attain justice.

For instance, in the Shell Petroleum case, the Dutch corporation through its local subsidiary in Nigeria (Shell Petroleum Development Company ('SPDC') of Nigeria) for decades had been exposed to multiple domestic litigations brought by victims of oil spillages in the Niger Delta. In 2010, one of such claims (***Agbara and ors v. SPDC and ors***) led to a domestic multi-million dollar judgement against SPDC before a Nigerian High Court.[231] A decade later, the local claimants' still had not reaped the fruit of the local judgment meant to remedy the destruction of their local communities. For 9 years, the SPDC resisted compliance with the local judgment after several unsuccessful attempts to annul it up to the Nigerian Supreme Court. In December 2019, the SPDC successfully resisted enforcement of the Nigerian court judgement before an English High Court.[232] Subsequently in November 2020, the Nigerian Supreme Court rejected another attempt by SPDC to have the apex court review its earlier decision on the 2010 lower court judgement.[233]

In 2021, as enforcement efforts resumed in Nigeria to claim the proceeds of the 2010 judgement, Shell Petroleum and SPDC directly challenged the Nigerian state by initiating an ICSID arbitration.[234] As reported by IA*Reporter*, the ICSID case related to disputes surrounding the oil spillages in the Niger Delta and the ensuing court proceedings.[235] In October 2022, the ICSID case was discontinued.[236] According to a press report, this discontinuation followed Shell Petroleum's

---

[230] *Ibid.*, p. 139 f.

[231] *Agbara and ors v. SPDC and ors.*, [2001] FHC/ASB/CS/231/2001.

[232] *Agbara and ors v. SPDC and ors*, [2019] EWHC 3340 (QC).

[233] Premium Times Report, Supreme Court dismisses Shell's application to review N17bn Ogoni judgement, available at: https://www.premiumtimesng.com/news/headlines

[234] Reuters, Shell files international arbitration against Nigeria over oil spill case, available at: https://www.reuters.com/article/uk-shell-nigeria-arbitration-

[235] IA*Reporter*, Shell lodges ICSID claim against Nigeria, (11 February 2021), https://www.iareporter.com/articles/shell-lodges-icsid-claim-against-nigeria/

[236] *Shell Petroleum N.V. and The Shell Petroleum Development Company of Nigeria Limited v. Federal Republic of Nigeria*, ICSID Case No. ARB/21/7, Order taking note of the discontinuance (13 October 2022).

successful review, based on an out-of-court settlement, of the amount including interest to be paid to the Niger Delta claimants.[237]

Significantly, had the ICSID claim proceeded, the absence of any investor obligation in the invoked Netherlands-Nigeria BIT (1992) raises doubts about whether human rights or environmental considerations would have influenced the tribunal's interpretation of Nigeria's obligations to Shell Petroleum under the BIT. If going by the *von Pezold v. Zimbabwe*[238] decision, the best Nigeria could have received was sympathy. As in that case, although the tribunal recognised and empathised with Zimbabwe regarding the human rights implications of the case, it reaffirmed that its adjudicative mandate was limited to resolving the dispute in accordance with the ICSID convention and the applicable law, which does not include human rights considerations.[239]

Furthermore, although the ICSID case was discontinued following Shell Petroleum's final out-of-court settlement with the Niger Delta claimants,[240] the protracted time it took before the claimants could get any form of relief cannot be ignored. Arguably, had the Niger Delta claimants' possessed an international award having the enforcement characteristics of an ICSID award,[241] it is quite conceivable that relief could have arrived much earlier.

Notably, attempts to hold not just Shell Petroleum but other multinational oil corporations accountable for their atrocities in the Niger Delta have also played out in multiple domestic forums abroad—from the USA to the United Kingdom and the Netherlands. While it is not the focus of this thesis to review those cases, one study that examined selected domestic cases related to Niger Delta claims reveals the uncertainty in securing justice for victims of human rights abuses committed by multinational oil corporations, even in the most advanced judicial systems abroad.[242]

Significantly, it will be inapposite to conclude this analysis without acknowledging a few instances in ISDS history where the investors' conduct was considered relevant in the resolution of a BIT dispute, even when the BIT did not explicitly establish an investor obligation. Although no direct accountability in the sense of direct claims against the investors was possible in these cases, a form of accountability was found acceptable either through counterclaims or denial of treaty protection.

---

[237] Africa Intelligence, Pollution: behind the scenes of the abandonment of Shell vs Abuja Arbitration, https://www.africaintelligence.fr/afrique-ouest/2022/11/08/pollution%2D%2Dles-coulisses-de-l-abandon-de-l-arbitrage-shell-vs-abuja,109841510-art

[238] *Bernhard von Pezold and Others v. Republic of Zimbabwe*, ICSID Case No. ARB/10/15, (Award, 28 July 2015).

[239] *Ibid.*, para. 2 ff.

[240] IA*Reporter*, Shell discontinues ICSID case against Nigeria, (6 December 2022), https://www.iareporter.com/articles/w; *Africa News*, Justice at last: Shell agrees to pay $110 M over oil spills in Nigeria, https://www.africanews.com/2021/08/12/justice-at-last

[241] See in this regard, Schreuer et al. (2009), p. 1096 ff.

[242] Adetula and Jaiyebo (2020), p. 166 ff.

For instance, in *Urbaser v. Argentina,*[243] when assessing the merits of the respondent's counterclaim against the claimant, the tribunal dismissed the claimant's submissions that sought to interpret the BIT as 'a closed system strictly preserving investors rights under the BIT'.[244] For the tribunal, the BIT's explicit reference to international law as an applicable law suggests the contracting parties could not have intended to apply the BIT in isolation from other rules of international law.[245] Relying on the BIT's reference to 'international law', the tribunal drew from a number of international law sources to determine whether the investor had an obligation to guarantee the human right of access to water.[246] The tribunal later concluded in the negative that no such duty is imposed on a corporation under international law.[247] However, it agreed such a duty may be derived from contract or under a state's civil or commercial law.[248]

Importantly, the tribunal also recognised that, although non-state actors have no duty to guarantee international human rights, they do have one not to violate them. According to the *Urbaser* tribunal:

> The situation would be different in case an obligation to abstain, like a prohibition to commit acts violating human rights would be at stake. Such an obligation can be of immediate application, not only upon States, but equally to individuals and other private parties.[249]

The *Urbaser* tribunal offered no examples of human rights violations that may fall under this exception. However, in another counterclaim decision in *David Aven v. Costa Rica,*[250] sharing the *Urbaser* view, the tribunal considered the protection of the environment as one of those international obligations that a foreign investor cannot claim immunity from based on being a non-state actor.[251] Accordingly, the tribunal reasoned that the investor was equally a subject of international law that could be held accountable under the treaty for violating international environmental protection policies.[252]

Besides using the reference to international law as a tool to counterclaim against an investor for irresponsible conduct, tribunals also rely on international law to deny treaty protection to an abusive investor as a form of international accountability. For

---

[243] *Urbaser S.A. and Consorcio de Aguas Bilbao Bizkaia, Bilbao Biskaia Ur Partzuergoa v. The Argentine Republic,* ICSID Case No. ARB/07/26, (Award 8 December 2016).

[244] *Ibid.,* para. 1191.

[245] *Ibid.,* para. 1191 f.

[246] *Ibid.,* para. 1193 ff.

[247] *Ibid.,* para. 1208 ff.

[248] *Ibid.,* para. 1210.

[249] *Ibid.*

[250] *David R. Aven and Others v. Republic of Costa Rica,* ICSID Case No. UNCT/15/3, Award (18 September 2018).

[251] *Ibid.,* para. 738.

[252] *Ibid.,* para. 737 ff.

example, in *World Duty Free v. Kenya*,[253] at issue was a contract for the construction, maintenance, and operation of duty-free complexes at two Kenyan airports, which the claimant alleged was unlawfully expropriated through the acts of Kenya's executive and judicial agent.[254] In response, Kenya *inter alia* contended that the case must be dismissed with prejudice because the contract at issue was procured after a bribe of 2 million U.S. Dollars was paid to the President of Kenya at the time.[255]

Upon establishing the existence of bribery,[256] the tribunal relying on various domestic and international jurisprudence held that bribery is contrary to international public policy of most if not all nations, thus a contract tainted in bribery and corruption cannot be protected by the tribunal.[257] Although this was a contractual dispute where both the private and state parties share obligations, it is instructive that the investor's obligation in this case to abstain from corruption was not read as a duty under the contract but as a duty under international law that affected the enforceability of the contract. The *World Duty Free* tribunal reasoning has since been relied upon by several ISDS tribunals, including in treaty claims.[258]

Additionally, 'compliance with domestic law' is another tool that has been deployed by arbitral tribunals to check against irresponsible investor conduct that is detrimental to the host state's sustainable development. This duty is applied notwithstanding the silence of the relevant IIA on the investor's duty to comply with local law.[259] For example, in *Cortec Mining v. Kenya*,[260] the claimant of British nationality had brought an ICSID arbitration against Kenya for multiple BIT

---

[253] *World Duty Free Company v Republic of Kenya*, ICSID Case No. Arb/00/7, Award (4 October 2006).

[254] *Ibid.*, para. 74.

[255] *Ibid.*, para. 105.

[256] *Ibid.*, paras. 130–136.

[257] *Ibid.*, paras. 138–157.

[258] See, *Fynerdale Holdings B.V. v. Czech Republic*, PCA Case No. 2018-18, Award (29 April 2021), para. 550; *Chevron Corporation (U.S.A.) and Texaco Petroleum Corporation (U.S.A.) v. Republic of Ecuador II*, PCA Case No. 2009-23, Second Partial Award on Track II (30 August 2018), para. 9.16; *Krederi Ltd. v. Ukraine*, ICSID Case No. ARB/14/17, Excerpts of Award (2 July 2018), para. 386; *Metal-Tech Ltd. v. Republic of Uzbekistan*, ICSID Case No. ARB/10/3, Award (4 October 2013), para. 292; *Waguih Elie George Siag and Clorinda Vecci and the Arab Republic of Egypt*, ICSID Case No. ARB/05/15, Dissenting Opinion of Professor Francisco Orrego Vicuña (1 June 2009), para. 17; *Phoenix Action, Ltd. v. Czech Republic*, ICSID Case No. ARB/06/5, Award (15 April 2009), para. 112; *Plama Consortium Limited v. Republic of Bulgaria*, ICSID Case No. ARB/03/24, Award (27 August 2008), para. 142.

[259] *Phoenix Action, Ltd. v. The Czech Republic*, ICSID Case No. ARB/06/5, Award (19 April 2009), para. 101; *Plama Consortium Limited v. Republic of Bulgaria*, ICSID Case No. ARB/03/24, Award (27 August 2008), paras. 138 ff; *SAUR International v. Argentine Republic*, ICSID Case No. ARB/04/4, Decision on Jurisdiction and Liability (6 June 2012), paras. 307 ff; *David Minnotte and Robert Lewis v. Republic of Poland*, ICSID Case No. ARB(AF)/10/1, Award (16 May 2014), para. 131; *Saluka Investments BV (The Netherlands) v. Czech Republic*, PCA Case No. 2001-04, Partial Award (17 March 2006), para. 204.

[260] *Cortec Mining Kenya Limited, Cortec (Pty) Limited and Stirling Capital Limited v. Republic of Kenya*, ICSID Case No. ARB/15/29, Award (22 October 2018).

breaches under the Kenya-United Kingdom BIT (1999). At the center of the dispute was the revocation of the claimant's mining license which the claimant argued amounts to an unlawful expropriation of its investment.

In its defence, Kenya argued that the claimant had made no investment because the purported investment was made in violation of Kenyan law which cannot be protected under the BIT or the ICSID convention.[261] In particular, the license was granted at the eleventh hour by the responsible government minister, before a change of government in Kenya, without the necessary environmental impact assessment (EIA) report. Reading a legality requirement into the Kenya-UK BIT (1999),[262] the tribunal held the mining license was void due to the claimant's failure to comply with the statutory EIA requirement.[263] According to the tribunal, *'[n]on-compliance with the protective regulatory framework was a serious matter'*,[264] especially one that concerns the protection of the environment.[265] Hence, the proportionate response to such grave misconduct should be the denial of protection to the investment under the BIT and the ICSID convention.[266]

Although the above instances where tribunals have indirectly held investors accountable either through counterclaims or denial of treaty protection are laudable, such instances are not common. Achieving such results remains an uphill task under old-generation IIAs that are solely focused on the protection of foreign investment. For instance, as opined by the tribunal in *Al-Warraq v. Indonesia*,[267] *[c]ounterclaims are problematic in investment arbitration because of the 'inherently asymmetrical character' of an investment treaty.*[268] Most importantly, counterclaims must be closely connected and not independent of the investor's claim.[269] Consequently, even if an investor breaches a recognised international or domestic legal obligation, a counterclaim would not be actionable, save the breach is connected to the investor's claim.

Furthermore, although the denial of treaty protection for abusive investments might stop the investor from benefiting from its own misconduct, this will not remedy the loss or damage inflicted on the state or its ordinary citizens who have suffered the direct consequence of the investor's abuse.

---

[261] *Ibid.*, para. 318.

[262] *Ibid.*, para. 319 ff.

[263] *Ibid.*, para. 332 ff.

[264] *Ibid.*, para. 348.

[265] *Ibid.*, para. 364.

[266] *Ibid.*, para. 365.

[267] *Hesham Talaat M. Al-Warraq v. Republic of Indonesia*, UNCITRAL, Final Award (15 December 2014).

[268] *Ibid.*, para. 659.

[269] *Saluka Investments BV (The Netherlands) v. Czech Republic*, PCA Case No. 2001-04, Decision on Jurisdiction over the Czech Republic's Counterclaim (7 May 2004), para. 61; *Oxus Gold plc v. Republic of Uzbekistan*, UNCITRAL, Final Award (17 December 2015), para. 954; *Marco Gavazzi and Stefano Gavazzi v. Romania*, ICSID Case No. ARB/12/25, Decision on Jurisdiction Admissibility and Liability (21 April 2015), para. 154 ff.

Therefore, despite the creative approaches arbitral tribunals have employed to hold investors accountable for their misconduct in host territories, this has not proven sufficient to ensure a fair balance in protecting the interest of investors, states, and affected individuals/host communities (third-parties) often at stake in an investor-state relationship. Hence, there is a need to do more in order to protect the rights and interests of all stakeholders involved. This will necessitate a recalibration of the substantive law on investment protection to better safeguard the rights and interests of all stakeholders, including states and affected third parties.

3.2 The Undesirable Effect of ISDS Clauses as Applied by Arbitral Tribunals

As earlier highlighted, the principal and most important procedural guarantee in an IIA is the ISDS clause, which ensures investors' access to international arbitration through a variety of arbitral forums, with ICSID topping the list ($\rightarrow$ Chap. 3). Notably, arbitration as a dispute resolution method has certain unique characteristics including: the 'exclusivity of arbitral jurisdiction', 'before a neutral forum', with the power to adjudicate 'through a confidential process' and issue a 'final and binding award', with 'limited review possibilities'.[270]

Overtime, these unique characteristics which promoted the popularity of arbitration as the preferred choice of ISDS are now reasons for its criticism in Africa and beyond. The criticism includes *inter alia*: the failure to foster the development of local courts by requiring first recourse to local remedies (3.2.1); the failure to foster the usage and development of alternative dispute resolution ('ADR') (3.2.2); including limited transparency and third party participation concerns (3.2.3).

3.2.1 Failure to Foster the Development of Local Courts by Requiring First Recourse to Local Remedies

Given the exclusive nature of an arbitration clause,[271] its inclusion in an IIA circumvents the jurisdiction of local courts over an investment dispute that may be covered by the consent to arbitration, save the contracting parties agreed otherwise. No doubt, it may be argued that this is the natural result of a state's unqualified consent to arbitration, as arbitration is purposed to provide a neutral forum for the adjudication of investment disputes detached from any state control, save for certain

---

[270]Born (2021), p. 2 ff; Blackaby et al. (2023), para. 2.01 ff; Article 53 and 54, ICSID Convention; Article 34, UNCITRAL Model Law.

[271]Article 26, ICSID Convention; Article 8, UNCITRAL Model Law.

limited judicial oversight.[272] While this is accurate, it is important to also contextualise this understanding of arbitration within the public nature of investment disputes, which differs from disputes stemming from purely commercial transactions.

To appreciate this context, it is important to recognise that the arbitration system in force today was primarily designed to resolve commercial law disputes involving private contracts, which is now being used in adjudicating public law matters.[273] However, unlike commercial arbitration where arbitral tribunals focus on disputes arising out of commercial contracts between private parties with decisions having no consequence outside the privity of contract, investment arbitration decisions on the other hand produce consequences outside privity because the disputes arise out of the exercise of states' public authority,[274] which is intended to serve the citizens interests. Therefore, investment arbitration tribunals through their decisions have the effect of restraining or shaping states public policies, having a direct impact on ordinary citizens.[275] Giving this public nature of ISDS and its effect on a state's sovereign authority over its territorial affairs, the practice of denying local courts, which serve as an independent and impartial instrument of the state, the first right to resolve investment disputes before recourse to international arbitration, has generated public discontent with the traditional ISDS system.

Significantly, initial recourse to local remedies is the established rule under CIL before an alien can initiate an international claim against its host state, commonly referred to as the 'exhaustion of local remedies' ('ELR') rule. The ELR rule is precisely aimed at safeguarding a state's sovereign authority by requiring aggrieved aliens to seek local redress first before recourse to international remedy can be sought.[276] However, in investment arbitration, the prevailing view has been that the ELR rule is inapplicable to investment disputes, save explicitly required under the relevant IIA.[277] As provided in Article 26 of the ICSID Convention, consent of the parties to ICSID arbitration shall be to the exclusion of any other remedy, save a contracting party require the exhaustion of local remedies as a condition to its consent. The same position is followed in principle by tribunals in non-ICSID arbitration disputes.[278]

Although, direct recourse to international arbitration has its advantages, including the avoidance of politically influenced local courts, unnecessary delays, costs, or a

---

[272] Article 54, ICSID Convention; Article 34, UNCITRAL Model Law.

[273] Butler and Subedi (2017), p. 44.

[274] Vadi (2015), p. 473.

[275] Kim (2011), p. 253 ff.

[276] Brauch (2017), p. 1; see also, UNCTAD (2018), p. 51; See also, Article 14, International Law Commission (ILC)'s Articles on Diplomatic Protection ('ADP') with commentaries.

[277] *PL Holdings S.A.R.L. v. Republic of Poland*, SCC Case No V2014/163, Partial Award (28 June 2017), para. 441; *Gavrilovic and Gavrilovic d.o.o. v. Republic of Croatia*, ICSID Case No. ARB/12/39, Award (26 July 2018), para. 889; *Patrick Mitchell v. Democratic Republic of the Congo*, ICSID Case No. ARB/99/3, Excerpts of Award (9 February 2004), para. 33.

[278] Douglas (2009), p. 98 f; Paparinskis (2013), p. 642.

potential denial of justice, its detrimental effect on the development and capacity-building of domestic judicial systems also cannot be overlooked. While investment arbitration cases are often times treaty claims that justify the bypass of local courts directly to an international tribunal, it is also a valid argument that most times treaty claims have an equivalent remedy under national law, which should be exhausted when available.[279] For example, the right to the protection of private property is a constitutionally guaranteed right in all civilised domestic legal systems, which may be limited only in public interest under certain constitutionally specified conditions.[280] Therefore, a claim for an unlawful expropriation or denial of full protection and security to an investment will typically be actionable in a domestic court under the local law on the protection of private property.

Crucially, regardless of an international arbitration clause, domestic courts remain the default forum for ISDS.[281] Therefore, a situation in which the current system encourages an unrestricted bypass of local courts in favour of international arbitration does not foster but undermines the development of local judicial capacity in the field of ISDS. This, in turn, hinders the development of the rule of law in the host state, if the effectiveness of local laws regarding the protection of private property, including foreign investments, is not being tested by local judicial authorities. Hence, a need to ensure an ISDS system that preserves the access of foreign investors to international remedies, without hindering the host state's capacity to develop effective local remedies for resolving investment disputes. Striking this balance is what African states aim to achieve as part of the reforms required to enhance the legitimacy and credibility of the ISDS system.

3.2.2   Failure to Foster the Usage and Development of ADR

Traditionally, ADR is regarded as a dispute settlement process secured through means other than a binding court decision. However, since arbitration is the dominant means of settling investment disputes, the term ADR is also used to qualify an ISDS process not involving a binding arbitral award or court decision. ADR involves the intervention of a third party who assists the disputants in reaching an **amicable settlement** of their dispute.[282] These alternatives to arbitration or domestic court

---

[279] ELR is deemed available under international law provided such an effort is not futile, see— Article 15(a), ADP with commentaries; *Swissbourgh Diamond Mines (Pty) Limited and others v. Lesotho*, PCA Case No. 2013-29, Judgment of the Singapore Court of Appeal (27 November 2018), para. 211.

[280] For examples see, Article 14, Basic Law for the Federal Republic of Germany (1949); Fifth Amendment, Constitution of the United States of America (1788); Article 44(1) Constitution of the Federal Republic of Nigeria (1999); Article 25, Constitution of the Republic of South Africa (1996); Article 300A, Constitution of India (1949).

[281] Kaufmann-Kohler and Potestà (2020), p. 36, para. 68.

[282] UNCTAD (2010), p. 50.

litigation include: negotiation, mediation, conciliation, or any other amicable settlement process agreed by the parties.[283]

ADR is not a strange process to ISDS. In fact, a majority of the IIAs underlying investment disputes make room for a **cooling-off period** when disputants are expected to attempt an **amicable settlement** of their dispute within a specified period of time.[284] An example of this provision in an extra-African BIT is found in Article VII of the Egypt-Turkey BIT (1996), which provides:

> 1. Disputes between one of the Parties and an investor of the other Party [. . .] shall be notifies in writing [. . .]. As far as possible, the investor and the concerned party shall endeavour to settle these disputes by consultations and negotiations in good faith.
>
> 2. If these disputes cannot be settled in this way within six months following the date of the written notification mentioned in paragraph 1, the dispute can be submitted, as the investor may choose, to:

[. . .]

Also, Article 8 of the Tanzania-Italy BIT (2001) provides:

> Any dispute which may arise between one of the Contracting Parties and the investors of the other Contracting Party on investments [. . .], shall be settled through consultations and negotiations, as far as possible.
>
> In the event that such dispute cannot be settled as provided in paragraph (1) of this Article within six months of the date of the written application for settlement, the investor in question may submit at his choice the dispute for settlement to:
>
> [. . .]

While a mutually agreed solution is generally foreseen in most IIAs, ADR remains largely underutilised in ISDS. For example, based on ICSID statistics as of December 2023, only 14 cases had been registered under the ICSID Convention Conciliation Rules (including, the Additional Facility Conciliation Rules), compared to the 953 cases registered under both the ICSID Arbitration Rules and Additional Facility Rules.[285] This underutilisation of ADR in ISDS can be attributed to several factors, including the dominant nature that arbitration has played in the field of ISDS over the years, resulting in limited knowledge or understanding of alternative approaches to arbitration. Also, until recently, concerns about the enforceability of ADR decisions were an issue, since unlike arbitration, there was no mechanism to ensure the enforcement of ADR outcomes.[286] This has fostered a perceived ineffectiveness, stirring parties to often bypass ADR for arbitration.

Besides the systemic challenges, the interpretation of ADR clauses by arbitral tribunals has also downplayed rather than enhanced its usage and development.

---

[283] ICSID, Other Alternative Dispute Resolution Mechanisms, https://icsid.worldbank.org/services-arbitration-other-adr-mechanisms

[284] See, Ganesh (2017), p. 2.

[285] See ICSID, Case Load Statistics (Issue 2024-1), p. 2, https://icsid.worldbank.org/sites

[286] ADR outcomes resulting from mediation can now be enforced through the: United Nations Convention on International Settlement Agreements Resulting from Mediation (Singapore Convention on Mediation), August 7 2019, U.N. Doc. 73/198.

Particularly, several arbitral tribunals have treated the IIAs' requirement to pursue amicable settlement of investment disputes through negotiations or other ADR options as a mere directory, rather than a mandatory jurisdictional requirement.[287] The *Biwater v. Tanzania*[288] case is one example of a dispute involving an African party where the tribunal had declined to give a mandatory effect to the BIT's amicable settlement clause. In contention was the 6-months amicable settlement period contemplated under Article 8(3) of the Tanzania-UK BIT (1994). Ruling on Tanzania's jurisdictional objection that it did not consent to arbitration without fulfilment of the 6-month cooling-off requirement,[289] the tribunal held that:

> [. . .] properly construed, this six-month period is procedural and directory in nature, rather than jurisdictional and mandatory [. . .], therefore, does not preclude this Arbitral Tribunal from proceeding.[290]

Similarly in *Al-Kharafi v. Libya*,[291] where the underlying contract to the dispute contained a pre-arbitration amicable settlement clause, the tribunal held that it is established in arbitral jurisprudence that this clause is only a procedural requirement that does not constitute a prerequisite to the arbitral tribunal's jurisdiction.[292]

However, in contrast to the abovementioned decisions, there are other tribunals that have taken the position that the amicable settlement clause in IIAs' constitutes a mandatory jurisdictional requirement.[293] One case example involving an African

---

[287] *SGS Société Générale de Surveillance S.A. v. Islamic Republic of Pakistan*, ICSID Case No. ARB/01/13, Award on Jurisdiction (6 August 2003), para. 184; *Republic of Italy v. Republic of Cuba*, Preliminary Award (15 March 2005), para. 70 f; *Bayindir Insaat Turizm Ticaret Ve Sanayi AS v. Islamic Republic of Pakistan I*, ICSID Case No. ARB/03/29, Decision on Jurisdiction (14 November 2005), para. 102; *El Paso Energy International Company v. Argentine Republic*, ICSID Case No. ARB/03/15, Decision on Jurisdiction (27 April 2006), para. 38; *Spyridon Roussalis v. Romania*, ICSID Case No. ARB/06/1, Award (1 December 2011), para. 335.

[288] *Biwater Gauff (Tanzania) Limited v. United Republic of Tanzania*, ICSID Case No. ARB/05/22, Award (24 July 2008).

[289] *Ibid.*, para. 297.

[290] *Ibid.*, para. 343.

[291] *Mohamed Abdulmohsen Al-Kharafi & Sons Co. v. State of Libya and others*, Final Arbitral Award (22 March 2013).

[292] *Ibid.*, para. 245.

[293] *Noble Energy Inc. and MachalaPower Cía. Ltd. v. Republic of Ecuador and Consejo Nacional de Electricidad*, ICSID Case No. ARB/05/12, Decision on Jurisdiction (5 March 2008), para. 212; *Enron Creditors Recovery Corporation (formerly Enron Corporation) and Ponderosa Assets, L.P. v. Argentine Republic*, ICSID Case No. ARB/01/3, Decision on Jurisdiction (14 January 2004), para. 88; *Generation Ukraine Inc. v. Ukraine*, ICSID Case No. ARB/00/9, Final Award (16 September 2003), para. 14.3; *Burlington Resources Inc. v. Republic of Ecuador*, ICSID Case No. ARB/08/5, Decision on Jurisdiction (2 June 2010), para. 312, 315; *Murphy Exploration and Production Company International v. Republic of Ecuador I*, ICSID Case No. ARB/08/4 Award on Jurisdiction (15 December 2010), para. 132, 148 ff; *Tulip Real Estate and Development Netherlands B.V. v. Republic of Turkey*, ICSID Case No. ARB/11/28, Decision on Bifurcated Jurisdictional Issue (5 March 2013), para. 71 f, 92; *Louis Dreyfus Armateurs SAS v. Republic of India*, PCA Case No. 2014-26, Decision on Jurisdiction (22 December 2015), para. 94 ff; *Almasryia for Operating & Maintaining Touristic Construction Co. L.L.C. v. State of Kuwait*, ICSID Case

party is *Salini v. Morocco*.[294] In interpreting the amicable settlement provision in Article 8(2) of the Morocco-Italy BIT (1990), the tribunal concluded that the requirement to attempt amicable settlement prior to initiating arbitration was compulsory.[295]

From the above cases, it can be observed that amicable dispute settlement through ADR options can be treated as optional or mandatory. Although the scrutiny of an IIA's ADR provision under Article 31 VCLT may well justify the divergent interpretation of its effect across treaties, the concern is that such justification is not always provided. As observed in UNCITRAL Working Group III, the interpretation of the cooling-off requirement by arbitral tribunals—contemplating amicable settlement within a designated period before arbitration, is one of the procedural inconsistencies in traditional ISDS worth addressing.[296]

Without clarity in the relevant IIA, there is no guarantee that a future MIC will treat ADR provisions any differently from how arbitral tribunals currently do, raising questionable interpretations. From the UNCITRAL Working Group III ISDS reform discussions, there is a general support among delegates for increased ADR usage, including support from the EU and its member states.[297] This reflects the widespread acknowledgement that adversarial modes of dispute resolution may not always be the most effective or suitable method for settling investment disputes, and that ADR can offer valuable alternatives.

The efficiency of ADR in terms of cost-effectiveness, preservation of relationships, flexibility, and potential for creative and tailored solutions that align with the cultural values and development objectives of states, are all values that align with the interest of African states' regarding an efficient and legitimate ISDS process. However, despite these attractive factors, the present reality is that the overall usage and development of ADR in ISDS remains comparatively limited, due to the factors discussed above amongst several others.[298]

No. ARB/18/2, Award on the Respondent Application under Rule 41(5) of the ICSID Arbitration Rules (1 November 2019), para. 39.

[294] *Salini Costruttori S.P.A. and Italstrade S.P.A. v. Kingdom of Morocco*, ICSID Case No. ARB/00/4, Decision on Jurisdiction (16 July 2001).

[295] *Ibid.*, para. 16.

[296] UNCITRAL, *Possible Reform of Investor-State Dispute Settlement (ISDS): Consistency and Related Matters*: Note by the Secretariat of 28/8/2018, A/CN.9/WG.III/WP.150, para. 18.

[297] UNCITRAL, *Submission from the European Union and its Member States* of 24/1/2019, A/CN.9/WG.III/WP.159/Add.1., para. 12.

[298] For further readings on the underutilisation of ADR in ISDS see in general: Rasilla (2023), p. 169 ff; Ubilava (2022), p. 131 ff; Claxton (2020), p. 84 ff.

3.2.3   Limited Transparency and Third-Party Participation Concerns

For several years, transparency and third-party participation concerns have been a major contributor to the backlash against the traditional ISDS system. This specific backlash arises out of the need for better **'openness'** and **'accessibility'** of the ISDS process to the public.[299] Given its confidential nature, the suitability of arbitration to ISDS, a process historically designed for settling commercial disputes has come under increased scrutiny and criticism.[300] While a commercial dispute may run its course behind closed doors, the appropriateness of applying the same approach to a dispute that challenges a government policy with significant implications for the public is quite controversial.

Sticking to its historical roots, investment arbitration like commercial arbitration is often conducted behind closed doors, with limited or no public access. Consequently, the public directly or indirectly impacted by an arbitration process has no right to access the arbitration documents, nor the hearings. Further, traditionally, access to ISDS is limited to the claimant-investor and the respondent-host state, meaning that third parties whose interests may be affected by the proceedings are excluded from participation. Albeit, transparency and third party participation is not absolutely absent in ISDS, the extent of openness and access to the public is still largely dependent on the will of the parties, the arbitration rules and the tribunal's discretion. Overall, this closed-door approach has exposed the legitimacy of the current ISDS system to questioning. In this context, legitimacy refers to the acknowledgment and willingness of individuals residing within a legal framework to embrace and utilize it due to their perception of its fairness and suitability for their good.[301]

Notably, unlike other critiques of the traditional ISDS system, the need to improve transparency and third party participation is one matter where states have managed at a multilateral level on multiple occasions to implement desirable ISDS reforms. One example is the UNCITRAL Rules on Transparency in Treaty-based Investor-State Arbitration ('UNCITRAL Rules on Transparency').[302] The UNCITRAL Rules on Transparency applies to all cases initiated under the UNCITRAL Arbitration Rules pursuant to a treaty, concluded on or after 1 April 2014, save the Parties to the treaty agree otherwise.[303] Sequel to this, multiple states signed the United Nations Convention on Transparency in Treaty-based

---

[299] See, Douglas (2015), p. 112.

[300] OECD (2005), p. 2, para. 1.

[301] Hurst (1971), p. 224; See also Brower and Schill (2009), p. 471.

[302] United Nations Commission on International Trade Law Rules on Transparency in Treaty-based Investor-State Arbitration and Arbitration Rule ('UNCITRAL Rules on Transparency'), 16 December 2013.

[303] Article 1(1), UNCITRAL Rules on Transparency 2013.

Investor-State Arbitration ('Mauritius Convention'),[304] consenting to apply the UNCITRAL Rules on Transparency to disputes under investment treaties concluded before 1 April 2014.[305] As the name suggests, the UNCITRAL Rules on Transparency introduced measures to increase the transparency of ISDS proceedings. This includes rules on the publication of arbitration-related documents,[306] participation of third parties,[307] and public hearings.[308] Likewise, the most recent update to the ICSID Arbitration Rules includes an entire chapter (i.e. Chap. X) specifically addressing the topic of transparency and third-party participation.[309]

Despite these laudable improvements, the adequacy of the UNCITRAL Rules on Transparency, or Chap. X of the ICSID Arbitration Rules 2022 is still in question. For instance, while the former does not foresee parties' consent for the publication of arbitration-related documents or the conduct of public hearings,[310] the latter still necessitates parties' consent before arbitration-related documents, including the award, can be made public.[311] Given that the ICSID arbitration procedure is the dominant procedure for ISDS, it can be inferred that ensuring transparency to the public remains largely uncertain. Basically, the ICSID arbitration procedure permits the parties to cherry-pick which documents are to be disclosed and which ones are not. While this concern may be downplayed by the fact that the majority of ICSID awards are made public, this is not the case with other arbitration-related documents such as: the written submissions of the parties, expert reports, witness statements, transcript of hearings, etc. Further, ICSID hearings are not open to the public, save agreed by the parties.

Regarding third-party participation, neither the UNCITRAL Rules on Transparency nor the ICSID Arbitration Rules 2022 allows affected third-parties active participation in the ISDS process. Third-party participation in ISDS refers to the involvement of non-disputing parties ('NDPs') in the arbitral proceedings. Typically, there are two categories of NDPs recognised in arbitral practice i.e. a 'non-disputing treaty party', and a 'non-disputing private party' (non-state actor). The former includes the home state of the investor or another treaty party with an interest in the dispute, while the latter relates to private non-state actors with an interest in the dispute e.g. affected communities, environmental groups, and other non-governmental public interest groups, etc.

---

[304] United Nations Convention on Transparency in Treaty-based Investor-State Arbitration ('Mauritius Convention'), 10 December 2014.

[305] Article 1(1), Mauritius Convention 2014.

[306] See. Article 2 and 3, UNCITRAL Rules on Transparency 2013.

[307] See. Article 4 and 5, UNCITRAL Rules on Transparency 2013.

[308] See. Article 6, UNCITRAL Rules on Transparency 2013.

[309] Chapter X, ICSID Arbitration Rules 2022, (Publication, Access to Proceedings and Non-Disputing Party Submissions).

[310] See. Article 2 and 3, UNCITRAL Rules on Transparency 2013.

[311] See, Rule 62–64, ICSID Arbitration Rules 2022.

As earlier stated, NDPs are not allowed any form of active participation in ISDS, like the ability to initiate or defend a claim in order to safeguard their interests. In essence, the designation of their role as NDPs literally excludes such possibilities. However, one specific form of NDP participation that is allowed in ISDS is the submission of '*amicus curiae*' briefs. This is a legal brief or submission made by a person or organisation that is not a party to a case but has an interest in its outcome.[312] Primarily, the *amicus curiae* is regarded as a 'friend of the court' whose role is to provide their special perspective, expertise, and arguments to assist the tribunal in reaching its decision.[313] Both the ICSID Arbitration Rules and the UNCITRAL Rules on Transparency contain explicit rules on *amicus curiae* submissions,[314] and likewise the arbitration rules of the SCC and SIAC.[315] Further, some recent IIAs also incorporate provisions on *amicus curiae* submission.[316]

Undoubtedly, the inclusion of *amicus curiae* briefs in ISDS is a commendable mechanism for addressing the potential imbalance caused by the closed nature of the system. This mechanism is particularly valuable in considering the interests of third parties that may otherwise be overlooked without the allowance of an *amicus* brief. Since ISDS cases often involve matters of public interest, such as environmental protection, human rights, or other sustainable development concerns, *amicus curiae* briefs offer an avenue for organisations or bodies representing these interests to present their arguments and concerns. This is particularly important when these interests may not be adequately represented by the disputing parties. By allowing amicus curiae briefs, the tribunal gains a comprehensive understanding of the issues involved, enabling them to make well-informed decisions.

Despite this important role, NDPs have no unhindered access to submit *amicus curiae* briefs in ISDS. First, the majority of IIAs do not have explicit provisions for *amicus* submissions.[317] This creates uncertainty regarding the acceptance and possible room for inconsistencies in the requirements for accepting these submissions. Second, where permitted under an IIA or the procedural rules governing an arbitration, the acceptance of an *amicus* submission is still contingent upon the tribunal's discretion and the fulfilment of certain stringent conditions.[318] One common

---

[312] See in general, Sands and Mackenzie (2008).

[313] *Suez, Sociedad General de Aguas de Barcelona S.A. and Interagua Servicios Integrales de Agua S.A. v. Argentine Republic*, ICSID Case No. ARB/03/17, Order in response to a Petition for Participation as Amicus Curiae (17 March 2006), para. 13.

[314] Rule 67, ICSID Arbitration Rules 2022; Article 4, UNCITRAL Rules on Transparency 2013.

[315] Article 3, SCC Arbitration Rules Appendix III; Article 29, SIAC Investment Arbitration Rules.

[316] Annex 29-A (para. 43–46), Canada-EU, Comprehensive Economic and Trade Agreement ('CETA'), signed 30 October 2016; Annex 14-A(para. 42–44), EU-Singapore FTA, signed 15 October 2018; Article 9.16(3) and (4) Australia-China FTA, entered into force 20 December 2015.

[317] Lamb et al. (2017), p. 74.

[318] See for example, Rule 67(2) ICSID Arbitration Rules 2022; Article 4, UNCITRAL Transparency Rules 2013.

condition is that the *amicus* must address a matter within the scope of the dispute.[319] However, there are instances where the interests represented by *amici* do not necessarily fall within the scope of the tribunal's adjudicatory mandate. This is particularly true for interests that are traditionally not covered under international investment law, such as human rights which the disputing parties have also failed to raise as an issue in contention.

The *Pezold v. Zimbabwe*[320] case provides an illustrative example of the denial of an *amicus* submission for failing to address a matter within the scope of the dispute. As earlier analysed, the dispute involved the alleged unlawful expropriation of the claimants' farm land investments in Zimbabwe (→ Sect. 3.1.1.3), whereas the NDP had proposed to address 'putative rights of the indigenous communities as 'indigenous peoples' under international human rights law.[321] For the tribunal, human rights considerations were outside the scope of its adjudicatory mandate. To buttress its conclusion, the tribunal determined that the rights of indigenous communities under international law were not raised by the disputing parties as relevant to the factual or legal issues in question.[322] As a result, the tribunal deemed the amicus submission out of scope and irrelevant to the determination of the case.

Even when allowed to make a submission, an *amici* typically does not have procedural rights ensured, such as access to case files or participation in oral hearings.[323] While the recent ICSID Arbitration Rules recognise the right of NDPs to access arbitration documents, this right can be revoked if any of the disputing parties object to it.[324] Notably, these restrictions may not prevent an NDP from accessing the benefits provided by other transparency rules to which the disputing parties are obliged e.g. the UNCITRAL Rules on Transparency. In any case, there is no guarantee that the tribunal will accept the NDP's submission and the amici cannot contest the tribunal's decision on its application.[325] As a result of these aforementioned constraints, there are concerns about whether the current rules and jurisprudence regarding *amicus* submissions adequately ensure the participation of interested third-parties in ISDS.[326]

Particularly from an African perspective, there has been a growing demand for greater transparency and involvement of third parties in ISDS processes.[327] This call

---

[319]Rule 67(2)(a) ICSID Arbitration Rules 2022; Article 4(1), UNCITRAL Rules on Transparency 2013.

[320]*Bernhard von Pezold and Others v. Republic of Zimbabwe*, ICSID Case No. ARB/10/15, Procedural Order No. 2 (26 June 2012).

[321]*Ibid.*, para. 60.

[322]*Ibid.*, para. 59.

[323]Hornkohl and Melikyan (2022), p. 13.

[324]Rule 67(6) ICSID Arbitration Rules 2022.

[325]Hornkohl and Melikyan (2022), p. 14.

[326]Coleman et al. (2019), p. 7.

[327]UNCITRAL, *Submission from the Government of South Africa* of 17/7/2019, A/CN.9/WG.III/WP.176, paras. 17,32,52–54.

for change stems from the recognition of the need to establish a more equitable investment framework that considers the interests of all stakeholders, including local communities, the environment, and public welfare which underlie investment disputes. The *von Pezold* case is a classic example of how an investor's claim could have a significant impact on the rights of third-parties who are given no opportunity to participate or present their concerns in ISDS proceedings.

Besides the *Pezold* case, the Shell Nigeria case serves as another illustrative example of the disparity within ISDS when it comes to the impact on third parties. While the Dutch claimant had the power and resources to initiate arbitration against Nigeria, following local efforts to enforce a judgment against it for environmental damage caused by oil spillages in its host communities (→ Sect. 3.1.3), the affected host communities, on the other hand, had no direct access to the tribunal to remedy their grief. While they could have potentially participated as *amicus curiae*, there is no record of such an attempt before the case was discontinued.[328] However, the previously mentioned limitations, including whether the interests of the affected communities fall within the scope of the dispute, could potentially lead to the denial of access to the tribunal as *amicus curiae*.

This imbalance has been another major source of discontent with the traditional ISDS system from an African perspective, leading to the demand for a more balanced and inclusive investment protection framework that considers the interests of all stakeholders, including that of affected local communities.[329] As the call for reforms gains momentum, it underscores the pressing need to establish an ISDS system that fosters fairness, equity, and a more comprehensive approach to investment protection, ultimately aiming to address the concerns and aspirations of all those impacted by international investments.

3.3 Interim Conclusion

As highlighted at the beginning of this chapter, the African criticism of the traditional ISDS system arises from substantive and procedural concerns not unique to Africa, but a global challenge. Recognising the global discourse that has ensued regarding these challenges, this chapter takes a region-specific approach, focusing on understanding why African countries have become increasingly disenchanted with the traditional ISDS framework.

To shed light on the African dilemma with traditional ISDS, this chapter utilizes pertinent case examples to highlight two fundamental aspects: *First*, how the

---

[328] *Shell Petroleum N.V. and The Shell Petroleum Development Company of Nigeria Limited v. Federal Republic of Nigeria*, ICSID Case No. ARB/21/7, order taking note of the discontinuance (13 October 2022).

[329] UNCITRAL, *Submission from the Government of South Africa* of 17/7/2019, A/CN.9/WG.III/ WP.176, paras. 52–54.

application of the substantive standards of treatment in old-generation IIAs has yielded undesirable outcomes for African nations, threatening a regulatory chill, uncertainty regarding their treaty obligations due to conflicting outcomes, and failure to guarantee investor accountability. *Second*, this chapter considers how the ISDS procedure conceived in old-generation IIAs has been applied by arbitral tribunals in a manner that threatens the development of local courts competence in ISDS, fails to foster the use of ADR mechanism in settling investment disputes, including the unsatisfactory transparency and participation of third parties in ISDS.

By highlighting the African story of disenchantment with traditional ISDS, this chapter sets the stage for the forthcoming discussion in Chap. 4, focusing on a deeper examination of those crucial considerations that need to be accounted for in the foundations of a future MIC. How these crucial considerations subsequently discussed are addressed will ultimately decide the answer to the question at the heart of this research: i.e., whether African states would find an MIC attractive as a suitable alternative to traditional ISDS.

Other Documents

International Law Commission (ILC)'s Articles on Diplomatic Protection ('ADP') with commentaries

UNCITRAL, Possible Reform of Investor-State Dispute Settlement (ISDS): Consistency and Related Matters: Note by the Secretariat of 28/8/2018, A/CN.9/WG. III/WP.150

UNCITRAL, Report of Working Group III (Investor-State Dispute Settlement Reform) of 14/5/2018, A/CN.9/935

UNCITRAL, Report of Working Group III (Investor-State Dispute Settlement Reform) of 26/2/2018, A/CN.9/930/Add.1/Rev.1

UNCITRAL, *Submission from the European Union and its Member States* of 24/1/ 2019, A/CN.9/WG.III/WP.159/Add.1

UNCITRAL, *Submission from the Government of South Africa* of 17/7/2019, A/CN.9/WG.III/WP.176

References

Adetula V, Jaiyebo O (2020) Electoral democracy, foreign capital flows and the human rights infrastructure in Nigeria. In: Hodu YN, Mbengue MM (eds) African perspectives in international investment law. Manchester University Press, Manchester, pp 153–172

Akinkugbe OD (2019) Reverse contributors? African State Parties, ICSID and the development of international investment law. ICSID Rev FILJ 34(2):434–454

Alschner W (2022) Ensuring correctness or promoting consistency? Tracking policy priorities in investment arbitration through largescale citation analysis. In: Behn D, Fauchald K, Langford M (eds) The legitimacy of investment arbitration: empirical perspectives. Cambridge University Press, Cambridge, pp 230–255

Amnesty International (2011) UN confirms massive oil pollution in Niger Delta, https://www. amnesty.org/en/un-confirms-massive-oil-pollution-niger-delta/

Blanco SM (2019) Full protection and security in international investment law. Springer, Cham

Berge TL (2020) Dispute by design? Legalization, backlash, and the drafting of investment agreements. ISQ 64(4):919–928

Blackaby N, Partasides C, Redfern A (2023) Redfern and hunter on international arbitration: student version, 7th edn. Oxford University Press, Oxford

Born G (2021) International arbitration: law and practice, 3rd edn. Kluwer Law International, Alphen aan den Rijn

Brauch MD (2017) Exhaustion of local remedies in international investment law (IISD). https:// www.iisd.org/system/files

Brower CN, Schill S (2009) Is arbitration a threat or a boom to the legitimacy of international investment law? CJIL 9(2):471–498

Butler N, Subedi S (2017) The future of international investment regulation: towards a world investment organisation? NILR 64:43–72

Calatayud JT, Candelas JC, Fernández PP (2008) The accountability of multinational corporations for human rights' violations. CCCFFC 64:171–186

Claxton JM (2020) Compelling parties to mediate investor-state disputes: no pressure, no diamonds? PDRLJ 20(1):78–100

Coleman J, Johnson L, Güven B, Cotula L, Berger T (2019) Third-party rights in investor-state dispute settlement: options for reform (CCSI). https://scholarship.law.columbia.edu/sustain able_investment_staffpubs/150/

Deroche L (2020) War clauses in international investment law: a need for clarity. McGill JDR 7:34–67

Douglas M (2015) The importance of transparency for legitimising investor-state dispute settlement: an Australian perspective. New Zealand Association of Comparative Law, Hors Serie XIX:111–121

Douglas Z (2009) The international law of investment claims. Cambridge University Press, Cambridge

Ganesh A (2017) Cooling-off period (investment arbitration). MPILux Working Paper 7. https:// www.mpi.lu/fileadmin/mpi/

Hildebrand T (2021) The fighting's done, now pay me: investment treaties, war, and state liability. VJTL 54(4):995–1040

Hober K (2018) Investment treaty arbitration. Elgar, Cheltenham

Hodgson M, Kryvoi Y, Hrcka D (2021) 2021 empirical study: cost, damages and duration in investor-state arbitration. https://www.biicl.org/documents/136_isds-costs-damages-duration_ june_2021.pdf

Hornkohl L, Melikyan A (2022) Legitimisation through participation: can third-party participation cure the sustainable development wounds of ISDS. https://papers.ssrn.com/sol3/papers.cfm? abstract_id=4188372

Hurst JW (1971) Problems of legitimacy in the contemporary legal order. OLR 24(2):224–238

Jones A (2021) The Sinister Turn: the Decolonized African State in ICSID expropriation arbitration. https://papers.ssrn.com/sol3/papers.cfm?abstract_id=3983221

Junngam N (2018) The full protection and security standard in international investment law: what and who is investment fully[?] Protected and secured from? ABLR 7(1):1–100

Kaufmann-Kohler G, Potestà M (2020) Investor-state dispute settlement and National Courts: current framework and reform options. Springer, Cham

Kaushal A (2009) Revisiting history: how the past matters for the present backlash against the foreign investment regime. HILJ 50:491–534

Kim D (2011) The Annulment Committee's role in multiplying inconsistency in ICSID arbitration: the need to move away from an annulment-based system. NYLR 86:242–279

Lamb S, Harrison D, Hew J (2017) Recent developments on the law and practice of amicus briefs in investor-state arbitration. IJAL 5(2):72–92

Le Cannu PJ (2018) Foundation and innovation: the participation of African States in the ICSID dispute resolution system. ICSID Rev FILJ 33(2):456–500

Leibold AM (2016) The friction between investor protection and human rights: lessons from Foresti v. South Africa. HJIL 38:215–268

Mavroidis PC, Adams CC, Schreuer C, Wang G (2011) Preventing a backlash against investment arbitration: could the WTO be the solution. JWIT 12(3):425–446

Montineri C (2021) UNCITRAL Reform Process on ISDS. In: Hobe S, Scheu J (eds) Evolution, evaluation and future developments in international investment law. Nomos, Baden-Baden, pp 157–172

Newcombe AP, Paradell L (2009) Law and practice of investment treaties: standards of treatment. Kluwer Law International, Alphen aan den Rijn

OECD (2005) Transparency and third party participation in investor-state dispute settlement procedures. https://doi.org/10.1787/524613550768

Paparinskis M (2013) Investment treaty arbitration and the (new) law of state responsibility. EJIL 24(2):617–647

Parra A (2017) The history of ICSID, 2nd edn. Oxford University Press, Oxford

Pérez-Aznar F (2017) Investment protection in exceptional situations: compensation-for-losses clauses in IIAs. ICSID Rev FILJ 32(3):696–720

Pohl J, Mashigo K, Nohen A (2012) Dispute settlement provisions in international investment agreements: a large sample survey. OECD Working Papers on International Investment. https://www.oecd.org/investment/investment-policy/WP-2012_2.pdf

Polanco R (2018) The return of the home state to investor-state disputes: bringing back diplomatic protection? Cambridge University Press, Cambridge

Rasilla I (2023) 'The greatest victory'? Challenges and opportunities for mediation in investor-state dispute settlement. ICSID Rev FILJ 38(1):169–200

Reinisch A, Schreuer C (2020) International protection of investments: the substantive standards. Cambridge

Sands PJ, Mackenzie R (2008) International Courts and Tribunals, Amicus Curiae, Max Planck Encyclopedia of Public International Law. https://opil.ouplaw.com/display/

Schefer KN (2020) International investment law: text, cases and materials, 3rd edn. Elgar, Cheltenham

Schreuer C (2019) War and peace in international investment law. In: Gómez KF, Gourgourinis A, Titi C (eds) International investment law and the law of armed conflict. Springer, Cham, pp 1–21

Schreuer C, Malintoppi L, Reinisch A, Sinclair A (2009) The ICSID convention: a commentary, 2nd edn. Cambridge University Press, Cambridge

Sinclair A (2004) The origins of the umbrella clause in the international law of investment protection. Arb Int 20(4):411–434

Spears S, Agius MF (2019) Protection of investments in war-torn states: a practitioner's perspective on war clauses in bilateral investment treaties. In: Gómez KF, Gourgourinis A, Titi C (eds) International investment law and the law of armed conflict. Springer, Cham, pp 283–317

Transnational Institute (2019) ISDS in numbers: impact of investment arbitration against African States. https://www.tni.org/files/publication-downloads/isds

Ubilava A (2022) Underutilisation of ADR in ISDS: resolving treaty interpretation issues. UCLA JILFA 26(2):131–168

UN News (2011) Cleaning up Nigerian Oil Pollution could take 30 years. Cost Billions. https://news.un.org/en/story/2011/08/383512

UNCTAD (1998) Bilateral investment treaties in the mid-1990's. United Nations Publication, United Nations

UNCTAD (2010) Investor-state disputes: prevention and alternatives to arbitration. https://unctad.org/system/files/official-document/diaeia200911_en.pdf

UNCTAD (2017) Special update on investor-state dispute settlement: facts and figures. https://unctad.org/system/files/official-document/diaepcb2017d7_en.pdf

UNCTAD (2018) Reform package for the international investment regime. https://investmentpolicy.unctad.org/uploaded-files. Accessed 24 June 2024

UNEP (2011) United Nations, environmental assessment of ogoniland report. https://www.unep.org/explore-topics/disasters-conflicts/where-we-work/nigeria/ogoniland

Vadi V (2015) Global cultural governance by investment arbitral tribunals: the Making of a Lex Administrativa Culturalis. BUILJ 33(2):457–492

Yannaca-Small (2006) Interpretation of the umbrella clause in investment agreements, OECD Working Papers on International Investment. https://www.oecd.org/investment

Chapter 4
The Proposed MIC: Crucial Considerations for Acceptance by African States

As highlighted in Chap. 1, African states became active participants in the international investment law system starting from the 1960s onward when decolonisation gained full momentum on the continent. During the decolonisation period, newly independent African states recognised FDI as a crucial factor for their development agenda. Consequently, many African governments sought to attract FDI by entering into BITs that included ISDS provisions.

Over the years, numerous literatures have debated without consensus the question of whether BITs and ISDS clauses do lead to increased FDI,[1] which in turn propels economic development.[2] While this point can also be debated in Africa given the level of underdevelopment still prevalent in most nations in the continent,[3] what is not in doubt is how the BITs and FDI inflow have propelled ISDS claims against African states from the 1990s till the present. Although various factors have contributed to this upsurge, including blatant-inappropriate conduct of public officials,[4] one factor that cannot be ignored are the sweeping BIT guarantees, which enable protected investors to challenge legitimate public interest measures that may contradict investors' interests, potentially exposing the concerned state to financial liability in ISDS.

Recognising the need to reassess their approach to ISDS, several responses have been undertaken by African governments ranging from fixing to replacing the existing system.[5] Some states, for example, South Africa and Morocco have gone as far as terminating their BITs with foreign governments to curtail the undesirable effects of the traditional ISDS procedure and the substantive guarantees it is

---

[1] Ahmad et al. (2022), p. 2; Salacuse and Sullivan (2005), p. 67 ff; Busse et al. (2010), p. 147 ff.
[2] See generally, Colen et al. (2013), p. 70 ff.
[3] See generally, Cleeve et al. (2015), p. 1 ff.
[4] Laryea and Fabusuy (2019), p. 29.
[5] Ofodile (2014), p. 340 ff.

designed to enforce.[6] While this fact may suggest there is no uniform approach to ISDS reform in Africa, there is nevertheless a shared objective among African nations. This shared objective is to restore equilibrium in the relationship between foreign investors and states, creating an ISDS framework that effectively safeguards investor interests while also prioritising national interests for sustainable development in an increasingly interconnected global economy.

As previously highlighted in the general introduction, reforming the traditional ISDS system is indeed a global concern that has triggered ongoing reform debates within UNCITRAL Working Group III. So far, these reform debates have yielded numerous procedural reform proposals, including the MIC. Since the MIC proposal is the primary focus of this thesis, its acceptability as a suitable alternative to traditional ISDS for African states cannot be assured if the shortcomings of the traditional ISDS system are replicated in the MIC. Therefore, the purpose of this chapter is to identify those crucial interests that must be taken into consideration within the framework of an MIC, and how to address them in order to attract African states' participation.

Building upon the contextual background presented in the preceding chapters, this chapter will proceed as follows: *Firstly*, it will provide an introduction to the MIC system proposed by the EU (Sect. 4.1); *secondly*, it will delve into the crucial considerations necessary to secure African states' support for an MIC (Sect. 4.2); and lastly, how those crucial interest could be addressed to attract African states participation in a future MIC (Sect. 4.3).

4.1 What Is the MIC (The EU MIC Proposal)?

The EU's proposal for a Multilateral Investment Court (MIC) is part of a larger shift away from its previously acclaimed 'gold standard' approach to international investment protection.[7] The member states' BIT templates, which have played a significant role in negotiating and concluding the majority of investment treaties across the globe, were previously regarded as representing the EU's gold standard in investment treaty-making. However, this has changed since the EU assumed FDI treaty-making powers under Article 207 of the Treaty of Lisbon.[8] Although the EU Commission is committed to negotiating investment treaties inspired by the gold standard,[9] the documents and negotiating mandates that have emerged from the

---

[6] South Africa has terminated its BITs with Spain (1998), Netherlands (1995), Belgium (1998), Luxembourg (1998), Germany (1995), Switzerland (1995); also Morocco terminated its BITs with Germany (1961), Spain (1989), France (1975), Belgium (1965).

[7] See in this regard, Bungenberg and Reinisch (2021), p. 443 ff.

[8] Treaty of Lisbon Amending the Treaty on European Union and the Treaty Establishing the European Community [2007] OJ C 306/01.

[9] European Commission (2010), p. 6.

Union post-Lisbon Treaty suggest that the model BITs of member states have played a less significant role in the EU's investment treaty negotiations.[10] The EU's advocacy for an MIC is a testament to this fact.

The EU's proposal for an MIC marks a significant shift from the investment arbitration system earlier regarded by its member states as the gold standard for investment dispute resolution. In contrast to the traditional ISDS system, which consists of various arbitration forums established under different institutional and non-institutional (*ad-hoc*) bodies operating independently,[11] the MIC is envisioned as a centralized body for resolving investor-state disputes. It would be composed of full-time judges, serving in both the first and second instance courts, organised into multiple chambers, with long-term appointments.[12]

The EU's advocacy for an MIC system came against the backdrop of growing public criticism of the traditional ISDS system within Europe. Over time, the investment arbitration system initially promoted to safeguard the investment interest of European citizens abroad, has resulted in European states themselves being frequent subjects to ISDS claims. According to the UNCTAD's ISDS database as of December 31, 2023, EU member states have been named as respondents in a total of 301 ISDS cases, out of which 208 cases occurred within the last decade.[13] This significant surge in ISDS claims against EU states heightened public awareness and scrutiny of the system, exposing its flaws to the citizens.[14]

In 2014, the EU Commission initiated a public consultation process to gather opinions on investment protection and ISDS in the context of the Transatlantic Trade and Investment Partnership ('TTIP') negotiation with the United States. The outcome of this public consultation, which received almost 150,000 replies, echoed the citizens' desire for a new approach to ISDS.[15] In response to the TTIP consultation and obvious disenchantment with the traditional ISDS system, the European Commission came up with the proposal for an Investment Court System ('ICS') for the TTIP and other EU trade and investment negotiations.[16] Fundamentally, the ICS represents the EU and its member states' approach to replacing the one-off arbitration system within their contracted IIAs with a permanent two-tiered court system.

Although the TTIP negotiation was later suspended indefinitely in 2016,[17] the concept of an ICS would later materialise in subsequent EU investment agreements

---

[10]Titi (2015), p. 640 ff.

[11]See, Schefer (2020), p. 371 ff.

[12]Bungenberg and Reinisch (2020), p. 4; EI-IILCC Study Group on ISDS Reform (2022), p. 27; European Commission (2017), p. 29.

[13]UNCTAD ISDS database, https://investmentpolicy.unctad.org/investment-dispute-settlement/advanced-search.

[14]See, Danish and Uribe (2022), p. 12.

[15]European Commission (2015).

[16]European Commission Press (2015).

[17]European Parliament (2016).

with third countries.[18] The EU and its member states, together with their recent IIA partners, now seek to replicate the ICS idea at a global level through the creation of an MIC. They aim to achieve this through future cooperation in establishing a multilateral investment tribunal and appellate mechanism for resolving investment disputes, ultimately replacing the ICS.[19]

In March 2018, the European Commission received the negotiating directives for an MIC from the European Council.[20] In January 2019, the EU submitted to UNCITRAL Working Group III its detailed position and rationale for endorsing the MIC option as the most pragmatic solution to holistically address the identified concerns associated with traditional ISDS.[21] The EU also put forward its suggestions on the fundamental elements that should be taken into account when establishing a future MIC, which include, among others:[22]

- A standing mechanism that encourages amicable settlement;
- A two-tiered system with a first and second instance (appellate) court, Composed of full-time adjudicators;
- Adjudicators subject to strict ethical requirements ensuring independence and impartiality from parties;
- Adjudicators qualification requirements comparable to those of other international courts;
- An objective appointment process by the contracting parties;
- Inclusive representation, fostering geographical and gender diversity;
- Application of the UNCITRAL Rules on Transparency as a minimum standard, and ability of affected third parties to participate in investment disputes.
- An effective enforcement mechanism, with no possibility to review MIC awards at a domestic level;
- An MIC application to existing and future investment treaties;
- The availability of an assistance mechanism.

The above-mentioned characteristics of an MIC are now a subject of debate in UNCITRAL Working Group III. The UNCITRAL Secretariat has provided an initial draft on a standing multilateral mechanism assisting the member states

---

[18] See, Article 8.27–8.28, Canada-EU CETA, signed 30 October 2016; Article 3.38–3.39, EU-Vietnam IPA, signed 30 June 2019; Article 3.9–3.10, EU-Singapore IPA, signed 15 October 2018; Article 11–12, Investment Dispute Resolution, EU-Mexico Agreement in Principle (2018); Article 10.33–10.34, EU-Chile Advanced Framework Agreement (Investment Chapter) (2022).

[19] See, Article 8.29, Canada-EU CETA, signed 30 October 2016; Article 3.41, EU-Vietnam IPA, signed 30 June 2019; Article 3.12, EU-Singapore IPA, signed 15 October 2018; Article 14, Investment Dispute Resolution, EU-Mexico Agreement in Principle (2018); Article 10.36, EU-Chile Advanced Framework Agreement (Investment Chapter) (2022).

[20] *European Council*, Negotiating Directives for a Convention Establishing a Multilateral Court for the Settlement of Investment Disputes, 12981/17 ADD 1.

[21] UNCITRAL, *Submission from the European Union and its Member States* of 24/1/2019, A/CN.9/WG.III/WP.159/Add.1, para. 40 ff.

[22] *Ibid.*, para. 11 ff.

discussions.[23] As of the completion of this thesis, the initial draft only consisted of 11 draft provisions, with topics primarily related to the establishment, composition, and jurisdiction of the court.[24] Negotiating these terms, along with other crucial considerations that need to be taken into account will require extensive international cooperation, to achieve the consensus necessary to bring an MIC into reality.

Notably, the MIC proposal has not started out with overwhelming support from member states in Working Group III. Indeed, major trading partners of the EU, such as the USA and Japan have refrained from endorsing the creation of an MIC.[25] In Africa, a major EU trading partner such as South Africa has been one of the most vocal critics of the proposed MIC system in Working Group III.[26] While no other African state has openly criticised the MIC proposal in written submissions to the working group, the lack of interest in such a system can be deduced from the ISDS reform policies being implemented in the continent both regionally and bilaterally,[27] none of which includes the consideration for an MIC system.

Notably, two recent Africa-EU member states' BITs foresee a future participation in an MIC.[28] However, it is noteworthy that, unlike other recent EU IIAs with non-African counterparts, the Cabo Verde-Hungary BIT (2019) and Côte d'Ivoire-Portugal BIT (2019) do not foresee a common provision obliging the contracting parties to *'pursue with other trading partners the establishment of a multilateral investment tribunal and appellate mechanism for the resolution of investment disputes'.*[29] Rather, the aforementioned BITs only contemplate that an MIC will replace the treaty's ISDS clause if such a multilateral court system enters into force between the contracting parties in the future.[30] This indicates that the respective African states are currently unwilling to undertake an obligation to pursue the establishment of an MIC with the EU and other trading partners, but would not rule out the possibility of joining such a court system in the future.

Despite the apparent lack of enthusiastic interest, it would be inaccurate to conclude that African states are not in favour of an MIC system. The recent BITs

---

[23] UNCITRAL, *Standing Multilateral Mechanism: Selection and Appointment of ISDS Tribunal Members and Related Matters*: Note by the Secretariat of 8/12/2021, A/CN.9/WG.III/WP.213.

[24] *Ibid.*

[25] European Parliament, Legislative train: Multilateral Investment Court, p. 3, https://www.europarl.europa.eu/l.

[26] UNCITRAL, *Submission from the Government of South Africa* of 17/7/2019, A/CN.9/WG.III/WP.176, para. 88 ff.

[27] See, Ofodile (2014), p. 1, 3; Tarawali (2019), p. 4.

[28] See, Article 9(11), Cabo Verde-Hungary BIT (2019), entered into force 02 February 2020; Article 25, Côte d'Ivoire-Portugal BIT (2019), signed 13 June 2019.

[29] Article 8.29, CETA; Article 34(1), EU-Vietnam IPA, signed 30 June 2019; Article 3(12), EU-Singapore IPA, signed 15 October 2018; Article 14, Investment Dispute Resolution, EU-Mexico Agreement in Principle (2018); Article 10(36), EU-Chile Advanced Framework Agreement (Investment Chapter) (2022).

[30] Article 9(11), Cabo Verde-Hungary BIT (2019), signed 28 March 2019; Article 25, Côte d'Ivoire-Portugal BIT (2019), signed 13 June 2019.

between Cabo Verde and Côte d'Ivoire with EU states, as mentioned above, suggest that African states may be open to participating in an MIC system, provided it aligns with their expectations for a desirable ISDS mechanism. Essentially, they seek a dispute resolution system that not only focuses on protecting foreign investment but also safeguards the national interests of the states to promote sustainable development. The discussion below now delves into the crucial considerations necessary to achieve this critical balance.

4.2   Crucial Considerations for African States' Participation in an MIC

Considering the three interdependent pillars that uphold sustainable development in any given state, for an MIC to be accepted as a legitimate forum for ISDS involving Africa states, it must effectively safeguard the protection of foreign investment without jeopardising the rights of states to pursue their national interests within the three SD pillars, i.e.: economic development, social development, and environmental protection.

Significantly, sustainable development, the driving force behind the ISDS reform policies in Africa, is not an exclusive objective limited to the continent. This is a mandate found in several national constitutions[31] and one shared by all nations under the UN umbrella.[32] Given the universality of the SD objective, the EU as the primary proponent of the MIC undoubtedly aligns with the African call that investment protection policies required for fostering *'economic development'* should not be pursued to the detriment of *'social'* and *'environmental'* interests. The EU-Canada CETA affirms this submission. The preamble affirms the parties' commitment to:

> promote sustainable development and the development of international trade in such a way as to contribute to sustainable development in its economic, social, and environmental dimension.[33]

This preamble confirms the commitment of the CETA parties to contribute to sustainable development across its three pillars. Furthermore, in a Joint Interpretative Instrument ('JII') designed to function as an interpretive guide for CETA, the EU and Canada reaffirmed their dedication to sustainable development, emphasising that:

---

[31] Schrijver (2008), p. 326 ff.

[32] See generally, UNGA RES/70/1 *Transforming Our World: The 2030 Agenda for Sustainable Development* of 25/9/2015, UN DOC. A/RES/70/1.

[33] Ninth recital, Preamble to the CETA.

CETA reconfirms the longstanding commitment of Canada and the European Union and its Member States to sustainable development and is designed to foster the contribution of trade to this objective.[34]

Although both the CETA preamble and JII only referred to international trade and not investment, the broader understanding of international trade inherently encompasses investment.[35] The CETA further proceeds to dedicate a specific chapter (Chapter 22) to the subject of trade and sustainable development, emphasising the parties' acknowledgement that the three SD pillars:

[...] economic development, social development and environmental protection are interdependent and mutually reinforcing components of sustainable development, and reaffirm their commitment to promoting the development of international trade in such a way as to contribute to the objective of sustainable development, for the welfare of present and future generations.[36]

While the CETA Investment Chapter itself lacks any explicit reference to sustainable development, an interpretation of the treaty in accordance with Article 31 of the VCLT precludes an interpretation of the investment chapter in isolation of the preamble and other treaty chapters providing relevant context, including Chapter 22 CETA.[37] Therefore, the ICS implemented as the ISDS mechanism in CETA will inevitably need to take into account the three pillars of sustainable development while fulfilling its adjudicative role under the CETA investment chapter. In addition to the CETA, it is noteworthy that the EU has also included SD chapters in its various other Free Trade Agreements (FTAs).[38] Therefore, it can be asserted that incorporating SD chapters into FTAs has become a common treaty practice for the EU.[39] The foregoing analysis aims to demonstrate that the core principle propelling investment law reform in Africa represents a shared objective among the nations within UNCITRAL Working Group III debating the establishment of an MIC, including the EU and its member states as the chief proponents.

While foreign investors are granted certain investment protection guarantees to incentivize their contribution to economic development, this should be counterbalanced with effective local and international policies to avoid social and environmental harm.[40] This is exactly the interest African states seek to secure, a balancing that essentially mirrors the interest of other developing nations.[41]

---

[34] See, Joint Interpretative Instrument on the CETA, OJ L 11/3, 14/1/2017, para. 7(a).

[35] On the convergence between trade and investment, see Kurtz (2016), p. 10 ff; Schacherer (2019), p. 214.

[36] Article 22.1(1), CETA.

[37] See in this regard, Schacherer (2019), p. 220 ff.

[38] Chapter 13, EU-Vietnam FTA, signed 30 June 2019; Chapter 12, EU-Singapore FTA, signed 15 October 2018; Chapter 8, EU-UK FTA, entered into force 1 May 2021.

[39] Schacherer (2019), p. 214.

[40] Schill (2015), p. 6; UNCITRAL, *Submission from the Government of South Africa* of 17/7/2019, A/CN.9/WG.III/WP.176, para. 22.

[41] See, Kelsey and Mohamadieh (2021), p. 24 f.

Essentially, for an MIC to be deemed as a legitimate forum for ISDS in Africa, it must effectively safeguard the protection of foreign investment without jeopardising the rights of states to pursue their national interests within the three SD pillars. In specific details, this means the following: an MIC that safeguards the regulatory policy space of member states (Sect. 4.2.1); fosters both 'consistent' and 'correct' ISDS decisions (Sect. 4.2.2); investor accountability (Sect. 4.2.3); protection of third party interest (Sect. 4.2.4); development of local courts by requiring first recourse to local remedies (Sect. 4.2.5); and ADR (Sect. 4.2.6).

4.2.1   An MIC That Safeguards the Regulatory Policy Space of Member States

One common concern about the traditional ISDS system is its impact on the regulatory autonomy of sovereign states.[42] The most contentious aspect of this impact is on the host states' prerogative to implement public interest measures in pursuit of its sustainable development objectives. Equipped with broadly worded IIA guarantees mostly inspired by outdated western models, protected investors can challenge government public interest policies perceived as conflicting with their investment interests. As discussed in Chap. 3, African states have had their fair share of pecuniary exposure in ISDS for implementing measures aimed at promoting legitimate public welfare objectives such as human rights, environmental and public health protection (Sect. 3.1.1).

Although the old-generation IIAs are often silent on a state's right to regulate, it is noteworthy that this is a sovereign right, whether expressed in a treaty or not.[43] As held by the ICSID tribunal in *Feldman v. Mexico*,[44] a regulatory space is afforded to states under CIL to pursue legitimate public interest measures without having to compensate every investor adversely affected by such measures.[45] The *Methanex v. USA*[46] tribunal also confirmed that a state could implement measures tantamount to expropriation, provided it is done for a public purpose, non-discriminatory, and followed due process.[47] Such government measures will not be deemed expropriatory nor compensable, save the putative investor had been given a specific commitment by the state to refrain from such regulation.[48] Several ISDS tribunals

---

[42] Langford et al. (2020), p. 169; Menon and Issac (2018).

[43] Cf, Titi (2014), p. 32.

[44] *Marvin Roy Feldman Karpa v United Mexican States*, ICSID Case No ARB(AF)/99/1, Award (16 December 2002).

[45] *Ibid.*, para 103.

[46] *Methanex Corporation v United States of America*, UNCITRAL, Final Award of the Tribunal on Jurisdiction and Merits (3 August 2005), pt IV, ch D, paras 9, 15.

[47] *Ibid.*, Part IV, para. 6 f.

[48] *Ibid.*

have later followed the *Feldman* and *Methanex* case reasoning that investment treaties do not freeze the regulatory autonomy of host states under international law, save there is a specific commitment in that regard.[49]

However, while a state's right to regulate is acknowledged as an uncontested issue under international law, whether the adverse effect of a state's regulatory measure on an investor can go uncompensated remains an open question. When a state enters into an IIA, this action itself is considered a manifestation of the state's sovereign power to regulate its domestic affairs, by voluntarily committing to implement certain standards of investment protection, to the benefit of covered investors within its territory.[50] By the principle *pacta sunt servanda*, a state is under the obligation to comply with those commitments to the extent as bound under the contracted IIA.[51] It is upon this understanding that the ICSID tribunal in *ADC v. Hungary*[52] held that the state's right to regulate under international law is not unlimited but has boundaries, and the treaty obligations undertaken by the state provide such boundaries which must be honoured.[53]

Accordingly, whether a state can exercise its sovereign right to regulate—'-without pecuniary liability' to foreign investors, will depend on the four corners of the IIA obligations it has undertaken. This is the crux of the challenge because old-generation IIAs primarily concentrate on investment protection, encompassing broadly worded guarantees of protection from states to covered investors. The broadly phrased and unqualified nature of these guarantees restricts the capacity of governments to implement and enforce regulations deemed in public interest, as it exposes them to potential pecuniary liability in ISDS claims.

The *Foresti, et al v. South Africa*,[54] and *von Pezold v. Zimbabwe*[55] cases exemplify this vulnerability of African states to pecuniary liabilities under the old western styled IIAs when pursuing their legitimate public interest objectives. In the former case as earlier discussed, the claimants initiated a 350 million U.S. dollars ISDS claim against South Africa for implementing a legislation aimed at fostering

---

[49] *Saluka Investments BV (The Netherlands) v. Czech Republic*, PCA Case No. 2001-04, Partial Award (17 March 2006), para. 255; *Invesmart, B.V. v. Czech Republic*, UNCITRAL, Award (26 June 2009), para. 498; *EDF (Services) Limited v Romania*, ICSID Case No ARB/05/13, Award (8 October 2009) para 217; *AWG Group Ltd. v. Argentine Republic*, UNCITRAL, Decision on Liability (30 July 2010), para. 139; *Total SA v Argentine Republic*, ICSID Case No ARB/04/01, Decision on Liability (27 December 2010), paras 128 - 30; *Tza Yap Shum v. Republic of Peru*, ICSID Case No. ARB/07/6, Award (7 July 2011), para. 145; *El Paso Energy International Company v Argentine Republic*, ICSID Case No ARB/03/15, Award (31 October 2011), para 372.

[50] Titi (2022), p. 19.

[51] *Ibid.*

[52] *ADC Affiliate Limited and ADC & ADMC Management Limited v. Republic of Hungary*, ICSID Case No. ARB/03/16, Award (2 October 2006).

[53] *Ibid.*, para. 423.

[54] *Piero Foresti, Laura de Carli & Others v. The Republic of South Africa*, ICSID Case No. ARB (AF)/07/01, Award (4 August 2010).

[55] *Bernhard von Pezold and Others v. Republic of Zimbabwe*, ICSID Case No. ARB/10/15, Award (28 July 2015).

socio-economic inclusiveness for historically disadvantaged South Africans (HDSAs), who had long endured socio-economic marginalisation due to the country's apartheid history (Sect. 3.1.1.2). Although this claim was ultimately discontinued, this was only after the government reviewed the challenged legislation to a degree that significantly ameliorated the claimant's concern but significantly cut back on the benefits earlier intended for the HDSAs (Sect. 3.1.1.2). Implicitly, this compromise to its social development objective would not have been necessary if the state had felt secure in its safeguard from pecuniary liability under the IIAs invoked by the claimants, challenging the measure intended for its citizens' benefit.

This concern is substantiated by the later *von Pezold v. Zimbabwe*[56] case, where a decision was reached on the merits. Similar to the *Foresti* case, in question was another African government's policy intended to promote socio-economic inclusion for historically disadvantaged citizens, particularly regarding land ownership. Without restating the facts of the case earlier discussed (Sect. 3.1.1.3), what is worth noting is that the tribunal recognised the human rights considerations underlying Zimbabwe's land reform policies which resulted in losses to the claimants' investment.[57] However, the tribunal rejected Zimbabwe's argument for a wide margin of appreciation in pursuing its public interest objective under the IIA. For the tribunal, while such a wide margin is allowed under human rights law, it is not an established practice in international investment law.[58] Accordingly, the margin of appreciation allowed the respondent to implement its public interest measures remain within the confines of its treaty obligations, and under the treaty, the government has agreed to specific obligations which carried no (margin of appreciation) qualification.[59]

Due to the continued existence of outdated and broadly worded IIAs in Africa, the regulatory space of African governments to pursue public interest objectives without incurring financial liability in ISDS is uncertain even within an MIC framework. To address this concern, the modern IIAs emanating from the continent now incorporate explicit and much more precise provisions on investment protection standards—with clarity on the regulatory space of states to pursue their sustainable development objectives.[60] Notably, this reform towards a more balanced ISDS system has primarily occurred intra-Africa.[61] As recognised in several scholarly commentaries, evidence of this shift is manifest in the bilateral and sub-regional agreements

---

[56] *Ibid.*

[57] *Ibid.*, para. 2 ff.

[58] *Ibid.*, 465.

[59] *Ibid.*, 466.

[60] See for example, Article 23, Nigeria-Morocco BIT, signed 3 December 2016; Article 24, AfCFTA Investment Protocol; Article 14, SADC Protocol on Finance and Investment (2006); Article 20(8), Investment Agreement for the COMESA Common Investment Area (2007).

[61] Akinkugbe (2021), p. 31.

contracted post-2000 in the continent, as well as in domestic law reforms on investment protection.[62]

While the different levels of reform indicate divergent approaches to investment law reform in Africa, the February 2023 adoption of the African Continental Free Trade Area ('AfCFTA') Protocol on Investment[63] perhaps represents the current African consensus on an evenly balanced investment protection regime. The Protocol on Investment aims to establish a harmonized framework for protecting intra-African investments, replacing existing intra-African IIAs upon its entry into force.[64]

Unlike old-generation IIAs solely focused on investment protection, the Protocol on Investment has an investment protection chapter,[65] balanced with another dedicated chapter on sustainable development-related issues.[66] The latter includes *inter alia* a detailed provision on the 'right to regulate'[67] and the minimum standards on the environment, labour, and consumer protection that states must adhere to.[68] These provisions clarify that the main objective of the Protocol on Investment is not simply the 'protection of investment', but rather aimed at the protection of 'sustainable investment', that is—an investment that interdependently supports the three pillars of sustainable development.

To underscore this intention, the protocol provides the necessary qualifications to the substantive guarantees owed to covered investors. For example, while the protocol guarantees substantive standards such as non-discrimination[69] and guarantees against expropriation,[70] it further clarifies the exceptions to these guarantees, affirming the regulatory space of states to promote their sustainable development agenda within the clear margin provided under the protocol.[71]

Although the Protocol on Investment may signal the Pan-African ideal on how to strike the proper balance between the protection of foreign investment and safeguarding the policy space of states to regulate in public interest, the innovative characteristics of the protocol still have no place in the vast majority of IIAs in force in Africa. Therefore, from an African perspective, for any meaningful ISDS reform to take place, it has to be considered within the wider context of the outdated

---

[62] See generally, Akinkugbe (2021), pp. 7–33; Mbengue (2019), p. 463 ff; El-Kady and De Gama (2019), p. 483 ff; Mbengue and Schacherer (2017), p. 415 ff.

[63] AfCFTA Investment Protocol (Final Draft), https://www.bilaterals.org/IMG/pdf/en_.

[64] See Article 49, AfCFTA Investment Protocol; See also Lamprou and Iluezi-Ogbaudu (2023).

[65] Chapter 3, AfCFTA Investment Protocol.

[66] Chapter 4, AfCFTA Investment Protocol.

[67] Article 24, AfCFTA Investment Protocol.

[68] Article 25, AfCFTA Investment Protocol.

[69] See, Article 12 and 14, AfCFTA Investment Protocol.

[70] See, Article 19, AfCFTA Investment Protocol.

[71] See for instance, Article 13, 15 and 20, AfCFTA Investment Protocol (exceptions to: national treatment; most-favoured nation; and expropriation).

substantive guarantees that underlie ISDS claims.[72] Particularly, for participation in an MIC, it is crucial to consider how the MIC will interact with the existing old-generation IIAs that can be invoked in the court. If not, the fear is that an MIC will only concretise the inequities of the old IIA regime on a more permanent basis,[73] rather than to correct the imbalance that has rendered states susceptible to pecuniary liability in ISDS, threatening a regulatory chill.[74]

4.2.2 An MIC That Fosters Both 'Consistent' and 'Correct' ISDS Decisions

Considering the public interest nature of ISDS cases, as opposed to purely commercial disputes between private parties, it is crucial for MIC decisions having the potential to restrict or shape states' public policies and the exercise of regulatory authority to be consistent and correct. **Consistency** in this context refers to the uniform interpretation and application of the rules (substantive and procedural) that govern the protection of foreign investments as provided under the relevant IIAs or rules of international law.[75] **Correct decisions** on the other hand denote the accuracy of ISDS decisions to the applicable law and facts to a dispute.[76]

Regarding consistency, as revealed earlier, African states on multiple occasions have been confronted with conflicting decisions in similar ISDS cases without a clear rationale for the divergent outcomes (Sect. 3.1.2). Due to the *ad hoc* nature of arbitral tribunals, rendering decisions based on the facts and diverse applicable laws before them, with no precedential obligation,[77] achieving consistency in such a system is challenging.[78] The differences among the tribunals in terms of their establishment, composition, independent powers, qualifications, and backgrounds of arbitrators, coupled with the lack of interconnection, make it impractical to anticipate consistent outcomes in such a fragmented system.

Compared to the current decentralised system, it is argued that an MIC with judges appointed for long and staggered terms will foster ongoing collegiality and institutional memory in the court's bench, a factor crucial for retaining expertise and

---

[72] UNCITRAL, *Submission from the Government of South Africa* of 17/7/2019, A/CN.9/WG.III/WP.176, paras. 19, 111 ff.

[73] Kelsey and Mohamadieh (2021), p. 24.

[74] Chidede (2019), p. 463; Abimbola (2020).

[75] Adekemi (2021), p. 665.

[76] UNCITRAL, *Possible Reform of Investor-State Dispute Settlement (ISDS): Consistency and Related Matters*: Note by the Secretariat of 28/8/2018, A/CN.9/WG.III/WP.150, para. 8.

[77] *Ibid.*, para. 37.

[78] UNCITRAL, *Report of Working Group III (Investor-State Dispute Settlement Reform)* of 26/2/2018, A/CN.9/930/Add.1/Rev.1, para. 13.

cultivating a more consistent body of case law.[79] Moreover, a unified system such as an MIC is systematically positioned to ensure a consistent and coherent legal regime since it is inherently incentivised to accord deference to its earlier decisions (**precedents**), justified by the need to promote a coherent development of its case law.[80] Going by this argument, one may agree that an MIC is inherently better positioned to foster consistent outcomes.

However, while an MIC system is inherently better positioned to foster consistent outcomes, its primary objective remains the **correctness** i.e., the accuracy of ISDS decisions to the applicable law and facts to a case.[81] Therefore, clarity of the law is of paramount importance for states to avoid unintended outcomes in the interpretation of their treaty obligations. With the broad investment protection guarantees prevalent in old-generation IIAs, without corresponding safeguards for a state's sustainable development interest, it is possible to reach a correct decision in the legal sense but yet attract the disapproval of states. For instance, an MIC decision that does not consider the sustainable development interests of the respondent state, simply because such interests are not covered under the applicable IIA, may be technically correct but will set an undesirable precedent from the perspective of African states.

Notably, since a permanent court system has a higher incentive to follow its earlier decisions,[82] the major concern this poses is the risk of states being locked in a series of undesirable precedents. Notwithstanding the lack of binding precedent in the judicial practice of the MIC, the moral burden or weight that will be placed upon the court to uphold its precedent is of a significant degree that cannot be disregarded,[83] especially where the precedent is deemed consistent with the interpretation rules of Article 31 VCLT. This again underscores the point made earlier that it is crucial to address how the MIC will engage with the existing old-generation IIAs, in order not to solidify the inequities of the old system in a more permanent way.

---

[79] UNCITRAL, *Standing Multilateral Mechanism: Selection and Appointment of ISDS Tribunal Members and Related Matters – Initial Draft*: Comments of the EU and its Member States, p. 18 f, https://uncitral.un.org/sites/uncitral.un.org.

[80] Cate (2013), p. 463.

[81] Cf., UNCITRAL, *Possible Reform of Investor-State Dispute Settlement (ISDS): Consistency and Related Matters*: Note by the Secretariat of 28/8/2018, A/CN.9/WG.III/WP.150, para. 8.

[82] See, Butler and Subedi (2017), p. 59, opining that: ('[. . .] a dedicated investment court (with an appellate mechanism) would enable a solid body of jurisprudence to be built up, perhaps even based on the doctrine of formal legal precedent.').

[83] See, Schill (2011), p. 1101 f, (stating inter-alia that while precedent does not bind later investment treaty tribunals: '[. . .] it shifts the burden of argumentation by demanding a reasoned justification for departing from precedent. The more established precedent becomes, and the more investment treat tribunals align themselves with a certain line of jurisprudence, the more difficult it becomes to meet that burden and to convince tribunals to adopt solutions that deviate from prior practice'.).

4.2.3   An MIC that Fosters Investor Accountability

As discussed in Chap. 3, the lack of investor accountability in ISDS mechanisms is a pressing concern that has attracted significant attention and public criticism over the years. In reaction to this concern rooted in the asymmetric nature of traditional IIAs, a discernible trend has arisen in recent investment treaties, where investors' obligations are explicitly included to foster investor accountability.[84]

In Africa, the most recent notable example of this development is the AfCFTA Protocol on Investment. Therein, a chapter is specifically dedicated to the subject of investors' obligations to guarantee investor accountability for responsible investment.[85] Chapter five of the protocol explicitly incorporates investors' obligations pertaining to compliance with both national and international law,[86] human rights and labour standards,[87] environmental protection,[88] rights of indigenous peoples and local communities,[89] socio-political obligations,[90] anti-corruption,[91] corporate social responsibility,[92] corporate governance,[93] and taxation and transfer pricing obligations.[94]

Additionally, African treaties such as the SADC Protocol on Finance and Investment (2006),[95] the Investment Agreement for the Common Market for Eastern and Southern Africa (2007),[96] the Supplementary Act of the Economic Community of West African States,[97] and the Morocco-Nigeria BIT (2006),[98] collectively highlight the African preference for guaranteeing investor accountability through explicit provisions on investor obligations.[99] The aim of this policy shifts from a legal framework that foresees no investor obligation to one that does is to establish a fair balance between the protection of foreign investments on one hand, and upholding the host states' interests in safeguarding only those investments that align with their sustainable development objectives, on the other hand.

---

[84] Jarrett et al. (2021).

[85] See generally, Chapter 5, AfCFTA Investment Protocol.

[86] Article 32, AfCFTA Investment Protocol.

[87] Article 33, AfCFTA Investment Protocol.

[88] Article 34, AfCFTA Investment Protocol.

[89] Article 35, AfCFTA Investment Protocol.

[90] Article 36, AfCFTA Investment Protocol.

[91] Article 37, AfCFTA Investment Protocol.

[92] Article 38, AfCFTA Investment Protocol.

[93] Article 39, AfCFTA Investment Protocol.

[94] Article 39, AfCFTA Investment Protocol.

[95] Article 10, SADC Protocol on Finance and Investment (2006).

[96] Article 13, Investment Agreement for the COMESA Common Investment Area (2007).

[97] Chapter 3, Supplementary Act of the Economic Community of West African States (2008).

[98] Article 17-19, Morocco-Nigeria BIT (2016), signed 3 December 2016.

[99] Kern and Assefa (2020).

However, this hard law innovations taken in recent African IIAs towards promoting a balanced and fair investment protection regime for all stakeholders have not been replicated beyond the African continent.[100] The majority of IIAs in force in the continent remain one-sided, foreseeing no investor obligation. Consequently, the majority of IIAs that could be potentially invoked against African states in a future MIC has no provision on investor obligation, which is essential to strike a balance between the state's duty to provide investment protection and the investor's duty not to engage in activities that undermine the host state's sustainable development.

Given the significance of this topic in restoring the global legitimacy of the ISDS system, it was recently noted by the UNCITRAL Working Group III Secretariat that state delegates might wish to formulate provisions on investor obligations and methodologies for implementing such obligations within investment treaties, contracts or domestic laws on foreign investment.[101] Despite recognising its importance, suggestions to shelve this topic have prevailed for now based on the premise that the Working Group's mandate is restricted to procedural matters and does not encompass substantive law reform.[102] As South Africa's submission to UNCITRAL Working Group III rightly pointed out, the MIC proposal currently under consideration is silent on investor obligation or any legal instrument that could establish such.[103]

While recognising that tackling this matter primarily requires substantive law reform, an MIC, albeit a procedural reform approach, can still be devised in a manner to ensure that not only states but also 'investors' are accountable to certain standards in relation to their investment activities within the host state. Notably, the MIC need not reinvent the wheel to achieve this balance. Instead, as elaborated on below (Sect. 4.3.3), its procedural framework can simply integrate already recognised rules and procedures from existing practice to advance this purpose.

4.2.4 An MIC that Fosters the Protection of Third Party Interest

While the primary actors in the ISDS system are **'foreign investors'** and **'host states,'** disputes within this framework may also involve the interests of **'third parties,'** such as vulnerable individuals and host communities. Whereas, of these highlighted groups, only foreign investors benefit from specific IIA guarantees

---

[100] Akinkugbe (2021), p. 12 f.

[101] UNCITRAL, *Possible Reform of Investor-State Dispute Settlement (ISDS) – Multiple proceedings and counterclaims*: Note by the Secretariat of 22/1/2020, A/CN.9/WG.III/WP.193, para. 41.

[102] *Ibid.*, para. 42.

[103] UNCITRAL, *Submission from the Government of South Africa* of 17/7/2019, A/CN.9/WG.III/WP.176, para. 84.

provided by the host state, including the exclusive right to initiate ISDS claims, an asymmetry that has become a cause for concern.[104]

Hence, another crucial consideration in the African vision for an ideal ISDS system – including an MIC, is the realisation of an inclusive system that guarantees access to all parties whose interests are at stake in the ISDS process.[105] Inclusivity ensures that the voices and concerns of all stakeholders are heard and considered. This includes besides the primary actors: affected local communities, civil society organisations, and other affected third parties. By including diverse perspectives, ISDS in an MIC can better balance the interests of different stakeholders and promote much fairer and more equitable outcomes than the current system.

While the primary actors in ISDS have the opportunity to defend their interests within the confined scope of the relevant IIA, third parties such as individuals or host communities whose interests are intertwined with an ISDS claim have no equal opportunity.[106] Although where the applicable rules permit, *amicus curiae* submissions may serve as a gap-filling tool for this lacunae, however, this tool still falls short of providing effective and meaningful participation for third parties in ISDS because of its limitations,[107] including the limitation to address only matters within the scope of the dispute (Sect. 4.3.4). Moreover, arbitrators ultimately decide who they will listen to, thus at liberty to decide without question which *amicus* petition they choose to allow or reject.[108]

Consequently, there is no guarantee that the third party interest at stake in an investment dispute will be accounted for in the current ISDS system. This is even more challenging when the respondent host state does not share the third party's interest as an issue in dispute. In that case, the chances of being heard as an *amicus curia* go from difficult to nearly impossible. An illustrative example is *von Pezold v. Zimbabwe*,[109] where a request for third party participation as an *amicus curiae* was submitted on behalf of the affected indigenous host communities. Besides rejecting the application because the human rights interests raised by the *amicus* were not covered by the applicable IIA, the tribunal also found it instructive to reject the *amicus* because the respondent state did not raise human rights considerations as relevant to its defense or the tribunal's determination of the case.[110]

---

[104] Fan (2018), Chaudhuri (2020), p. 4; Client Earth (2019).

[105] UNCITRAL, *Submission from the Government of South Africa* of 17/7/2019, A/CN.9/WG.III/WP.176, para. 52.

[106] See, Coleman et al. (2019), p. 4 f, (describing how the rights or interests of third parties may be at stake in ISDS).

[107] See, Coleman et al. (2019), p. 6; UNCITRAL, *Submission from the Government of South Africa* of 17/7/2019, A/CN.9/WG.III/WP.176, para. 53.

[108] Saei (2017), p. 289.

[109] *Bernhard von Pezold and Others v. Republic of Zimbabwe*, ICSID Case No. ARB/10/15, Procedural Order No. 2 (26 June 2012).

[110] *Ibid.*, para. 59.

Notably, in contrast to the *von Pezold* case, the tribunal in *Methanex v. USA*[111] rightly acknowledged that there are disputes whereby the substantive issues at stake go 'far beyond' those raised by the disputing parties, and supporting an *amicus* participation in such instance is important for the transparency and fairness of the process.[112] For example, a respondent state may choose not to raise the human rights abuses of an investor in its host community in order not to expose its own human rights violations.[113] Therefore, the relevance of an *amicus curiae* should not be restricted to what the primary parties raise as the issues in dispute, as these may be influenced by factors not necessarily in the interest of affected third parties, whose rights and interests are nevertheless intertwined with the ISDS claim under scrutiny.

Significantly, as contended by South Africa in UNCITRAL Working Group III, allowing third party intervention in ISDS should also go beyond the mere possibility of submitting *amicus curiae* briefs.[114] A fair and just dispute settlement process should allow affected individuals or communities to intervene directly to protect their immediate and specific interests in ISDS cases.[115]

Today, the lack of inclusivity in traditional ISDS has become a significant concern, raising questions about the system's compatibility with sustainable development, due to its adverse effect on the right of access to justice for all affected stakeholders in ISDS.[116] Hence, to ensure an MIC that operates in a much more transparent and just manner, it is crucial to consider how an MIC could be designed as 'open' and 'accessible' to third parties for the direct protection of their immediate and specific interests in ISDS.

4.2.5   An MIC that Fosters the Development of Local Courts by Requiring First Recourse to Local Remedies

Although the advent of traditional ISDS through investment arbitration stemmed from the need to depoliticize investment disputes by removing them from intergovernmental control including the influence of local courts,[117] over the years, the justification for such a system has faced criticism, particularly for excluding investment disputes from the jurisdiction of local courts.[118]

---

[111] *Methanex Corporation v. United States of America*, UNCITRAL, Decision of the Tribunal on Petitions from Third Persons to Intervene as 'amici curiae' (15 January 2001).

[112] *Ibid.*, para. 49.

[113] IIED Briefing (2019), p. 3; see also, Peterson and Gray (2003), p. 16 f.

[114] UNCITRAL, *Submission from the Government of South Africa* of 17/7/2019, A/CN.9/WG.III/WP.176, para. 52.

[115] *Ibid.*

[116] See generally, CCSI and OHCHR (2018), p. 7 f.

[117] Kaufmann-Kohler and Potestà (2020), para. 30 ff, p. 17 ff.

[118] *Ibid.*, p. 8 ff.

Historically, the ability of foreign investors to have direct access to international arbitration tribunals was never intended to eradicate the settlement of investment disputes before local courts. Rather, this was meant to serve as a stopgap in cases of governmental maladministration, where a local remedy becomes unviable.[119] As stated by Aaron Broches, founding father of the ICSID Convention:

> International proceedings became important in the abnormal case, where the normal ways of dealing with disputes proved unsatisfactory, perhaps because of a lack of governmental or judicial stability; perhaps because new legal relationships were being created for which there was as yet no appropriate or competent local forum. **Implicit in the convention was the thought that it would be used only in these and other "appropriate cases".**[120]

This Broches' assertion is in fact reflected in the ICSID Conventions preamble which acknowledged that disputes are typically handled through national legal processes, but 'international methods of settlement **may be appropriate in certain cases**'.[121]

However, IIAs typically offer investors direct access to international arbitration without distinguishing between investment disputes that are appropriate for arbitration and those better suited for local remedies. The reason for this approach could be attributed to the perception that local courts are inefficient for ISDS due to some perceived flaws, such as delays, bias, increased costs, limited expertise in international law, etc.[122]

Therefore, even when local courts are well placed to offer adequate and effective access to justice, traditional IIAs permit investors to bypass the domestic legal system for international arbitration.[123] As earlier discussed, this practice is detrimental to the development of local courts' capacity in handling ISDS matters within their existing legal framework (Sect. 3.2.1). It is noteworthy that, regardless of an international arbitration clause in an IIA, local courts remain the default forum for ISDS.[124] Therefore, when investors can easily disregard local courts and directly resort to international arbitration without first seeking domestic remedies, it deprives the local judicial system of the opportunity to enhance their expertise in ISDS and demonstrate their commitment to the rule of law – by providing an independent and impartial legal system for resolving investment disputes.

Hence, from the perspective of African states, any meaningful ISDS reform, including the MIC option, must be designed in a way that does not undermine the capacity of local courts to resolve investment disputes within the existing domestic

---

[119] UNCITRAL, *Submission from the Government of South Africa* of 17/7/2019, A/CN.9/WG.III/WP.176, para. 37.

[120] ICSID (2006), p. 58.

[121] Third recital, Preamble to the ICSID Convention (1965).

[122] Kaufmann-Kohler and Potestà (2020), para. 35, p. 20; Schreuer (2011), p. 71 f; Bjorklund (2007), p. 253 ff.

[123] Harten (2010), p. 34; Republic of South Africa (2009), p. 45.

[124] Kaufmann-Kohler and Potestà (2020), para. 68, p. 36.

legal framework. This approach is crucial for bolstering the rule of law in the host states. As opined by the South African government:

> There is no compelling reason why review of an investor's claims against a state cannot be undertaken by the institutions of the state in question—**provided** these are independent of the public authority that is in dispute and they discharge their duties in accordance with basic principles of good governance, including an independent judiciary.[125]

Essentially, there is a need to recalibrate the ISDS clauses found in the majority of IIAs, akin to the idea conceived in the foundation of the ICSID Convention, as articulated by *Broches*.[126] The core idea is to grant access to international proceedings only as a last resort in **'appropriate cases'** when domestic remedies fall short. Crucially, there is no way to determine that a domestic remedy falls short if there is no attempt at it.

To ensure that this test is satisfied, a number of IIAs incorporate the **'exhaustion of local remedy'** ('ELR') or local litigation requirement within a stipulated timeframe. While the distinction between these clauses is not the focus here and is addressed in another study,[127] in effect they both serve a similar purpose, which is to obligate investors to seize local courts for remedy before resorting to an international forum. This aligns with the CIL rule that a state be allowed to remedy its own wrongdoing before international proceedings can be instituted,[128] save it will be futile to do so.[129] However, the vast majority of IIAs, including those contracted by African states, remain silent on the ELR rule.[130] Unless explicitly mandated in an IIA, there is no generalised ELR or local litigation requirement applicable in investment arbitration.[131]

Recognising the importance of local courts in ISDS, some African states are beginning to revert to the traditional ELR rule as a precondition for their consent to international arbitration.[132] States such as Morocco and South Africa have echoed this desire in their submissions to UNCITRAL Working Group III on ISDS

---

[125] Republic of South Africa (2009), p. 45.

[126] ICSID (2006), p. 58.

[127] Kaufmann-Kohler and Potestà (2020), para. 84 ff, p. 43 ff.

[128] *Interhandel Case (Switzerland. v. United States of America)*, Judgment [1959] ICJ Rep 6, p. 27; *Apotex Inc. v. The Government of the United States of America*, ICSID Case No. UNCT/10/2, Award on Jurisdiction and Admissibility (14 June 2013), para. 280; Brauch (2017), p. 2; Adler (1990), p. 641; Mollengarden (2019), p. 405.

[129] Article 15(a) International Law Commission, Draft Articles on Diplomatic Protection (2006); *Swissbourgh Diamond Mines (Pty) Limited and others v. Lesotho*, PCA Case No. 2013-29, Judgment of the Singapore Court of Appeal (27 November 2018), para. 211; Mollengarden (2019), p. 408.

[130] Brauch (2017), p. 7.

[131] *PL Holdings S.A.R.L. v. Republic of Poland*, SCC Case No V2014/163, Partial Award (28 June 2017), para. 441; *Gavrilovic and Gavrilovic d.o.o. v. Republic of Croatia*, ICSID Case No. ARB/12/39, Award (26 July 2018), para. 889.

[132] See for example, Article 36(3), Common Market for Eastern and Southern Africa (COMESA), Revised Investment Agreement for the COMESA Common Investment Area, adopted November

reform.[133] Though not generally regarded as a concern, delegates agree that '*requiring investors to exhaust local remedies before bringing their claims to investment arbitration was a tool to be considered in reforming ISDS*'.[134] However, despite this acknowledgement, the consideration of this tool particularly in relation to the introduction of an MIC remains to be seen. As observed in South Africa's submissions on the proposed MIC to the working group:

> There are no suggestions that investors would first need to exhaust local remedies or show that domestic courts would be unable to handle a particular case before they gain access to the investment court.[135]

As already stated, African states are now contracting IIAs with explicit provisions on local remedies before granting access to an international forum.[136] Under such treaties, an MIC is bound to enforce the local remedies requirement as a precondition to its jurisdiction. However, the challenge arises where a treaty's ISDS clause lacks an explicit reference to local remedies. In such cases, an MIC would be justified in not imposing such a condition.

Therefore, given the increasing emphasis on 'initial recourse to local remedies', it is important to address how the MIC will encourage recourse to local remedies in ISDS, particularly under old-generation IIAs silent on such conditions. Such consideration is vital to ensure that the development of local judicial competence in ISDS is not hampered due to direct recourse to an MIC, leading to a lack of local court experience in adjudicating investment disputes. The absence of experience in adjudicating investment disputes can hinder the growth of the rule of law in the host state, particularly in the area of investment protection. This could have a negative impact on the overall trajectory of sustainable development in any given state, as the lack of tested and trusted local remedies may discourage potential investors from entering the country, especially those wary of the potential cost of an international law firm if a need for an international remedy arises.

2017; Article 26(5), Nigeria-Morocco BIT, signed 3 December 2016; also see, Article 42(1)(c), PAIC (2016), https://au.int/sites/default/files/documents/.

[133] UNCITRAL, *Submission from the Government of South Africa* of 17/7/2019, A/CN.9/WG.III/WP.176, paras. 43-46; UNCITRAL, *Submissions from the Government of Morocco* of 11/2/2020, A/CN.9/WG.III/WP.161, para. 9.

[134] UNCITRAL, *Report of Working Group III (Investor-State Dispute Settlement Reform)* of 9/4/2019, A/CN.9/970, para. 30.

[135] UNCITRAL, *Submission from the Government of South Africa* of 17/7/2019, A/CN.9/WG.III/WP.176, para. 82.

[136] *See*, (fn. 132).

4.2.6   An MIC that Fosters the Development of ADR

As discussed in Chap. 3, ADR in relation to ISDS is used to describe an investment dispute resolution process that does not involve a binding arbitral award or court order (Sect. 3.2.2). Rather they entail *inter alia* amicable dispute settlement processes like negotiation, mediation, or conciliation, enabling the disputing parties to collaborate and find mutually beneficial solutions to their disagreements.

Historically, this collaborative method of dispute resolution has been the customary method of dispute resolution known to traditional African societies.[137] This approach stems from the recognition that the consequences of a dispute go beyond the perspectives of the disputing parties but extend to the overall peace and well-being of the community. As a result, the African traditional legal system embraces consensual dispute resolution, facilitated by the village elders or chiefs, focusing on achieving social peace by fostering peaceful co-existence in the community.[138] Given this background, it is not strange that African states are now emphasising the need to enhance the use of ADR in ISDS.

Considering the diverse interests often intertwined with investor-state disputes, it can be argued that amicable dispute settlement procedures are more suited for ISDS compared to other adversarial methods, such as domestic court litigation, arbitration, or potential dispute resolution within a future MIC. Unlike these adversarial procedures that promote win-lose outcomes, ADR methods prioritises win-win solutions, which can help preserve a peaceful co-existence between the investor, the host state and its populace at large. This makes the enhancement of ADR mechanisms in resolving investment disputes critical to African states, as it aligns with traditional African values regarding dispute resolution, benefiting both individuals and the society as a whole. This harmonious approach to dispute resolution is certainly a catalyst for inclusive socio-economic growth, a vital element for the sustainable development of any given state.

Notably, the need to promote the increased usage of ADR mechanisms in ISDS is not only shared by African states but is also widely supported by states engaged in the UNCITRAL Working Group III reform discussions.[139] There is a general consensus amongst delegates that ADR methods are less time-consuming and more cost-effective, with the added benefit of preserving long-term investor-state relationships.[140] Given this recognition, establishing an MIC that advances the use of ADR processes would undoubtedly enhance its global acceptability.

Considering the six crucial interests identified in the preceding discussions, which are rooted in both substantive and procedural concerns identified in the traditional

---

[137] Grande (1999), p. 64.

[138] *Ibid.*

[139] UNCITRAL, *Possible Reform of Investor-State Dispute Settlement (ISDS): Dispute Prevention and Mitigation - Means of Alternative Dispute Resolution*: Note by the Secretariat of 15/1/2020, A/CN.9/WG.III/WP.190, para. 29 ff.

[140] *Ibid.*

ISDS system, the following analysis now centers on how these essential interests could be effectively addressed within the constitutional framework of an MIC without replicating the traditional ISDS concerns, with the aim of attracting African states participation a future MIC.

4.3 Addressing the Crucial Considerations to Attract African States' Participation in a Future MIC

By focusing on the shared objective of sustainable development and the convergence in recent investment law policies contracted by prospective MIC members both on substantive and procedural rules, the ensuing discussions demonstrate the potential to design an MIC that effectively addresses the crucial interests of African states earlier discussed, thereby promoting the MICs acceptance as a suitable alternative to traditional ISDS.

4.3.1 Addressing the MIC's Interaction with Old-Generation IIAs through a Guiding Note on Treaty Interpretation

As the MIC is being considered as one possible reform option for ISDS, there exists the opportunity to incorporate a 'Guiding Note on Treaty Interpretation' ('GNTI') in the MIC's framework, even within the strictly procedural mandate of UNCITRAL Working Group III. Given that a significant apprehension regarding the MIC pertains to its interaction with old-generation IIAs that remain prevalent amongst its prospective members, the proposed GNTI in this thesis aims to furnish the MIC with the missing context necessary to address some critical gaps in old-generation IIAs. This would help foster interpretations consistent with the modern investment protection policies of the MIC members, as evident in recent IIAs.

Admittedly, the most suitable response to outdated IIAs is to either amend or completely overhaul and conclude new ones. However, the complex and elaborate process demanded by these options, as foreseen under the VCLT,[141] including the thousands of IIAs that would require amendment or replacement at a bilateral level, renders comprehensive IIA reform at state-to-state levels currently unlikely. However, rather than awaiting bilateral IIA reforms, the introduction of a GNTI within the MIC's framework provides states with an immediate avenue to collectively address major deficiencies in old-generation IIAs that an MIC would inevitably have to deal with. These include concerns regarding a state's right to regulate, what constitutes an expropriation, FET, FPS, or a breach of the MFN standard. By addressing these issues through a GNTI, there is an opportunity to significantly

---

[141] See, Part II and Part IV, VCLT.

curtail the recurrence of divisive outcomes within an MIC, thereby addressing a key factor that has contributed to the delegitimisation of traditional ISDS.

Notably, the GNTI proposal presented in this thesis can be viewed as an amendment to the investment protection guarantees in existing IIAs. This raises the question of the extent to which an MIC can be used for this purpose under international law. In this regard, it is important to emphasise that an attempt to amend existing IIAs through an MIC convention is in principle not prohibited under the law of treaties. Articles 39 and 40 of the VCLT set forth the default rules for treaty amendment under international law,[142] which are applicable unless a treaty specifies its own amendment procedure, a provision often absent in older IIAs.[143] Article 39 VCLT provides the general rule regarding the amendment of treaties (bilateral or multilateral), while Article 40 VCLT further contains specific rules on the amendment of multilateral treaties.[144]

According to Article 39 of the VCLT:

> **A treaty may be amended by agreement between the parties**. The rules laid down in Part II apply to such an agreement except in so far as the treaty may otherwise provide.

There are two significant points worth noting from the above provision. *First*, **an agreement between the treaty parties'** is the primary requirement for a treaty amendment. *Second*, the above provision does not stipulate any form or procedure in which such an agreement to amend must take,[145] save for multilateral treaties which in addition to the treaty parties' agreement to amend must comply with Article 40 VCLT. Notably, Article 40 of the VCLT also does not stipulate the form in which the agreement to amend a multilateral treaty must take or prohibit the amendment agreement from being formed in another international convention.

This factor allows states the flexibility to agree on their own procedure for implementing an amendment, especially when the underlying treaty is silent on this subject, which is the case with almost all old-generation IIAs in existence. Even when a treaty stipulates conditions to be followed for its amendment, subsequent unanimous agreement of the treaty parties can override such conditions.[146] Accordingly, as masters of their own treaties, the form or procedure for amending a treaty is determined by what the treaty parties consider appropriate.[147] Consequently, there is no legal barrier preventing prospective MIC members from adopting a GNTI within the MIC framework as an agreement to amend specific provisions of the IIAs shared among them.

As previously noted, the purpose of the GNTI would be to provide the missing context in old-generation IIAs, in order to facilitate interpretations in alignment with

---

[142] von der Decken (2018), Article 39, para. 2.

[143] Pathirana and Gathii (2022), p. 295.

[144] Villiger (2009), p. 512, 522; von der Decken (2018), Article 39, para 2.

[145] von der Decken (2018), Article 39, paras. 2, 10.

[146] Villiger (2009), p. 512.

[147] von der Decken (2018), Article 39, para. 10.

the current investment protection policies of the MIC members. For greater certainty on this point, an Annex to the MIC statute may be adopted, wherein IIA parties who are also members of the MIC can specify which IIAs they agree should be subject to the GNTI provisions. Members who do not desire the application of the GNTI may choose not to adopt or list any IIA within the GNTI Annex.

Importantly, the adoption of the GNTI, as proposed in this thesis should not be contentious, particularly for application to BITs between EU/member states and African states, including the EU's recent IIA partners such as Canada, Vietnam, Singapore, Japan, Mexico, and Chile. As revealed in the following discussions, the clarifications offered by the GNTI are grounded in commonly shared positions of the EU and African states, particularly as evinced in the CETA and AfCFTA. Notably, it should be emphasised that the CETA and AfCFTA are relied upon as primary reference points in the following analysis given the significant number of states behind these two instruments. This totals 82 prospective MIC members,[148] not including the aforementioned recent EU IIA partners that have adopted the CETA-styled provisions.

Given this significant number, the acceptance of MIC membership by African states is not farfetched if the convergence in substantive law evident in both the CETA and AfCFTA is leveraged by the prospective MIC members to incorporate a GNTI within the MIC statute. Doing so would significantly align their old-generation IIAs with their current investment protection policies, as reflected in new-generation IIAs. The following discussions now elaborate on how this can be achieved in order to address some major deficiencies in substantive law, thereby preventing the replication of controversies that have undermined the legitimacy of traditional ISDS within an MIC context.

4.3.1.1   Guiding Note Clarifying the State's Right to Regulate

While it is established under CIL that states may implement legitimate public interest measures without being obligated to provide compensation to every investor who might be adversely affected by such measures,[149] in principle, treaty law will prevail

---

[148] The cumulative count of '82' is derived from the combined total of EU parties to the CETA and the AfCFTA parties. Precisely, this encompasses 28 EU-CETA parties, consisting of 27 EU member states and the EU itself (1), in addition to 54 African Union Member States that are parties to the AfCFTA, resulting in a cumulative total of '82'.

[149] *Marvin Roy Feldman Karpa v United Mexican States*, ICSID Case No ARB(AF)/99/1, Award (16 December 2002), para 103; *Saluka Investments BV (The Netherlands) v. Czech Republic*, PCA Case No. 2001-04, Partial Award (17 March 2006), para. 255; *Invesmart, B.V. v. Czech Republic*, UNCITRAL, Award (26 June 2009), para. 498; *EDF (Services) Limited v Romania*, ICSID Case No ARB/05/13, Award (8 October 2009) para 217; *AWG Group Ltd. v. Argentine Republic*, UNCITRAL, Decision on Liability (30 July 2010), para. 139; *Total SA v Argentine Republic*, ICSID Case No ARB/04/01, Decision on Liability (27 December 2010) paras. 128-30; *Tza Yap Shum v. Republic of Peru*, ICSID Case No. ARB/07/6, Award (7 July 2011), para. 145; *El Paso*

over CIL due to its *lex specialis* nature.[150] Thus, since old-generation IIAs are famous for their broadly worded guarantees and lack of clarity on non-compensable public interest measures that states may adopt, a GNTI could provide valuable clarity on the margin of regulatory autonomy available to states without incurring financial liability within an MIC for conflicting with the IIA guarantees to investors.

Indeed, the CETA and AfCFTA have incorporated provisions clarifying legitimate public interest measures that state parties under the respective treaties may adopt without breaching their treaty commitments. Article 8.9(1) CETA provides:

> For the purpose of this Chapter, the Parties reaffirm their right to regulate within their territories to achieve legitimate policy objectives, **such as** the protection of public health, safety, the environment or public morals, social or consumer protection or the promotion and protection of cultural diversity.

The opening reference, **'for the purpose of this chapter'**, including the term **'such as'**—affirms that the entirety of CETA's Investment Chapter (Chapter 8) is subject to the parties' right to regulate in pursuit of a range of legitimate public policy objectives, the list of which is not exhaustive. In safeguarding their regulatory autonomy in pursuit of these non-exhaustive lists of 'legitimate policy objectives', the CETA parties further clarified that:

> For greater certainty, the mere fact that a Party regulates, including through a modification to its laws, in a manner which negatively affects an investment or interferes with an investor's expectations, including its expectations of profits, does not amount to a breach of an obligation under this Section.[151]

Therefore, Article 8.9 CETA provides interpretative guidance to adjudicators when interpreting the parties' investment protection obligations.[152] Most notably, a combined reading of Article 8.9(1)(2) CETA alongside the treaty's preamble[153] and the CETA JII[154] clearly establishes that the CETA parties have placed economic and

---

Energy International Company v Argentine Republic, ICSID Case No ARB/03/15, Award (31 October 2011), para 372.

[150] *ADC Affiliate Limited and ADC & ADMC Management Limited v. Republic of Hungary*, ICSID Case No. ARB/03/16, Award (2 October 2006), para. 481; Titi (2022), p. 64.

[151] Article 8.9(2), CETA.

[152] Schacherer (2019), Article 8.9, para. 14.

[153] Sixth recital, Preamble to the CETA ('RECOGNISING that the provisions of this Agreement preserve the right of the Parties to regulate within their territories and the Parties' flexibility to achieve legitimate policy objectives, such as public health, safety, environment, public morals and the promotion and protection of cultural diversity'); see also Ninth recital, Preamble to the CETA.

[154] Joint Interpretative Instrument on the CETA, OJ L 11/3, 14/1/2017, para. 2 ('CETA preserves the ability of the European Union and its Member States and Canada to adopt and apply their own laws and regulations that regulate economic activity in the public interest, to achieve legitimate public policy objectives such as the protection and promotion of public health, social services, public education, safety, the environment, public morals, social or consumer protection, privacy and data protection and the promotion and protection of cultural diversity'); see also, para. 7(a).

non-economic measures, including social and environmental interests, on an equal footing.[155] A clarification that is absent in older-generation European IIAs.

Turning to the AfCFTA, a similar pattern can be identified in Article 24 of the AfCFTA Investment Protocol. It provides:

1. In accordance with customary international law and other general principles of international law, each State Party has the right to regulate, including to take measures to ensure that investment in its territory is consistent with the goals and principles of sustainable development, and with other national environmental, health, climate action, social and economic policy objectives and essential security interests.
2. For greater certainty, measures taken by a State Party to comply with its international obligations under other relevant treaties shall not constitute a breach of this Protocol.
3. For avoidance of doubt, the exercise of the right to regulate under Paragraphs 1 and 2 cannot give rise to any claim by an investor for compensation.

Although worded differently from Article 8.9 CETA, the underlying meaning remains unchanged. The above provision equally clarifies that the investment protection guarantees provided under the AfCFTA are contingent upon the parties' prerogative to regulate in pursuit of legitimate public interest objectives that align with their sustainable development goals. The AfCFTA Investment Protocol further furnishes comprehensive provisions detailing specific sustainable development measures that the state parties are obligated to pursue.[156] While the CETA lacks such an extensive provision, this distinction is inconsequential due to the fact that Article 8.9 (1) of the CETA itself enumerates a non-exhaustive list of public interest measures that the CETA parties may undertake without being subject to challenge in ISDS.

Indeed, as evinced in Article 24(3) of the AfCFTA Investment Protocol, the position of African states is that no claim for compensation should arise against a state party's measure pursuing legitimate public interest objectives. This is the exact result contemplated in Article 8.9(2) CETA as confirmed by the Court of Justice of the European Union ('CJEU') that:

> [...] Parties have taken care to ensure that those tribunals have no jurisdiction to call into question the choices democratically made within a Party relating to, inter alia, the level of protection of public order or public safety, the protection of public morals, the protection of health and life of humans and animals, the preservation of food safety, protection of plants and the environment, welfare at work, product safety, consumer protection or, equally, fundamental rights.[157]

Accordingly, this shared understanding could form the basis of a GNTI clarifying the right to regulate in public interests that MIC judges must take into account when seized over an investment claim.

---

[155] Schacherer (2019), para. 18.

[156] See, Article 25–30, AfCFTA Investment Protocol.

[157] CJEU Opinion 1/17, ECLI:EU:C:2019:341, para. 160.

To avert any potential misuse of the members' regulatory powers, which the court cannot question, the MIC would retain the competence to determine its own jurisdiction. Thus, when a public interest measure comes under challenge, the respondent-member could seek an early dismissal from the MIC, akin to the remedy foreseen in Article 8.32 of the CETA or Rule 41(5) of the ICSID Arbitration Rules.[158] This would require the respondent-member to successfully argue that the claim is 'manifestly without legal merit', meaning 'clearly and obviously' unmeritorious,[159] for challenging a legitimately adopted public interest regulation, which the MIC holds no authority to scrutinise. Furthermore, the MIC may adopt the procedure analogous to Article 8.33 of the CETA, foreseeing an early dismissal on the ground that a claim is 'unfounded as a matter of law', 'even if the facts alleged were assumed to be true'.[160]

The foregoing discussion is intended to substantiate the assertion that African states and their EU counterparts share the view that IIA guarantees should not hinder states from pursuing their legitimate public interest objectives without being exposed to financial liability in ISDS. The incorporation of a GNTI into the MIC framework, drawing inspiration from the shared understanding evident in Article 24 of the AfCFTA and Article 8.9 of the CETA, could effectively address the gaps present in outdated IIAs among the MIC members pertaining to the right to regulate.

4.3.1.2   Guiding Note Clarifying the Expropriation Guarantee

As revealed in Chap. 2, the IIA expropriation guarantee is the second most-invoked standard in ISDS proceedings against African states. Although a treaty-based claim, its origin is rooted in CIL.[161] Traditionally, states are not prohibited from expropriating a foreign property provided it is done for:

- Public purpose (Sect. 2.2.1);
- Non-discriminatory (Sect. 2.2.2);

---

[158] Cf, Stifter (2022), Article 8.32, para. 54 ff.

[159] *Trans-Global Petroleum, Inc. v. Hashemite Kingdom of Jordan*, ICSID Case No. ARB/07/25, Decision on the Respondent's Objection under Rule 41(5) of the ICSID Arbitration Rules (12 May 2008), para. 88; *Brandes Investment Partners, LP v. Bolivarian Republic of Venezuela*, ICSID Case No. ARB/08/3, Decision on the Respondent's Objection Under Rule 41(5) of the ICSID Arbitration Rules (2 February 2009), para. 62; *Global Trading Resource Corp. and Globex International, Inc. v. Ukraine*, ICSID Case No. ARB/09/11, Award (1 December 2010), para. 35; *PNG Sustainable Development Program Ltd. v. Independent State of Papua New Guinea*, ICSID Case No. ARB/13/33, Decision on Respondent Article 41(5) Objections (28 October 2014), para. 88; *Álvarez y Marín Corporación S.A. and others v. Republic of Panama*, ICSID Case No. ARB/15/14, Decision on Respondent Preliminary Objections pursuant to ICSID Arbitration Rule 41(5) (4 April 2016), para. 79.

[160] See, Stifter (2022), Article 8.33, para. 32 ff.

[161] See, Reinisch and Schreuer (2020), p. 5, para. 4.

– In accordance with due process (Sect. 2.2.3); and
– Compensated (Sect. 2.2.4)

This traditional understanding of what constitutes a lawful expropriation present in the vast majority of IIAs has not changed either in the CETA[162] or AfCFTA.[163] Notably, of the four conditions, the duty to compensate has generated the most contentious debate in practice, particularly regarding the question of the amount due for a lawful expropriation.[164] This thesis does not attempt to answer this question that has confounded stakeholders for the past century. Perhaps the most fundamental question demanding clarity is if at all an expropriation has occurred, because only then may the question of compensation arise.

While the notion of direct expropriation is generally acknowledged as the forceful transfer of an investor's asset title to the state,[165] or outright physical seizure of an investor's property,[166] the notion of indirect expropriation has generated varying interpretations from arbitral tribunals. The challenge lies in the fact that an indirect expropriation does not involve a transfer of title, but rather a regulatory measure that diminishes the benefits an investor derives from its investment.[167] Since this concerns a regulatory measure that does not deny the investor ownership of its investment but rather its benefits, tribunals have had to distinguish between a regulatory measure equivalent to an expropriation (indirect/regulatory expropriation) and one that falls legitimately within a state's regulatory authority not equivalent to an expropriation.

Arbitral tribunals have addressed this question using mainly three different tests. These are:

---

[162] See, Article 8.12(1), CETA.

[163] See, Article 19(1), AfCFTA Investment Protocol.

[164] Reinisch and Schreuer (2020), p. 226, paras. 1090–1101.

[165] *BG Group Plc. v. Republic of Argentina*, UNCITRAL, Award (24 December 2007), para. 259; *National Grid P.L.C. v. Argentina Republic*, UNCITRAL, Award (3 November 2008), para. 145; *Waguih Elie George Siag & Clorinda Vecchi v. Arab Republic of Egypt*, ICSID Case No. ARB/05/15, Award (1 June 2009), para. 427; *Suez, Sociedad General de Aguas de Barcelona S.A. and Vivendi Universal S.A v. Argentine Republic*, ICSID Case No. ARB/03/19, Decision on Liability (30 July 2010), para. 132; *Quiborax S.A. and Non Metallic Minerals S.A. v. Plurinational State of Bolivia*, ICSID Case No. ARB/06/2, Award (16 September 2015), para. 200.

[166] *Caratube International Oil Company LLP and Devincci Salah Hourani* v. Republic of Kazakhstan, ICSID Case No. ARB/13/13, Award (27 September 2017), para. 822; *JSC Tashkent Mechanical Plant and others v. Kyrgyz Republic*, ICSID Case No. ARB(AF)/16/4, Award (17 May 20239), para. 546.

[167] *Suez, Sociedad General de Aguas de Barcelona S.A. and Vivendi Universal S.A v. Argentine Republic*, ICSID Case No. ARB/03/19, Decision on Liability (30 July 2010), paara. 132; *National Grid P.L.C. v. Argentina Republic*, UNCITRAL, Award (3 November 2008), para. 149; *Gemplus, S.A., SLP, S.A. and Gemplus Industrial, S.A. de C.V. v. United Mexican States*, ICSID Case No. ARB(AF)/04/3 & ARB(AF)/04/4, Award (16 June 2010), paras. 8–23.

(a) the sole effect doctrine, which focuses on the impact of the state regulation on the investor, irrespective of the reason why it was adopted;[168]
(b) the police power doctrine, which focuses on the public interest, due process, and non-discriminatory nature of the measure;[169] and lastly
(c) the balancing approach, which basically involves a proportionality test, weighing the government's public measure against the sole effect on the investor.[170]

Except a treaty provides clarity on this issue, it is impossible to predict which of these tests a tribunal would apply to determine whether a measure crosses the threshold from a legitimate public regulation to an indirect expropriation subject to compensation. Moreover, these diverging approaches have been a catalyst for inconsistent interpretations regarding the meaning of indirect expropriation.

To address the dilemma posed by this lack of clarity, both the CETA and AfCFTA parties have provided specific guidance to tribunals on what would constitute either a direct or indirect expropriation. This again reveals a shared understanding of this concept between the EU and African states as underlined below.

According to Article 8.12 CETA, the treaty's expropriation guarantee *'shall be interpreted in accordance with Annex 8-A'*.[171] This Annex defines what the CETA parties consider as amounting to a direct or indirect expropriation:

The Parties confirm their shared understanding that:

1. Expropriation may be direct or indirect:

   (a) direct expropriation occurs when an investment is nationalised or otherwise directly expropriated through formal transfer of title or outright seizure; and
   (b) indirect expropriation occurs if a measure or series of measures of a Party has an effect equivalent to direct expropriation, in that it substantially deprives the

---

[168] *Técnicas Medioambientales Tecmed, S.A. v. United Mexican States*, ICSID Case No. ARB (AF)/00/2, Award (29 May 2003), para. 116; *Saipem S.p.A. v. People's Republic of Bangladesh*, ICSID Case No. ARB/05/07, Award (30 June 2009), para. 133; *Siemens A.G. v. Argentine Republic*, ICSID Case No. ARB/02/8, Award (6 February 2007), para. 270; *Burlington Resources Inc. v. Republic of Ecuador*, ICSID Case No. ARB/08/5, Decision on Liability (14 December 2012), para. 396 f.

[169] *Saluka Investments BV (The Netherlands) v Czech Republic*, UNCITRAL Partial Award (17 March 2006), para 255; *Methanex Corporation v. United States of America*, UNCITRAL, Final Award (3 August 2005), part iv – para. 15; *Crompton (Chemtura) Corp. v. Government of Canada*, PCA Case No. 2008-01, Award (2 August 2010), para. 266.

[170] *Técnicas Medioambientales Tecmed, S.A. v. United Mexican States*, ICSID Case No. ARB (AF)/00/2, Award (29 May 2003), para. 122; *LG&E Energy Corp., LG&E Capital Corp. and LG&E International Inc. v. Argentine Republic*, ICSID Case No. ARB/02/1, Decision on Liability (3 October 2006), para. 195; *Azurix Corp. v. Argentine Republic*, ICSID Case No. ARB/01/12, Award (14 July 2006), para. 311 f; *Deutsche Bank AG v. Democratic Socialist Republic of Sri Lanka*, ICSID Case No. ARB/09/2, Award (31 October 2012), para. 522; *M. Meerapfel Sohne AG v. Central African Republic*, ICSID Case No. ARB/07/10, Excerpts of Award (12 May 2012), para. 334.

[171] See, Article 8.12(1), CETA.

investor of the fundamental attributes of property in its investment, including the right to use, enjoy and dispose of its investment, without formal transfer of title or outright seizure.

For further clarity, Annex 8-A CETA provides that:

2. The determination of whether a measure or series of measures of a Party, in a specific fact situation, constitutes an indirect expropriation requires a case-by-case, fact-based inquiry that takes into consideration, among other factors:

   (a) the economic impact of the measure or series of measures, although the sole fact that a measure or series of measures of a Party has an adverse effect on the economic value of an investment does not establish that an indirect expropriation has occurred;
   (b) the duration of the measure or series of measures of a Party;
   (c) the extent to which the measure or series of measures interferes with distinct, reasonable investment-backed expectations; and
   (d) the character of the measure or series of measures, notably their object, context and intent.

Zooming in on the sister-provision under the AfCFTA, a nearly identical wording to Annex 8-A(1)(2) CETA can be found in Article 19(2) of the AfCFTA Investment Protocol. This provides that:

2. For the purposes of this Protocol:

a. direct expropriation occurs when an investment is nationalised or expropriated directly, through a formal transfer of ownership or outright seizure;
b. indirect expropriation results from a measure or a series of measures having an equivalent effect of direct expropriation without formal transfer of title or outright seizure. The sole fact that a measure or a series of measures has an adverse effect on the economic value of an investment does not establish that an indirect expropriation has occurred; and
c. the determination of whether a measure or a series of measures have an effect equivalent to expropriation requires a case-by-case, fact-based inquiry, that takes into consideration among others:

   i. the duration of the measure or series of measures of a State Party; and
   ii. the character of the measure or series of measures, notably their object, context and intent.

The underlined wordings indicate that both the CETA and AfCFTA instruments largely convey an identical understanding of factors to be taken into account when determining what constitutes an indirect expropriation. The only minor exception is that the CETA includes the legitimate expectation of an investor as one of the factors to consider.[172] The apparent fact that this factor is lacking in the AfCFTA should not

---

[172] Annex 8-A(2)(c) CETA, ('the extent to which the measure or series of measures interferes with distinct, reasonable investment-backed expectations').

be problematic for African states to approve, since it is counterbalanced by the other factors a tribunal must take into account, including: the economic impact with an **equivalent effect of a direct expropriation**;[173] the **duration of the measure**,[174] and **character of the measure**, particularly the object, context and intent.[175] Evidently, both the CETA and AfCFTA parties have embraced the balancing approach when determining a regulatory measure that qualifies as an indirect expropriation. They have also outlined a specific list of economic and non-economic factors that tribunals must consider while conducting the balancing exercise.

To further secure their regulatory authority, both the CETA and AfCFTA parties reaffirm that non-discriminatory measures aimed at protecting certain legitimate public policy objectives will not constitute an indirect expropriation.[176] Although worded differently, with the AfCFTA appearing more detailed, the qualifying phrase 'such as', adopted in both instruments suggests no difference in meaning. The parties simply stipulated a list of non-exhaustive public interest measures they may pursue, albeit non-discriminately, without constituting an indirect expropriation. This regulatory exception further narrows the discretion an investment tribunal may accord to an investor's legitimate expectation when in conflict with a state's legitimate public interest measure.[177]

Notably, the provisions of Annex 8-A of CETA and Article 19(2) of the AfCFTA Investment Protocol are not novel, as the US[178] and Canada[179] Model BIT, predating the CETA and AfCFTA adopts a similar approach. It can thus be asserted that the CETA and AfCFTA parties modelled their approach on expropriation after that of their North American counterparts. This further reinforces the notion that the common position shared between the EU and African states regarding the determination of compensable expropriation extends beyond the boundaries of Europe and Africa.

Therefore, a GNTI employed by MIC judges to determine compensable expropriation could potentially be integrated into the MIC system without contentious

---

[173] Cf, Annex 8-A(1)(b) CETA and Article 19(2)(b) AfCFTA Investment Protocol.

[174] Cf, Annex 8-A(2)(b) CETA and Article 19(2)(c)(i) AfCFTA Investment Protocol.

[175] Cf, Annex 8-A(2)(d) CETA and Article 19(2)(c)(ii) AfCFTA Investment Protocol.

[176] Annex 8-A(3) CETA, ('For greater certainty, except in the rare circumstance when the impact of a measure or series of measures is so severe in light of its purpose that it appears manifestly excessive, non-discriminatory measures of a Party that are designed and applied to protect legitimate public welfare objectives, such as health, safety and the environment, do not constitute indirect expropriations');
similarly:
Article 20(2), AfCFTA Investment Protocol, ('Non-discriminatory regulatory actions by a State Party designed to protect legitimate public policy objectives, such as public morals, public health, prevention of diseases and pests in animals or plants, climate action, essential security interests, safety and the protection of the environment, labour rights or to comply with other international obligations, shall not constitute indirect expropriation').

[177] Kriebaum (2022), Article 8.12, para. 78.

[178] Annex B, United States of America Model BIT (2012).

[179] Annex B.13(1), Canada Model BIT (2004).

debate. This inclusion would tackle the ambiguity in old-generation IIAs, where investment tribunals are afforded broad discretion to define expropriation. This, in turn, curtails the risk of a regulatory chill among states, stemming from the fear of an expansive interpretation of ambiguously worded expropriation guarantees in old-generation IIAs that might be invoked within the MIC.

4.3.1.3   Guiding Note Clarifying Fair and Equitable Treatment Guarantee

The FET guarantee is another widely adopted treaty standard that has no settled interpretation regarding its definition or precise content.[180] Due to its diversely and vaguely worded forms across treaties, arbitral tribunals have either interpreted the FET standard broadly,[181] or restrictively.[182] Consequently, arbitral tribunals differ on whether the FET standard is equivalent to or autonomous from the CIL minimum standard of treatment. This has rendered the FET standard as one of the most inconsistently applied treaty standards by ISDS tribunals.[183]

When treated as equivalent to CIL, the treaty's FET standard is restricted to the content of FET recognised under the CIL, including 'gross denial of justice, manifest arbitrariness, blatant unfairness, a complete lack of due process, evident discrimination, or a manifest lack of reasons'.[184] Further, any of these acts must be *sufficiently egregious and shocking'*, indicating a very high threshold to establish a breach of FET under CIL.[185] This is the position taken by most NAFTA tribunals[186] and

---

[180] *Oxus Gold plc v. Republic of Uzbekistan*, UNCITRAL, Final Award (17 December 2015), para. 313; *Joseph Charles Lemire v. Ukraine II*, ICSID Case No. ARB/06/18, Decision on Jurisdiction and Liability (14 January 2010), para. 247 f; *Invesmart, B.V. v. Czech Republic*, UNCITRAL, Award (26 June 2009), para. 200; *Consortium R.F.C.C. v. Kingdom of Morocco*, ICSID Case No. ARB/00/6, Final Award (22 December 2003), para. 51.5.

[181] *Técnicas Medioambientales Tecmed, S.A. v. The United Mexican States*, ICSID Case No. ARB (AF)/00/2, Award (29 May 2003), para. 154 ff; *Metalclad Corporation v. The United Mexican States*, ICSID Case No. ARB(AF)/97/1, Award (30 August 2000), para. 74 ff; *William Ralph Clayton, William Richard Clayton, Douglas Clayton, Daniel Clayton and Bilcon of Delaware Inc. v. Government of Canada*, Award on Jurisdiction and Liability (17 March 2015), para. 437 ff.

[182] *Waste Management Inc. v United Mexican States ("Number 2")*, ICSID Case No. ARB(AF)/00/3, Award (30 April 2004), para. 89 ff; *Saluka Investments B.V. v. Czech Republic*, UNCITRAL, Partial Award (17 March 2006), para. 291 ff.

[183] See further on this, UNCITRAL, *Possible Reform of Investor-State Dispute Settlement (ISDS): Consistency and Related Matters*: Note by the Secretariat of 28/8/2018, A/CN.9/WG.III/WP.150, para. 16.

[184] *Glamis Gold, Ltd. v. United States*, UNCITRAL, Award (8 June 2009), para. 627.

[185] *Ibid.*

[186] See, *Cargill, Inc. v. Mexico*, ICSID No. ARB(AF)/05/02, Award (18 September 2009), para. 296; *Mobil Investments Canada Inc. & Murphy Oil Corporation v. Canada*, ICSID No. ARB(AF)/07/4, Decision on Liability and on Principles of Quantum (22 May 2012), para. 152; *William Ralph Clayton, William Richard Clayton, Douglas Clayton, Daniel Clayton and Bilcon of Delaware, Inc. v Canada*, UNCITRAL PCA Case No. 2009-04, Award on Jurisdiction and Liability (17 March

confirmed by the NAFTA's FTC Note on FET[187] after some conflicting decisions.[188] On the other hand, when treated as autonomous from CIL, the prevailing conclusion in non-NAFTA cases, the interpretation of the FET provision can extend beyond the content recognised under the MST. For example, in *Biwater v. Tanzania* (Sect. 3.1.1.1), the ICSID tribunal rejected Tanzania's contention that the BIT's FET standard is no more than what is contemplated under the CIL-MST. According to the tribunal, Article 2(2) of the Tanzania-UK BIT (1994) shows the contracting parties intended to adopt an autonomous standard from CIL.[189] The tribunal further reinforced this conclusion with the opinion of *Christoph Schreuer*, stating that:

> [I]t is inherently implausible that a treaty would use an expression such as "fair and equitable treatment" to denote a well-known concept such as the "minimum standard of treatment in customary international law". If the parties to a treaty want to refer to customary international law, it must be presumed that they will refer to it as such rather than using a different expression.[190]

Several other tribunals have adopted the same reasoning that the FET standard is autonomous CIL in the absence of express treaty language to treat it as such.[191] In a more recent decision involving another African party, the PCA tribunal in *Bahgat v. Egypt*[192] rejected Egypt's argument to reduce the BIT's FET clause to the MST. Relying on the treaty formulation, the tribunal interpreted Article 2(1) of the Egypt-

---

2015), para. 442; *Mesa Power Group, LLC v. Canada*, UNCITRAL PCA Case No. 2012-17, Award (24 March 2016), para. 502; *Eli Lilly and Company v Canada*, UNCITRAL Case No. UNCT/14/2, Final Award (16 March 2017), para. 222; See, in contrast, the tribunal's reasoning in *Windstream Energy Llc v. Canada*, UNCITRAL, Award (27 September 2016), para. 347 ff, (which does not follow this approach).

[187] Notes of Interpretation of Certain Chapter 11 Provisions (NAFTA Free Trade Commission, July 31, 2001), https://files.pca-cpa.org/pcadocs/bi-c/2.%20Canad.

[188] See, Dumberry (2022), Article 8.10, para. 4.

[189] *Biwater Gauff (Tanzania) Limited v. United Republic of Tanzania*, ICSID Case No. ARB/05/22, Award (24 July 2008), para. 591.

[190] *Ibid.*

[191] *OKO Pankki Oyj and others v. Republic of Estonia*, ICSID Case No. ARB/04/6, Award (19 November 2007), paras. 230, 238; *Inmaris Perestroika Sailing Maritime Services GmbH and others v. Ukraine*, ICSID Case No. ARB/08/8, Excerpts of Award (1 March 2012), para. 265; *Crystallex International Corporation v. Bolivarian Republic of Venezuela*, ICSID Case No. ARB (AF)/11/2, Award (4 April 2016), para. 530 ff; *Philip Morris Brand Sàrl (Switzerland), Philip Morris Products S.A. (Switzerland) and Abal Hermanos S.A. (Uruguay) v. Oriental Republic of Uruguay*, ICSID Case No. ARB/10/7, Award (8 July 2016), para. 316; *Cervin Investissements S.A. and Rhone Investissements S.A. v. Republic of Costa Rica*, ICSID Case No. ARB/13/2, Award (7 March 2017), para. 452 f; *Tethyan Copper Company Pty Limited v. Islamic Republic of Pakistan*, ICSID Case No. ARB/12/1, Decision on Jurisdiction and Liability (10 November 2017), para. 804 ff; *RREEF Infrastructure (G.P.) Limited and RREEF Pan-European Infrastructure Two Lux S.à r.l. v. Kingdom of Spain*, ICSID Case No. ARB/13/30, Decision on Responsibility and on the Principles of Quantum (30 November 2018), para. 236.

[192] *Mohamed Abdel Raouf Bahgat v. Arab Republic of Egypt I*, PCA Case No. 2012-07, Final Award (23 December 2019).

Finland BIT (1980) as autonomous, meaning the FET clause has a broader scope beyond the CIL-MST.[193]

Since traditional European-styled IIAs typically do not incorporate a FET standard explicitly linked to CIL, for IIAs modelled in this fashion, which is the case for the majority of IIAs in force in Africa, it is impossible to determine how broad a tribunal might interpret an autonomous FET clause beyond the treatment recognised under CIL. Moreover, an autonomous FET clause does not require a government's conduct to be 'gross or shocking' to constitute a FET breach.[194]

During the CETA negotiations, the formulation of the agreement's FET clause was one of the most contentious debates, as Canada wanted to stick to its NAFTA style by linking the FET clause to what existed under CIL. The EU was, however, reluctant to accept this position for fear of reducing significantly the investment protection afforded by the FET standard.[195]

Nevertheless, recognising the risk of an uncircumscribed FET standard and an MST susceptible to unpredictable evolution, the CETA parties agreed to explicitly delimit the FET clause to an exhaustive-closed list of elements, as an effective alternative to expressly linking the standard to the CIL-MST. Hence Article 8.10 (2) CETA provides:

A Party breaches the obligation of fair and equitable treatment referenced in paragraph 1 if a measure or series of measures constitutes:

(a) denial of justice in criminal, civil or administrative proceedings;
(b) fundamental breach of due process, including a fundamental breach of transparency, in judicial and administrative proceedings;
(c) manifest arbitrariness;
(d) targeted discrimination on manifestly wrongful grounds, such as gender, race or religious belief;
(e) abusive treatment of investors, such as coercion, duress and harassment; or
(f) a breach of any further elements of the fair and equitable treatment obligation adopted by the Parties in accordance with paragraph 3 of this Article.

As described by *Patrick Dumberry*, Article 8(10) CETA simply reflects 25 years of NAFTA case law on the recognised elements of a FET breach under Article 1105 NAFTA.[196] In contrast to a direct reference to CIL, the CETA parties omitted the term CIL and instead adopted a closed list of specific elements of FET protection that

---

[193] *Ibid.*, para. 246 f.

[194] *Inmaris Perestroika Sailing Maritime Services GmbH and others v. Ukraine*, ICSID Case No. ARB/08/8, Excerpts of Award (1 March 2012), paras. 263-265; *Crystallex International Corporation v. Bolivarian Republic of Venezuela*, ICSID Case No. ARB(AF)/11/2, Award (4 April 2016), para. 543; *Eureko B.V. v. Republic of Poland*, UNCITRAL, Partial Award and Dissenting Opinion (19 August 2005), para. 234; *RREEF Infrastructure (G.P.) Limited and RREEF Pan-European Infrastructure Two Lux S.à r.l. v. Kingdom of Spain*, ICSID Case No. ARB/13/30, Decision on Responsibility and on the Principles of Quantum (30 November 2018), para. 263.

[195] Dumberry (2022), Article 8.10, para. 13.

[196] *Ibid.*, para. 9 f.

have gained acknowledgment from NAFTA tribunals, originating from the CIL-MST. As a result, the EU/member states and Canada have established certainty for all stakeholders under the CETA framework on what to expect concerning the agreement's FET standard. This action curtails the risk of an overly broad interpretation of the FET clause by the CETA ICS that goes beyond the intended scope of Article 8.10(2) CETA.

Furthermore, recognising the evolutionary nature of the FET standard, the CETA parties adopted a periodic review mechanism to update the closed list of elements that constitutes a FET violation.[197] As confirmed in the CETA JII, the periodic review is to ensure that Article 8.10(2) CETA continues to reflect the intention of the parties and that the FET clause is not interpreted in a broader manner than the parties intended.[198]

Turning to Africa, as seen in the *Biwater v. Tanzania* (Sect. 3.1.1.1) and *Bahgat v. Egypt* (Sect. 4.3.1) case examples, one major frustration of African states within their old-generation IIAs is the susceptibility of the FET clauses to overly broad interpretation owing to their imprecise scope. This unpleasant fact has resulted in the exclusion of the FET standard in recent investment law policies emanating from the continent. For instance, we can observe this exclusion in the 2016 Pan-African Investment Code ('PAIC') and the 2018 Economic Community of West African States ('ECOWAS') Common Investment Code.[199] Notably, the AfCFTA also excludes the FET standard. Instead, the AfCFTA adopted the 'Administrative and Judicial Treatment' ('AJT') standard.[200] This approach is likely influenced by the 'fair judicial and administrative treatment' provided in the revised COMESA Investment Agreement.[201] Precisely, Article 17(1) of the AfCFTA Investment Protocol provides:

> Each State Party shall ensure that, in administrative and judicial matters, investors and investments of another State Party are not subject to treatment which constitutes a fundamental denial of justice in criminal, civil and administrative adjudicative proceedings, an evident denial of due process, a manifest arbitrariness, a discrimination based on gender, race or religious beliefs, or an abusive treatment in administrative and judicial proceedings.

Significantly, a comparison of the underlined texts with Article 8.10(2) CETA reveals that the AJT shares identical elements with the FET standard enshrined in the CETA. Akin to the CETA, Article 17(1) of the AfCFTA Investment Protocol is

---

[197] See, Article 8.10(2)(f) and (3), CETA.

[198] Joint Interpretative Instrument on the CETA, OJ L 11/3, 14/1/2017, para. 6(d).

[199] Pasipanodya and Olmedo (2021).

[200] See, Article 17, AfCFTA Investment Protocol.

[201] Article 14, Common Market for Eastern and Southern Africa (COMESA), Revised Investment Agreement for the COMESA Common Investment Area, adopted November 2017. https://www.comesa.int/wp-content.

also motivated by the need to narrow down the parties' international responsibility to a closed list of fair treatment obtainable under the CIL-MST.[202]

Despite being phrased differently, and with the parties' emphasis that the article should not be treated as FET,[203] the essential takeaway from the comparison between Article 8.10(2) of CETA and Article 17(1) of the AfCFTA Investment Protocol is that it could serve as a viable foundation for a GNTI to be employed by MIC judges, addressing the gap prevalent in the majority of older generation IIAs with vague FET clause permitting expansive interpretation. Essentially, instead of leaving the MIC to interpret the FET standard in old-generation IIAs in their vague form, risking broad interpretations to the displeasure of states, the MIC could incorporate a GNTI clarifying that the FET treatment contained in the members' old-generation IIAs encompasses an exhaustive list of prohibited treatments. The exhaustive list of prohibited treatments as previously highlighted and commonly shared by both the CETA and AfCFTA parties, could serve as a valuable model for prospective MIC members to adopt or build on.

This is another way to boost the confidence of African states that the MIC is effectively designed to deliver decisions that are in tune with the current investment law policies of its members, even when adjudicating under old-generation IIAs.

4.3.1.4 Guiding Note Clarifying the Full Protection and Security Guarantee

Like the preceding treaty guarantees already examined, the FPS guarantee is another treaty provision that is widely incorporated across IIAs. Traditionally, this standard obliges host states to take all necessary measures to safeguard the physical security of foreign investors and their assets,[204] protecting them from unlawful third party harm.[205] Despite its fundamental importance, the lack of clarity regarding the scope of the FPS standard in IIAs has led to conflicting interpretations by ISDS tribunals.

The diverging interpretation of the FPS standard primarily stems from two ambiguous issues regarding its scope:

---

[202] See, Article 17(2), AfCFTA Investment Protocol: ('[...]. For further certainty, Paragraph 1 includes the minimum standard of treatment under customary international law and does not allow for an interpretation and application of such a standard that would go beyond the elements contained in Paragraph 1'), (accordingly, though the parties have linked the AJT clause to the MST, they have made sure a tribunal cannot interpret the standard beyond the MST elements expressed in paragraph 1).

[203] See, Article 17(2), AfCFTA Investment Protocol, stating: ('For greater certainty, Paragraph 1 shall not be interpreted as equivalent to fair and equitable treatment').

[204] *Saluka Investments BV (The Netherlands) v. Czech Republic*, PCA Case No. 2001-04, Partial Award (17 March 2006), para. 483; *OI European Group B.V. v. Venezuela*, ICSID Case No. ARB/11/25, Award (10 March 2015), para. 580; *Reinisch, Schreuer*, p. 558, para. 79 ff.

[205] Schefer (2020), p. 384.

- *First*, whether the FPS scope is limited to physical protection; and
- *Second*, whether the FPS scope is limited to harmful acts from third parties (private citizens).

Without repeating the extensive discussion on this matter already presented in Chap. 2, it is crucial to underscore the need for clarity to enhance legal certainty for both investors and host states. This is particularly important given that the FPS guarantee is one of the most frequently invoked standards by foreign investors against African states in ISDS. Acknowledging the significance of addressing the ambiguity surrounding the FPS standard, the CETA and AfCFTA parties have eliminated any risk of conflicting interpretation by clarifying the precise scope of the standard, particularly with respect to the first contentious issue mentioned above.

Alongside the FET standard, Article 8.10(1) CETA obliges the treaty parties to provide FPS to investors with respect to their covered investments. However, unlike traditional IIAs, Article 8.10(5) CETA further clarifies that:

> For greater certainty, 'full protection and security' refers to the Party's obligations relating to the physical security of investors and covered investments.

This clarification curtails expansive interpretation of the FPS standard, as seen in cases like *Azurix v. Argentina*.[206] In that instance, the tribunal capitalised on the adjective 'full' to extend the FPS standard beyond its CIL understanding of physical security to encompass legal security.[207] This undesirable reasoning has subsequently been adopted by several other tribunals,[208] including those dealing with African-related disputes such as *Biwater v. Tanzania*,[209] and *Oztas v. Lybia*.[210] In addition to relying on the adjective 'full', the FPS standard could also be construed to encompass both physical and legal security when formulated in conjunction with the FET standard, which is not confined to physical protection.[211] Notably, a majority of IIAs

---

[206] *Azurix Corp. v. The Argentine Republic*, ICSID Case No. ARB/01/12, Award (14 July 2006).

[207] *Ibid.*, para. 408, ('when the terms 'protection and security' are qualified by 'full' and no other adjective or explanation, they extend, in their ordinary meaning, the content of this standard beyond physical security').

[208] *Krederi Ltd. v. Ukraine*, ICSID Case No. ARB/14/17, Award (2 July 2018), para. 652; *Global Telecom Holding S.A.E. v. Canada*, ICSID Case No. ARB/16/16, Award (27 March 2020), para. 665 f; *Anglo American PLC v. Bolivarian Republic of Venezuela*, ICSID Case No. ARB(AF)/14/1, Award (18 January 2019), para. 482; *Toto General Construction SpA v. Republic of Lebanon*, ICSID Case No. ARB/07/12, Award (7 June 2012), para. 169; *El Paso Energy International Company v. Argentine Republic*, ICSID Case No. ARB/03/15, Award (31 October 2011), para. 228; *AWG Group Ltd. v. Argentine Republic*, UNCITRAL, Decision on Liability (30 July 2010), para. 168.

[209] *Biwater Gauff (Tanzania) Ltd. v. Tanzania*, ICSID Case No. ARB/05/22, Award (24 July 2008), para. 729.

[210] *Oztas Construction, Construction Materials Trading Inc. v. Libyan Investment Development Company and State of Libya*, ICC Case No. 21603/ZF/AYZ, Dissenting Opinion of Dr. Tolga Ayoglu (14 June 2018), para. 24.

[211] See, *National Grid plc v. The Argentine Republic*, UNCITRAL, Final Award (3 November 2008), para. 187.

incorporate the FET and FPS standards together,[212] either separated by a comma, or the word 'and'.[213] Interestingly, Article 8.10(1) CETA follows this pattern.[214]

However, with the clarification offered in Article 8.10(5) CETA, there is no ambiguity with respect to what the parties' intentions are concerning their FPS obligation. As aptly opined by *Patrick Dumberry*, the EU/member states and Canada simply codified an important distinction that has been established by several tribunals (albeit not all) that the FPS obligation specifically concerns the 'physical protection and security of investors'.[215]

Significantly, this is the exact clarification that the AfCFTA parties thought crucial to provide in their agreement. In fact, to avoid any expansive reading, the parties completely avoided the use of the adjective 'full' and titled the relevant standard **'Physical Protection and Security'** in Article 18 of the AfCFTA Investment Protocol. The provision states:

> A State Party shall, subject to its capabilities, accord to investors and their investments **physical protection and security** no less favourable than that which it accords to the investments of its own investors or to the investments of the investors of any other State Party or Third Party.

> For greater certainty, the expression "subject to its capabilities" refers to the obligation of due diligence that a State Party shall exercise on its territory in accordance with customary international law and does not allow for an interpretation and application of such a standard that would go beyond the elements contained in this Paragraph.

Although the formulation of the above provision differs noticeably from the FPS standard in the CETA, the significant similarity is that it equally confirms the AfCFTA parties' intention to unequivocally restrict their FPS exposure to physical security. Therefore, it is evident that both the CETA and AfCFTA parties prefer an FPS application that is limited to physical protection.

This shared position in the CETA and AfCFTA suggests that at least 83 prospective MIC members could potentially agree to a GNTI clarifying that the FPS standard is limited to physical security.[216] This figure does not account for other

---

[212] Reinisch and Schreuer (2020), p. 550, para. 48.

[213] *Ibid*, para. 52.

[214] Article 8.10(1), CETA, ('Each Party shall accord in its territory to covered investments [. . .] fair and equitable treatment **and** full protection and security [. . .]').

[215] Dumberry (2022), Article 8.10, para. 33; see on tribunals limiting the FPS standard to physical security, *Saluka Investments BV (The Netherlands) v. Czech Republic*, PCA Case No. 2001-04, Partial Award (17 March 2006), para. 484; *Enron Creditors Recovery Corporation (formerly Enron Corporation) and Ponderosa Assets, L.P. v. Argentine Republic*, ICSID Case No. ARB/01/3, Award (22 May 2007), para. 286; *Sempra Energy International v. Argentine Republic*, ICSID Case No. ARB/02/16, Award (28 September 2007), para. 323; *BG Group Plc. v. Republic of Argentina*, UNCITRAL, Award (24 December 2007), para. 323 ff; *Rumeli Telekom A.S. and Telsim Mobil Telekomunikasyon Hizmetleri A.S. v, Republic of Kazakhstan*, ICSID Case No. ARB/05/16, Award (29 July 2008), para. 668 f; *AWG Group Ltd. v. Argentine Republic*, UNCITRAL, Decision on Liability (30 July 2010), para. 174 ff.

[216] The cumulative count of '83' is derived from the combined total of parties in both CETA and AfCFTA. Precisely, this encompasses 29 CETA parties, consisting of 27 EU member states, the EU

states that have adopted the same clarification in recent IIAs with the EU.[217] Certainly, such a clarification would address the lack of precision present in old-generation IIAs, curtailing the potential for an MIC to interpret the FPS clause beyond the duty to provide physical security to encompass legal security. This aligns with African states' interests which the CETA implies the EU and its recent IIA partners do not oppose. Hence, such clarification could be potentially adopted in a GNTI to clarify the expected FPS duty under vaguely worded old-generation IIAs.

4.3.1.5   Guiding Note Clarifying the 'Most Favoured Nations' ('MFN') Clause

The MFN clause is another investment protection guarantee widely incorporated across IIAs. This standard obliges contracting parties to treat investors and investments from the other contracting party(ies) no less favourable than investors and investments from third countries.[218] Therefore, unlike the national treatment standard that focuses on non-discrimination between foreign and domestic investors (i.e. with nationality of the host state),[219] the MFN standard strictly focuses on non-discriminatory treatment between foreign investors operating within the host state market.

Generally, arbitral tribunals recognise three essential conditions for an MFN claim to succeed:[220]

- *Firstly*, the existence of a more favourable treatment;
- *Secondly,* the treatment is offered to another foreign investor in a similar/like situation (comparator); and
- *Thirdly,* the differential treatment is without any objective justification.

While this three-step test has been widely embraced by ISDS tribunals to asses an MFN claim, the precise scope of treatment to which it is applicable remains unsettled. Specifically, arbitral tribunals are divided on whether the MFN clause encompasses procedural rights, such as dispute resolution methods, or is limited solely to substantive rights. While certain tribunals have concluded that it extends to

---

itself (1), and Canada (1), in addition to 54 African Union Member States that are parties to the AfCFTA, resulting in a cumulative total of '83'.

[217] See, Article 2.5(5), EU-Vietnam IPA, signed 30 June 2019; Article 2.4(5), EU-Singapore IPA, signed 15 October 2018; Article 15(3), Investment, EU-Mexico Agreement in Principle (2018); Article 10.15(4), EU-Chile Advanced Framework Agreement (Investment Chapter) (2022).

[218] Reinisch and Schreuer (2020), p. 686, para. 1.

[219] See, on national treatment, *Ibid.*, p. 587 ff.

[220] See, *Parkerings-Compagniet AS v. Republic of Lithuania*, ICSID Case No. ARB/05/8, Award (11 September 2007), para. 366 ff; *Pawlowski AG and Project Sever s.r.o. v. Czech Republic*, ICSID Case No. ARB/17/11, Award (1 November 2021), para. 534.

the former,[221] others have disagreed.[222] This conflicting interpretation has rendered the MFN clause one of the most controversial topics in the international investment law community.[223]

To avoid an extension of this controversy into the CETA, the contracting parties have made sure to clarify the scope of the MFN treatment provided in Article 8.7 CETA:

1. Each Party shall accord to an investor of the other Party and to a covered investment, treatment no less favourable than the treatment it accords in like situations, to investors of a third country and to their investments with respect to the establishment, acquisition, expansion, conduct, operation, management, maintenance, use, enjoyment and sale or disposal of their investments in its territory.

2. For greater certainty, the treatment accorded by a Party under paragraph 1 means, with respect to a government in Canada other than at the federal level, or, with respect to a government of or in a Member State of the European Union, treatment accorded, in like situations, by that government to investors in its territory, and to investments of such investors, of a third country.

3. [. . .].

4. For greater certainty, the 'treatment' referred to in paragraphs 1 and 2 does not include procedures for the resolution of investment disputes between investors and states provided for in other international investment treaties and other trade agreements. Substantive obligations in other international investment treaties and

---

[221] *Emilio Agustín Maffezini v. Kingdom of Spain*, ICSID Case No. ARB/97/7, Decision on Jurisdiction (25 January 2000), para. 54 ff; *Siemens A.G. v. Argentine Republic*, ICSID Case No. ARB/02/8, Decision on Jurisdiction (3 August 2004), para. 85 f, 103; *Camuzzi International S.A. v. Argentine Republic II*, ICSID Case No. ARB/03/7, Decision on Objections to Jurisdiction (10 June 2005), paras. 25, 34; *Gas Natural SDG, S.A. v. Argentine Republic*, ICSID Case No. ARB/03/10, Decision of the Tribunal on Preliminary Questions on Jurisdiction (17 June 2005), para. 26 ff; *Austrian Airlines v. Slovak Republic*, UNCITRAL, Separate Opinion of Charles N. Brower (20 October 2009), para. 4 f; *RosInvestCo UK Ltd. v. Russia*, SCC Case No. Abr. V 079/2005, Award on Jurisdiction (5 October 2007), para. 132 ff; *Garanti Koza LLP v. Turkmenistan*, ICSID Case No. ARB/11/20, Decision on the Objection to Jurisdiction for Lack of Consent (3 July 2013), para. 96.

[222] *Salini Costruttori S.p.A. and Italstrade S.p.A. v. Hashemite Kingdom of Jordan*, ICSID Case No. ARB/02/13, Decision on Jurisdiction (9 November 2004), para. 106 ff; *CME Czech Republic B.V. v. Czech Republic*, UNCITRAL, Separate Opinion of Ian Brownlie (14 March 2003), para. 11; *Plama Consortium Limited v. Republic of Bulgaria*, ICSID Case No. ARB/03/24, Decision on Jurisdiction (8 February 2005), para. 217 ff; *Telenor Mobile Communications A.S. v. Republic of Hungary*, ICSID Case No. ARB/04/15, Award (13 September 2006), para. 91 ff; *Vladimir Berschader and Moïse Berschader v. The Russian Federation*, SCC Case No. 080/2004, Award (21 April 2006), para. 185; *Austrian Airlines v. Slovak Republic*, Award (20 October 2009), para. 129 ff; *Tza Yap Shum v. Republic of Peru*, ICSID Case No. ARB/07/6, Decision on Jurisdiction and Competence (19 June 2009), para. 216; *H&H Enterprises Investments, Inc. v. Arab Republic of Egypt*, ICSID Case No. ARB/09/15, Award (6 May 2014), para. 358.

[223] *Daimler Financial Services AG v. Argentine Republic*, ICSID Case No. ARB/05/1, Award (22 August 2012), para. 160.

other trade agreements do not in themselves constitute 'treatment', and thus cannot give rise to a breach of this Article, absent measures adopted or maintained by a Party pursuant to those obligations.

The paragraph 4 above particularly provides the necessary clarification significant to this discourse. *Firstly*, the highlighted provision unequivocally rejects the application of the MFN clause to procedural treatments, thereby preventing the importation of more favourable dispute resolution clauses from other IIAs into the CETA. This eliminates the potential for a *Maffezini v. Spain* reasoning or similar decisions cited earlier to gain traction within the context of the CETA.[224]

Secondly, paragraph 4 narrows down the application of the MFN clause by clarifying that substantive obligations in other IIAs *'do not in themselves constitute treatment'*, except for actual *'measures adopted or maintained by a party pursuant to those obligations'*. Consequently, the CETA parties have effectively precluded the potential for importing substantive obligations, such as FET, from other IIAs solely on the premise that it is a more advantageous treatment offered by the responding CETA party within a third-country IIA. For such an MFN claim to be successful, the claimant-investor would have to proof actual *de facto* treatment pursuant to the more favourable FET clause in the third country IIA.[225]

Significantly, African states have provided a similar level of clarity aimed at averting the jurisprudential controversy surrounding the application of the MFN clause within the AfCFTA. As provided in Article 14 of the AfCFTA Investment Protocol:

1. Each State Party shall accord to investors of another State Party and their investments treatment no less favourable than it accords, in like circumstances, to investors of any other State Party or Third Parties with respect to the management, conduct, operation, use, expansion and sale or other disposition of their investments.
2. [...].
3. For greater certainty, the "treatment" referred to in Paragraphs 1 and 2 does not include dispute settlement procedures, including, but not limited to, those related to admissibility and jurisdiction, provided for in other treaties. Substantive obligations in other investment treaties, do not in themselves constitute "treatment", and cannot give rise to a breach of this Article.

Paragraph 3 above specifically reflects the convergence between the CETA and AfCFTA parties regarding the pertinent application of the MFN clause, which is relevant to this discourse. First, as underlined above, paragraph three equally reflects the African states' interest in preventing the *Maffezini*-like precedents[226] from taking root within the AfCFTA framework. Thus, like the CETA parties, African states

---

[224] *See*, (fn. 221).

[225] *See*, Reinisch (2022), Article 8.7, para. 55 ff.

[226] *See*, (fn. 221).

made sure to clarify that their MFN commitment under Article 14(1) of the AfCFTA Investment Protocol *'does not include dispute settlement procedures'*.

Secondly, the AfCFTA parties clarified that the substantive obligations in other IIAs *'do not in themselves constitute treatment'* that could breach the MFN clause. Although, unlike the CETA, paragraph 3 above lacks clarity on the exact 'treatment' that could constitute an MFN breach, it can be inferred that the AfCFTA parties likely intended *de facto* and not merely *de jure* treatment as the decisive factor.

Generally, arbitral tribunals have accepted that MFN clauses allow the importation of more favourable substantive treatments available by legal provision *(de jure)* in other IIAs,[227] even if such treatments do not factually *(de facto)* exist. However, the explicit limitation of the MFN clause in both the CETA and AfCFTA effectively preclude such interpretation, since it is settled that something more than a written down legal provision in another IIA is required to establish an MFN breach.

Notably, the above clarification regarding the application of the MFN clause is not limited to the CETA and AfCFTA, but also found in other new generation IIAs.[228] With the mutual understanding being unveiled across new generation IIAs, it is plausible to agree on a GNTI for use by MIC judges clarifying the ambiguity concerning the MFN application present in old generation IIAs. The GNTI could simply affirm that the application of the MFN clause in force between the MIC members is to be interpreted as excluding procedural treatment, and its extension to substantive treatment only applies when there is an actual measure adopted or maintained pursuant to the more favourable substantive treatment provided in a third-country IIA.

In rounding up this current discussion, admittedly, a GNTI alone may not comprehensively address all the gaps present in old-generation IIAs that have prompted public criticism against traditional ISDS and even raised concerns about the potential effectiveness of an MIC. However, considering that the MIC will have to interact with both old and new-generation IIAs, implementing a GNTI would make a substantial contribution to addressing the gaps in old-generation IIAs that have led to contentious interpretations due to their lack of clarity.

Rather than wait until the actual reform of old IIA guarantees takes place, whether, on a bilateral or multilateral basis, it is highly beneficial and possible for prospective MIC members to collectively agree on a GNTI within the MICs framework, providing the court with the necessary context missing in old-generation IIAs when interacting with such instruments. This is particularly pertinent since the GNTI

---

[227] *Vladimir Berschader and Moise Berschader v. The Russian Federation*, SCC Case No. 080/2004, Award (21 April 2006), para. 179; *Bayindir Insaat Turizm Ticaret Ve Sanayi A.S. v. Islamic Republic of Pakistan*, ICSID Case No. ARB/03/29, Award (27 August 2009), para. 155.

[228] See Article 8.9(5) EU-Japan Economic Partnership Agreement, entered into force 1 February 2019; Article 2.4(5) EU-Vietnam IPA, signed 30 June 2019; Article 7(4), PAIC (2016), https://au. int/sites/default/files/documents/; Article 5(7), Protocol of Cooperation and Intra-Mercosur Investment Facilitation, entered into force 30 July 2019; Article 8(4), Investment, EU-Mexico Agreement in Principle (2018).

topics discussed above address issues that are often at the heart of contention in ISDS claims. Hence, while the GNTI may not address all the shortcomings in old-generation IIAs, it will undoubtedly play a significant role in reducing the inherent deficiencies that have led to divisive outcomes in traditional ISDS within the context of an MIC.

4.3.2 Addressing the Concern of Achieving Both Consistent and Correct ISDS Decisions Within an MIC

To begin with, since a clear policy framework is necessary to facilitate judicial outcomes that align with the true intention of treaty makers, the preceding discussions regarding the introduction of a GNTI would also significantly foster the realisation of accurate treaty interpretation within an MIC. The additional context provided in the GNTI, especially in relation to old-generation IIAs, would help foster decisions in alignment with the modern-day investment protection objectives of the MIC members.

Importantly, while it was earlier stressed that ensuring the accuracy of decisions according to the applicable law and facts in a dispute remains the primary objective of an MIC (Sect. 4.2.2), the harmonious interpretation and application of these laws cannot be disregarded. This is particularly crucial in cases where the applicable laws and facts are identical or similar to those in previously decided cases. Given the convergence in investment protection standards prevalent in the vast majority of IIAs,[229] with the same trend observed in new generation IIAs as revealed in the discussions above, it becomes a valid argument that most existing IIAs raise similar interpretative questions.[230] Therefore, inconsistent treaty interpretation in such cases places stakeholders in a dilemma when trying to determine the scope of their rights and duties under the legal regime. The African ISDS cases discussed in Chap. 3 exemplify this dilemma, as they depict the uncertainty states could face concerning their international treaty obligations when disputes based on similar IIA guarantees are decided inconsistently, without a clear justification.

Significantly, a legal system that ensures consistency will *"support the rule of law, enhance confidence in the stability of the investment environment and further bring legitimacy to the regime".*[231] Noteworthy, besides being necessary attributes to safeguard sustainable development in a state, given the importance of a

---

[229] UNCITRAL, *Report of Working Group III (Investor-State Dispute Settlement Reform)* of 26/2/2018, A/CN.9/930/Add.1/Rev.1, para. 27. (noting that "[...] differences in treaty language had been exaggerated and that the vast majority of investment treaties contained very similar if not identical language")

[230] Diel-Gligor (2017), p. 141.

[231] UNCITRAL, *Possible Reform of Investor-State Dispute Settlement (ISDS): Consistency and Related Matters*: Note by the Secretariat of 28/8/2018, A/CN.9/WG.III/WP.150, para. 5.

predictable legal environment for fostering economic activities that facilitate development, these are equally fundamental attributes required to maintain the public legitimacy of a future MIC. A legal system (the MIC inclusive) that lacks consistency cannot enhance the rule of law to the satisfaction or reasonable expectation of its users and therefore risks losing its reputation as a proper and legitimate legal system.[232]

Therefore, given the importance of consistency and the lack of the common law rule of *stare decisis* (binding precedent) in international law to foster this goal,[233] the MIC's adjudicative mandate could be formally guided by the *jurisprudence constante* doctrine applied in civil law systems. This is a practice whereby a court is required to take past decisions into account in a matter where there exists sufficient uniformity in the previous case-laws.[234] Therefore, in contrast to the common law doctrine of *stare decisis* where a precedent has a binding effect on later cases,[235] *jurisprudence constante* only requires a court to take into account previous decisions in deciding a legal issue when there is sufficient uniformity in previous case law.

With this civil law doctrine, the statute remains the starting and final reference point for any legal analysis before a court. However, in between, non-binding judicial decisions that interpret the law wield a substantial influence on the court, as they represent the commonly accepted interpretation of the law in practice.[236] By applying this doctrine in an MIC, the court is inclined to maintain an interpretation that appears to be well-established, unless there is a justifiable reason not to do so. For instance, this might occur when a more accurate result is obtained through a well-reasoned, holistic interpretation of the applicable IIA pursuant to Article 31–33 of the VCLT.

An illustration of how the *jurisprudence constante* can be implemented in an MIC to facilitate consistency without compromising correctness can be found in Article 28(1)(d) of the "Draft Statute of the MIC" proposed by *Marc Bungenberg and August Reinisch*, providing:

> [...] By performing their duties, the judges of the MIC shall...
>
> (d) secure uniform and consistent interpretation of the law, taking into consideration previous decisions without establishing a doctrine of precedent, particularly where there exists sufficient uniformity in previous case law.[237]

---

[232] Diel-Gligor (2017), p. 122.

[233] See, *Lee-Chin v. Dominican Republic*, ICSID, Partial Award on Jurisdiction (15 July 2020), para.80, (*"[...]Tribunal cannot but recall that there is no stare decisis doctrine in international law"*); See also in this regard, *Micula v. Romania* (II) ICSID, Award (5 March 2020), para.352; *Sempra Energy International v. Argentine Republic*, ICSID Case No. ARB/02/16, Decision on the Argentine Republic's Request for a Continued Stay of Enforcement of the Award (Rule 54 of the ICSID Arbitration Rules) (5 Mar 2009), para. 94.

[234] Fon and Parisi (2006), p. 522.

[235] Born (2021), International Commercial Arbitration, p. 4182 ff.

[236] Bjorklund (2008), p. 272.

[237] Bungenberg and Reinisch, Draft Statute of the Multilateral Investment Court (2021), p. 62.

It is important to highlight that no other multilateral instrument related to ISDS, such as those under ICSID or UNCITRAL, incorporates a comparable provision. Although the *jurisprudence constante* doctrine has been informally recognised in arbitral practice,[238] its formal recognition in an MIC statute as conceived in the model provision above would guarantee the court has a duty to accord careful consideration to its existing line of case law on a similar legal issue before deciding whether deference to its precedents is appropriate or if rather a different outcome is justified to achieve the correct decision, which is the ultimate objective.

Importantly, being a court of law and not of precedent, judges must refrain from prematurely deferring to the MIC's existing body of case law when faced with similar interpretative questions. This is of particular importance to ensure that the primary focus of the court remains the interpretation of the treaty in each individual case. As noted by *Richard Chen*, although not with reference to an MIC, tribunals should refrain from embracing a consistent line of cases too quickly. Instead, they should view this as an opportunity to engage in a dialogue with past decisions, assess how a case aligns with broader discussions, and actively discuss potential solutions, rather than passively waiting for a solution to emerge from prior decisions.[239] Further, where the circumstances permit, they should provide more general reasoning to advance the dialogue.[240]

Although *Richard Chen's* comments were made in the context of *jurisprudence constante* in investment arbitration, his conception is equally applicable to the application of *jurisprudence constante* in an MIC. In lieu of deferring to past decisions simply based on a consistent line of interpretations, the MIC should rather defer to its consistent precedents after a rigorous dialogue with previous decisions, considering how they fit with the present case, and where possible, advance the dialogue on what future tribunals should consider when confronted with a related legal issue.

Fundamentally, at the core of this dialogue should be the balancing of the competing interests between predictability (consistency), accuracy (correctness), and legitimacy.[241] While there is a compelling ground for a tribunal to favour its consistent line of case law to foster predictability, a predictable but inaccurate decision to the law will consequently erode legitimacy. This is especially crucial since the applicable statutes remain the primary source for interpreting the legal

---

[238] On ISDS tribunals that has acknowledged the duty to adopt principles established in a series of consistent cases, see: *Iberdrola Energía, S.A. v. Republic of Guatemala (II)*, PCA Case No. 2017-41, Final Award (24 August 2020), para. 229; *Griffin Group v. Poland*, SCC Case No. 2014/168, Final Award (29 April 2020), para. 214; *AES Solar and others (PV Investors) v. Spain*, PCA Case No. 2012-14, Concurring and Dissenting Opinion of Charles N. Brower (28 February 2020), para. 16; *Swissbourgh and others v. Lesotho*, PCA Case No. 2013-29, Judgment of the High Court of Singapore on the Set Aside Application [2017] SGHC 195 (14 August 2017), para. 103; also see in general, Bjorklund (2008), p. 272.

[239] Chen (2019), p. 68.

[240] *Ibid.*

[241] *Ibid.* p. 72.

rights and liabilities of disputing parties.[242] Therefore, while a future MIC strives to offer consistency to its members through consistent decisions, it must with the same rigour pursue accuracy in the interpretation of the different treaties that come under its judicial scope notwithstanding their similarities. This approach would ensure that the MIC, in any case, provides a well-reasoned justification for either adhering to or deviating from its precedents, rather than making decisions without such reasoned justification.

Consequently, an MIC that engages in a rigorous dialogue with precedent, aiming to balance the concerns of consistency and correctness in each case, especially when dealing with similar interpretative issues will ensure that stakeholders are not confused as to the dynamics of the law and facts that may influence the decisions of the MIC in aligning or departing from its precedents. By so doing, the MIC will support the creation of a predictable legal environment for investment in its member states, fostering economic activities that are important to sustainable development. Moreover, this reduces the potential for conflicts, and in the event of one, ensures a clear understanding of the strengths and weaknesses of a claim or defence, allowing for a well-guided decision on the prudent course of action. In this way, the MIC would promote the broader goal of sustainable development in its respective member states.

4.3.3   Addressing the Concern of Investor Accountability in an MIC

Since the 1970s, reaching an agreement on a legal framework that mandates host states to safeguard foreign investments under specific standards, while foreign investors are also obliged to engage in investment activities meeting certain standards that contribute to the host's sustainable development, has been a debated topic without consensus between capital-exporting countries (mostly developed nations) and capital-importing countries (mostly developing nations).[243]

Although the current 'one-way' ISDS system solely focused on investment protection was originally intended to address a perceived imbalance between states and foreign investors, assuming that the latter is the weaker party that requires protection from the powerful sovereign.[244] Over time, this assumption has proven to be highly inaccurate, particularly when viewed from the perspective of small developing or least developed countries, which comprise the majority of African states.

For example, the largest FDI holders in Africa are multinational corporations from powerful European nations, led by investors from the United Kingdom, France,

---

[242] *Ibid.* p. 73.

[243] See, Perrone and Vásquez (2023).

[244] Papazoglou (2019), p. 48.

and the Netherlands.[245] The substantial financial resources, technological expertise, and global networks at the disposal of these multinationals give them significant leverage over most African economies with incomparable resources. Therefore, if possessing sovereignty does not automatically equate to being the dominant party in an investor-state relationship, the exclusive focus of the ISDS system on protecting investors against states, without reciprocal protection, is unjustifiable, as it only further weakens already vulnerable states against mighty multinationals. This inequity becomes especially concerning when it comes to restraining the misconduct of non-compliant multinational corporations or balancing the private interests of investors vis-à-vis the host state's public interest.

Notably, achieving this crucial balance within a future MIC is not impossible. There are, in particular, two approaches by which investor accountability for wrongful conduct can be guaranteed within the constitutional framework of an MIC. The *First* approach is **'indirect'**. As subsequently demonstrated, this can be achieved without substantive law reform by simply adopting existing procedural practices in traditional ISDS. The *Second* approach is **'direct'**. Albeit, this approach represents a significant shift from traditional ISDS, requiring both procedural and substantive law reform. Nevertheless, it is important to consider at least the procedural adaptation necessary to keep an MIC open for such member states willing to explore substantive law improvements related to 'direct' investor accountability.

4.3.3.1 Indirect Accountability for Investor Misconduct

Even though IIAs are typically silent on investor obligations, including how investment activities should be conducted and the penalties for violations, this does not imply that investors have the freedom to conduct their business in a manner detrimental to the host state's interests without facing any form of accountability. In traditional ISDS, a form of 'indirect accountability' is present to check irresponsible investor conduct. It is indirect because it does not involve a direct claim against the investor for misconduct. Rather, accountability is derived from the consequences that flow from an act of misconduct, which can be the forfeiture of access to arbitration for lacking a protected investment, or a lost or diminished right to compensation.[246] Additionally, in limited cases, arbitral tribunals have allowed indirect actions through counterclaims to address the harm caused to a host state due to investor misconduct.

Similarly, in an MIC, indirect accountability may be achieved in three ways consistent with already existing practice. Precisely, the forfeiture of MIC jurisdiction due to the absence of a protected investment (Sect. 4.3.3.1.1); or 'causality' resulting in a lost or diminished entitlement to compensation (Sect. 4.3.3.1.2); or through a counterclaim by the host state (Sect. 4.3.3.1.3).

---

[245] UNCTAD (2023).
[246] See, Jarrett et al. (2021).

4.3.3.1.1 Forfeiture of MIC Jurisdiction Due to Lack of a Protected Investment

While IIAs are established to offer specific investment protection assurances to foreign investors, guarantees such as the FET, FPS, and expropriation standards, *inter alia*—would hold no value if the intended beneficiaries (covered investors) lack the means to enforce them. In traditional ISDS, this will mean the lack of the host state's consent to arbitration. With consent being the cornerstone of all international treaty commitments including arbitration,[247] no tribunal will exercise jurisdiction over an investment dispute unless it is satisfied that the dispute falls within the treaty parties' scope of consent to arbitration.[248] Therefore, even though an investor has no direct treaty obligation towards the host state, the investor is indirectly obliged to refrain from actions that could place its investment outside the protective scope of the IIAs dispute resolution clause, as consented by the host state.

In investment arbitration, one of the claimant's primary burdens is to establish the tribunal's jurisdiction.[249] The same burden would be expected of a claimant before an MIC. Following the ICSID model, the most popular ISDS forum, to successfully seize a tribunal's jurisdiction, a claimant must satisfy the jurisdictional requirements foreseen under the Convention.[250] Particularly, the claimant must establish that it has fulfilled the condition for accessing arbitration both under the ICSID Convention and the relevant IIA.[251] Among these conditions is the necessity for the claimant to possess a qualified investment under both the ICSID Convention and the applicable IIA, often referred to as the 'double barrelled test'.[252]

---

[247] *Chevron Corporation and Texaco Petroleum Corporation v. Ecuador (II)*, PCA Case No. 2009-23, Third Interim Award on Jurisdiction and Admissibility (27 Feb 2012), para. 4.61; *Wintershall Aktiengesellschaft v. Argentine Republic*, ICSID Case No. ARB/04/14, Award (8 December 2008), para. 179; *Link-Trading Joint Stock Company v. Department for Customs Control of the Republic of Moldova*, UNCITRAL, Award on Jurisdiction (16 February 2001), para. 8.1; *Ethyl Corporation v. The Government of Canada*, UNCITRAL, Award on Jurisdiction (24 June 1998), para. 59; ICSID (1965), para. 23.

[248] As discussed earlier, consent to investment arbitration may be derived from other sources, including investment contracts and national law on foreign investment, but this thesis discussion proceeds on the basis of treaty based arbitration (Chap. 3).

[249] *National Gas S.A.E. v. Arab Republic of Egypt*, ICSID Case No. ARB/11/7, Award (3 April 2014), para. 118; *Philip Morris Asia Limited v. Commonwealth of Australia*, PCA Case No. 2012-12, Award on Jurisdiction and Admissibility (17 December 2015), para. 495; *ICS Inspection and Control Services Limited (United Kingdom) v. The Republic of Argentina*, UNCITRAL, PCA Case No. 2010-9, Award on Jurisdiction (10 February 2012), para. 280.

[250] See, ICSID (1965), para. 22 ff, p. 43; *Inceysa Vallisoletana S.L. v. Republic of El Salvador*, ICSID Case No. ARB/03/26, Award (2 August 2006), para. 169, 173.

[251] *Fábrica de Vidrios Los Andes, C.A. and Owens-Illinois de Venezuela, C.A. v. Bolivarian Republic of Venezuela (I)*, ICSID Case No. ARB/12/21, Award (13 November 2017), para. 261.

[252] *Koch Minerals Sarl and Koch Nitrogen International Sarl v. Bolivarian Republic of Venezuela*, ICSID Case No. ARB/11/19, Award (30 October 2017), para. 6.50; *Phoenix Action, Ltd. v. Czech Republic*, ICSID Case No. ARB/06/5, Award (15 April 2009), para. 74; *Toto Costruzioni Generali S.p.A. v. Lebanese Republic*, ICSID Case No. ARB/07/12, Decision on Jurisdiction (11 September

The double barrelled test which is a well-established principle within the ICSID system can similarly be adapted to the MIC system to strengthen investor accountability. Under this test, there will be no consent to the MIC's jurisdiction if no protected investment exists within the meaning of the MIC statute (Sect. 4.3.3.1.1.1) and the applicable IIA (Sect. 4.3.3.1.1.2).

4.3.3.1.1.1 Lack of a Protected Investment Under the MIC Statute

As already noted, the existence of an investment under Article 25 of the ICSID Convention must be objectively satisfied before a tribunal can exercise jurisdiction.[253] Likewise, an MIC can adopt this approach by denying jurisdiction if the claimant-investor lacks a protected investment within the meaning of the MIC statute.

It is noteworthy that no attempt was made to define an investment under the ICSID Convention.[254] To determine what constitutes an investment, tribunals have widely, although not exclusively, applied the so-called *Salini* four objective criteria.[255] In *Salini v. Morroco*,[256] the tribunal identified four characteristics that must be present to infer the existence of an investment under the ICSID convention. That is:

2009), para. 66; *Malicorp Limited v. Arab Republic of Egypt*, ICSID Case No. ARB/08/18, Award (7 February 2011), para. 107; *Abaclat and others (formerly Giovanna a Beccara and others) v. Argentine Republic*, ICSID Case No. ARB/07/5, Decision on Jurisdiction and Admissibility (4 August 2011), para. 344; *El Paso Energy International Company v. Argentine Republic*, ICSID Case No. ARB/03/15, Award (31 October 2011), para. 142.

[253] *Ambiente Ufficio S.P.A. and others (formerly Giordano Alpi and others) v. Argentine Republic*, ICSID Case No. ARB/08/9, Decision on Jurisdiction and Admissibility (8 February 2013), para. 438 f; *ABCI Investments Limited v. Republic of Tunisia*, ICSID Case No. ARB/04/12, Decision on Jurisdiction (18 February 2011), para. 65; *National Gas S.A.E. v. Arab Republic of Egypt*, ICSID Case No. ARB/11/7, Award (3 April 2014), para. 121.

[254] *Zhinvali Development Ltd. v. Republic of Georgia*, ICSID Case No. ARB/00/1, Award (24 January 2003), para. 351 ff; *Ambiente Ufficio S.P.A. and others (formerly Giordano Alpi and others) v. Argentine Republic*, ICSID Case No. ARB/08/9, Decision on Jurisdiction and Admissibility (8 February 2013), para. 448 ff; *Rasia FZE and Joseph K. Borkowski v. Republic of Armenia*, ICSID Case No. ARB/18/28, Award (20 January 2023), para. 371.

[255] *Bayindir Insaat Turizm Ticaret Ve Sanayi A.S. v. Islamic Republic of Pakistan (I)*, ICSID Case No. ARB/03/29, Decision on Jurisdiction (14 November 2005), para. 130 ff; *Compagnie d'Exploitation du Chemin de Fer Transgabonais v. Gabonese Republic*, ICSID Case No. ARB/04/5, Excerpts of Decision on Jurisdiction (19 December 2005), para. 27 f; *Jan de Nul N.V. and Dredging International N.V. v. Arab Republic of Egypt*, ICSID Case No. ARB/04/13, Decision on Jurisdiction (16 June 2006), para. 91 f; *Saipem S.p.A. v. People's Republic of Bangladesh*, ICSID Case No. ARB/05/07, Decision on Jurisdiction and Recommendation on Provisional Measures (21 March 2007), para. 99; *Ioannis Kardassopoulos v. The Republic of Georgia*, ICSID Case No. ARB/05/18, Decision on Jurisdiction (6 July 2007), para. 116.

[256] *Salini Costruttori S.P.A. and Italstrade S.P.A. v. Kingdom of Morocco*, ICSID Case No. ARB/00/4, Decision on Jurisdiction (16 July 2001), para. 52.

- a contribution of capital;
- for a certain duration of performance;
- participation in the risks of the transaction; and
- a contribution to the economic development of the host state of the investment.

These four characteristics have often formed the basis of the objective analysis for determining the existence of an investment under Article 25 of the ICSID Convention.

However, in contrast to the ICSID Convention where the definition of an investment is lacking, the definition of an investment could be explicitly provided under the MIC statute. Notably, such a definition can be adapted from the definition of an investment provided under the CETA. According to the CETA:

> investment means every kind of asset that an investor owns or controls, directly or indirectly, that has the characteristics of an investment, which includes a certain duration and other characteristics such as the commitment of capital or other resources, the expectation of gain or profit, or the assumption of risk [. . .].[257]

This CETA definition is followed by a non-exhaustive list of the various forms that an investment could take. For the purpose of this discussion, the focus is on the definition of an investment as underlined above, which shares characteristics similar to the *Salini* test. The only missing test is the *'contribution to the host state's economic development'*. However, the absence of this factor itself does not mean that an investment is not required to foster economic development. The apt argument is that this factor is already implicit in the other three characteristics, thus no need to consider it separately.[258] A contrary interpretation will be inapposite to the object and purpose of a treaty like the CETA which according to its preamble includes the contracting Parties:

> [. . .] commitment to promote sustainable development and the development of international trade in such a way as to contribute to sustainable development in its **economic**, social and environmental dimensions.

As earlier discussed (Sect. 4.2), the above preamble confirms that economic development as a pillar of sustainable development is not just critical to the CETA Parties, but also the other two pillars of SD i.e. social development and environmental protection.

As evinced in the AfCFTA, African states' understanding of what constitutes an investment is not so different from the CETA approach. The AfCFTA also adopts a non-exhaustive, asset-based approach with a *Salini*-like test to establish what qualifies as an investment within the treaty. The treaty states that:

---

[257] Article 8.1, CETA, (definition of an Investment).

[258] *Deutsche Bank AG v. Democratic Socialist Republic of Sri Lanka*, ICSID Case No. ARB/09/2, Dissenting Opinion of Makhdoom Ali Khan (31 October 2012), para. 40.

> For greater certainty, the investment must have the following characteristics: commitment of capital or other resources, the expectation of gain or profit, a certain duration, assumption of risk, and *a significant contribution to the Host State's sustainable development.*[259]

As underlined, the AfCFTA shares similar characteristics with the CETA on how to determine the existence of an investment. However, the AfCFTA takes an additional step by explicitly mandating a significant contribution to the host state's sustainable development. While the CETA does not explicitly mandate the same prerequisite, it can be argued that the CETA at least implicitly encompasses the need for an investment to 'contribute to the sustainable development of the host states, given that this aligns with one of the core objectives the CETA Parties are committed to pursuing.

Since there is evidence of mutual understanding between the CETA and AfCFTA Parties that the first three *Salini* tests apply to the determination of an investment: (i) commitment of capital, (ii) for a certain duration, (iii) risk assumption; including a shared commitment in principle to promoting sustainable development, this common ground could accordingly serve as the foundation for defining an investment eligible for protection under the MIC statute.

For example, for the purpose of exercising its jurisdiction, the MIC may necessitate the presence of an investment as defined in the court's statute by stipulating that:

> To qualify as an investment under this Statute, the investment must have the following characteristics: which includes a certain duration and other characteristics such as the commitment of capital or other resources, the expectation of gain or profit, or the assumption of risk [...], and a contribution to the Host State's sustainable development.

Only the fourth requirement will be a novel test without an existing precedent in ISDS practice. However, the inclusion of this requirement has become necessary to bridge the gap between the guarantee of investment protection on the one hand, and the guarantee of investment activities that do not undermine the sustainable development interests of the host nation on the other hand. In applying this test, certain guidance may be drawn from the jurisprudence on the legality requirement discussed *infra* (Sect. 4.3.3.1.1.2). For instance, arbitral tribunals faced with the question whether an investment has been 'made in accordance with the laws of the host state' have considered the seriousness or gravity of non-compliance with local law to conclude whether the suitable outcome is the rejection of jurisdiction.[260]

Similarly, failure to contribute to the host state's sustainable development should attract a denial of MIC jurisdiction only where the failure is of a severe gravity to warrant such an outcome. Otherwise, minor unintended errors, though constituting a

---

[259] Article 1, AfCFTA Investment Protocol, (definition of an investment).

[260] *Vladislav Kim and others v. Republic of Uzbekistan*, ICSID Case No. ARB/13/6, Decision on Jurisdiction (8 March 2017), para. 405 ff; *Krederi Ltd. v. Ukraine*, ICSID Case No. ARB/14/17, Excerpts of Award (2 July 2018), para. 384 ff; *Bank Melli Iran and Bank Saderat Iran v. Kingdom of Bahrain*, PCA Case No. 2017-25, Final Award (9 November 2021), para. 376; *Tokios Tokelés v. Ukraine*, ICSID Case No. ARB/02/18, Decision on Jurisdiction (29 April 2004), para 86.

misconduct, can still be effectively accounted for in the merit or compensation phase. This approach is necessary to establish a fair and equitable balance between the private and public interests that the MIC is tasked with safeguarding. Whether the threshold for denying jurisdiction is reached would therefore rely on an objective evaluation of the distinct facts and circumstances of each individual case.

Notably, within the context of the 'legality requirement' as applied in arbitral practice, a temporal restriction is also considered to determine the appropriate consequence for non-compliance with local law. Tribunals have held that such misconduct would affect jurisdiction only if it occurred when the investment was made, not afterward.[261] This interpretation is premised on the ground that the word 'made' is a past tense, implying that the legality requirement applies only when the investment is established, not after.[262] However, such a temporal consideration should hold no significance in determining the existence of an investment under the MIC statute. This is so because, unlike the 'legality requirement' obliging that an 'investment be **made** in accordance with the host state law', the operative word for a qualifying investment under the MIC statute, if modeled after the CETA or AfCFTA examples cited above, would be that— *'the investment must* **have** *the following characteristics: which includes [. . .]'*. The qualification **'have'** or **'has'** used in the CETA and AfCFTA respectively denotes a present perfect tense, in contrast to a past tense that the word 'made' would imply.

Hence, by requiring that an *'investment must have the following characteristics'*, which includes *inter alia* a contribution to the host state's sustainable development, this stipulates a present rather than a past condition. Therefore, a claimant-investor cannot contend that irresponsible conduct on its part cannot result in a jurisdictional bar for lacking a protected investment merely because the misconduct occurred after the investment was made. Since one of the main clamour of African states is to limit the jurisdiction of the MIC to claims by responsible investors who have not violated the sustainable development interest of their host nation,[263] this objective would be undermined if investors only needed to consider such a level of accountability at the time of making their investment, and not afterward.

Finally, on this discussion, it would also be beneficial to clarify the MIC's source for determining investor misconduct that excludes an investment from the protective

---

[261] *Bernhard von Pezold and others v. Republic of Zimbabwe*, ICSID Case No. ARB/10/15, Award (28 July 2015), para. 420; *Oxus Gold plc v. Republic of Uzbekistan*, UNCITRAL, Final Award (17 December 2015), para. 706 f; *Copper Mesa Mining Corporation v. Republic of Ecuador*, PCA Case No. 2012-2, Award (15 March 2016), para. 5.54; *Urbaser S.A. and Consorcio de Aguas Bilbao Biskaia, Bilbao Biskaia Ur Partzuergoa v. Argentine Republic*, ICSID Case No. ARB/07/26, Decision on Jurisdiction (19 December 2012), para. 260; *Teinver S.A., Transportes de Cercanías S.A. and Autobuses Urbanos del Sur S.A. v. Argentine Republic*, ICSID Case No. ARB/09/1, Decision on Jurisdiction (21 December 2012), para. 257; *Vannessa Ventures Ltd. v. Bolivarian Republic of Venezuela*, ICSID Case No. ARB(AF)/04/6, Award (16 January 2013), para. 167.

[262] *Vladislav Kim and others v. Republic of Uzbekistan*, ICSID Case No. ARB/13/6, Decision on Jurisdiction (8 March 2017), para. 374 ff.

[263] UNCITRAL, *Submission from the Government of South Africa* of 17/7/2019, A/CN.9/WG.III/WP.176, para. 55.

scope of the court, for being detrimental to the host state's sustainable development. Generally, ISDS tribunals have not found it difficult to deny treaty protection to claims arising out of a violation of 'international public policy'.[264] This means a violation of an *'international consensus as to universal standards and accepted norms of conduct that must be applied in all fora'*.[265] ISDS tribunals have applied these transnational norms of acceptable conduct to deny treaty protection to investment claims arising out of bribery, corruption, fraud or forgery.[266] It is expected that the same powers will be inherent in an MIC to decline jurisdiction over claims arising from any violation of international public policy. For greater certainty, the MIC may incorporate an already established provision from the CETA which excludes the submission of claims stemming from investments 'made through fraudulent misrepresentation, concealment, corruption, or conduct amounting to an abuse of process'.[267]

However, investor accountability for misconduct detrimental to the host state's sustainable development need not be limited to those aforementioned instances. Particularly, the lack of jurisdiction for not having a protected investment under the MIC could extend to violation of certain recognised international standards on the conduct of investors, which significantly compromised the host state's sustainable development interest. For this purpose, the MIC may draw reference from SD standards contained in international instruments such as the 2011 UN Guiding Principles on Business and Human Rights (UNGPs),[268] The Resolution of the United Nations General Assembly A/RES/76/300 ('The human right to a clean, healthy and sustainable environment'),[269] The ILO Declaration on Fundamental Principles and Rights at Work,[270] and other relevant international standards focused on the sustainable development of its members. Although these instruments by themselves do not create a binding legal obligation, prospective MIC members

---

[264] *Fraport AG Frankfurt Airport Services Worldwide v. Republic of the Philippines (I)*, ICSID Case No. ARB/03/25, Dissenting Opinion of Mr. Bernardo M. Cremades (16 August 2007), para. 40; *Vladislav Kim and others v. Republic of Uzbekistan*, ICSID Case No. ARB/13/6, Decision on Jurisdiction (8 March 2017), para. 593 ff; *Churchill Mining and Planet Mining Pty Ltd v. Republic of Indonesia*, ICSID Case No. ARB/12/14 and 12/40, Award (6 December 2016), para. 508; *Liman Caspian Oil BV and NCL Dutch Investment BV v. Republic of Kazakhstan*, ICSID Case No. ARB/07/14, Excerpts of Award (22 June 2010), para. 194.

[265] *World Duty Free Company Ltd v Republic of Kenya*, ICSID Case No ARB/00/07, Award (4 October 2006), para. 139.

[266] *Yukos Capital Limited (formerly Yukos Capital SARL) v Russian Federation*, PCA Case No. 2013-31, Final Award (23 July 2021), para. 514.

[267] See Article 8.18(3), CETA; see also, Article 41, Bungenberg and Renisch, Draft Statute of the Multilateral Investment Court (2021), p. 69.

[268] United Nations OHCHR (2011), p. 13 ff.

[269] UNGA RES/76/300 *The Human Right to A Clean, Healthy and Sustainable Environment* of 28/7/2022, UN DOC. A/RES/76/300.

[270] *International Labour Organisation (ILO)*, Declaration on Fundamental Principles and Rights at Work and its Follow-up, 1998, as amended (2022), https://www.ilo.org/declaration/lang%2D%2Den/index.htm.

may choose to adopt the standards and principles contained in them as applicable standards and principles to the interpretative mandate of an MIC under Article 31(3) (c) of the VCLT, which requires a contextual interpretation of an IIA that encompass the consideration of any relevant rule of international law applicable between the parties.

For greater certainty, considering the multitude of international instruments pertaining to responsible investor conduct and the concern that most are adopted as soft laws without binding effects, the MIC members may delineate, either in the Court's Statute or an annex to it, a specific list of international instruments aimed at promoting sustainable development, which the members could agree to treat as applicable within the meaning of Article 31(3)(c) of the VCLT.

Further, treating private persons as subjects without direct duties under international law is not a valid argument to exclude the consideration of investor conduct contrary to the international commitments on sustainable development shared by future MIC members. This includes investor accountability for any violation of established international human rights, labour, or environmental standards. For example, as held by the tribunal in *Urbaser v. Argentina*,[271] although non-state actors have no duty to guarantee international human rights, they do have one not to violate it.[272] Also endorsing the *Urbaser* view, the tribunal in *David Aven v. Costa Rica*[273] considered the protection of the environment as one of the international obligations that a foreign investor cannot claim immunity from, based on being a non-state actor.[274]

Accordingly, with a little bit of innovation complementing existing jurisprudence, there exists the potential to establish an MIC that exclusively protects responsible investments. This could be achieved by denying protection to investment activities that significantly compromise the sustainable development interests of its members through violation of international public policy or other notable international standards on investor conduct.

4.3.3.1.1.2   Lack of a Protected Investment Under the Applicable IIA

As earlier introduced, the ICSID double barrelled test approach to jurisdiction requires the existence of a protected investment both under the ICSID Convention and the applicable IIA. Adopting this ICSID approach, the existence of a protected investment under the MIC statute will only satisfy one limb of the test. The other limb that has to be satisfied to establish an MIC jurisdiction would be the existence of a protected investment under the applicable IIA.

---

[271] *Urbaser S.A. and Consorcio de Aguas Bilbao Bizkaia, Bilbao Biskaia Ur Partzuergoa v. The Argentine Republic*, ICSID Case No. ARB/07/26, (Award 8 December 2016).

[272] *Ibid.* para. 1210.

[273] *David R. Aven and Others v. Republic of Costa Rica*, ICSID Case No. UNCT/15/3, Award (18 September 2018).

[274] *Ibid.*, para. 738.

Unlike the ICSID convention, IIAs typically define the term investment. This is often done with broad terms such as 'all assets', followed by a non-exhaustive list of categories of such assets constituting an investment.[275] However, the mere fact that an investor's asset falls under the enumerated list does not automatically qualify such asset as a protected investment under the IIA. In addition to the broad definition of an investment, several IIAs contain a 'compliance clause' mandating that foreign investments are made in accordance with the laws of the host state.[276] This is also known as the **'legality requirement'**. By this clause, the protective scope of an IIA is limited to only lawful investments,[277] thereby excluding those that would otherwise meet the broad definition of an investment under the relevant IIA but denied treaty protection for being marred by illegality.

Notably, not all IIAs include an explicit reference to a compliance clause. Nevertheless, several tribunals have read this requirement as implicitly necessary,[278] while there are others that disagree.[279] With an MIC comes the advantage of affirming the former and applying it consistently. This follows the rationale that no state would intend to offer treaty protection to an investment made in contravention of its domestic law, regardless of whether this is explicitly stated in the treaty or not.[280]

Arbitral jurisprudence confirms that the source for finding an investment illegal under domestic law may be derived from both the local **substantive or procedural norms** applicable to the foreign investment. For example, regarding the domestic substantive norms, it is recognised that an investment may be denied treaty protection if made in contravention of the host state's substantive laws that limit foreign

---

[275] Dolzer and Schreuer (2008), p. 61.

[276] Diel-Gligor and Hennecke (2015), p. 566.

[277] *Ibid.*

[278] *Saluka Investments BV (The Netherlands) v. Czech Republic*, PCA Case No. 2001-04, Partial Award (17 March 2006), para. 204; *Plama Consortium Limited v. Republic of Bulgaria*, ICSID Case No. ARB/03/24, Award (27 August 2008), para. 138 ff; *SAUR International v. Argentine Republic*, ICSID Case No. ARB/04/4, Decision on Jurisdiction and Liability (6 June 2012), para. 307 ff; *David Minnotte and Robert Lewis v. Republic of Poland*, ICSID Case No. ARB(AF)/10/1, Award (16 May 2014), para. 131; *Blusun S.A., Jean-Pierre Lecorcier and Michael Stein v. Italian Republic*, ICSID Case No. ARB/14/3, Award (27 December 2016), paras. 264, 268; *South American Silver Limited v. Plurinational State of Bolivia*, PCA Case No. 2013-15, Award (22 November 2018), paras. 456, 469, 470.

[279] *Achmea B.V. (formerly Eureko B.V.) v. Slovak Republic (I)*, PCA Case No. 2008-13, Final Award (7 December 2012), para. 176 f; *MNSS B.V. and Recupero Credito Acciaio N.V. v. Montenegro*, ICSID Case No. ARB(AF)/12/8, Award (4 May 2016), para. 212; *Capital Financial Holdings Luxembourg S.A. v. Republic of Cameroon*, ICSID Case No. ARB/15/18, Award (22 June 2017), para. 467; *Bear Creek Mining Corporation v. Republic of Peru*, ICSID Case No. ARB/14/21, Award (30 November 2017), para. 319 f.

[280] *Mamidoil Jetoil Greek Petroleum Products Societe Anonyme S.A. v. Republic of Albania*, ICSID Case No. ARB/11/24, Award (30 March 2015), para. 359; *Cortec Mining Kenya Limited, Cortec (Pty) Limited and Stirling Capital Limited v. Republic of Kenya*, ICSID Case No. ARB/15/29, Decision on Application for Annulment (19 March 2021), para. 140; *Plama Consortium Limited v. Republic of Bulgaria*, ICSID Case No. ARB/03/24, para. 138 f.

shareholding in public utility enterprises,[281] or reserve certain activities for national entities, or safeguard specific sectoral or geographical areas from foreign investment activities.[282]

Notably, such material restrictions regulating the making of foreign investments are not uncommon in domestic legal systems, aimed at fostering specific national interest goals pivotal to the host state's sustainable development. Non-compliance with domestic environmental protection laws is another recognised source for declaring an investment as illegal, hence unworthy of treaty protection.[283] Therefore, as a form of indirect accountability, there is no reason why a tribunal cannot deny IIA protection to investments made in blatant disregard of the host state's domestic law restrictions. This includes public interest legislation such as environmental, human rights, and labour rights protection.[284]

Regarding the domestic procedural norms, an investment may be legal in substance, but may still be tainted by illegality if it is established or acquired through a fraudulent or corrupt process.[285] Consequently, in principle, procedural misconducts tainting the establishment or acquisition of an investment with comparable gravity to fraud or corruption are equally capable of excluding such investments from the protective scope of an IIA, as a matter of national law.

Ultimately, irrespective of treaty silence on this subject, investors are obliged to refrain from irresponsible conduct intended to undermine the substantive and procedural boundaries relating to the making of their investment in accordance with domestic law. Otherwise, on strong persuasive precedents, an MIC may indirectly ensure accountability from investments non-compliant with local law by declining jurisdiction over an investment claim for lack of protection under the applicable IIA.

It is however noteworthy that minor infractions with domestic law, whether substantive or procedural in nature may not necessarily be sanctioned with a denial of treaty protection. A *jurisprudence constante* appears to have emerged in arbitral practice that only significant and intended violations of fundamental principles of domestic laws by investors may serve as a ground for challenging jurisdiction.[286]

---

[281] *Fraport AG Frankfurt Airport Services Worldwide v. The Republic of the Philippines*, ICSID Case No. ARB/03/25, Award (16 August 2007), para. 396 ff.

[282] *Mamidoil Jetoil Greek Petroleum Products Societe Anonyme S.A. v. Republic of Albania*, ICSID Case No. ARB/11/24, Award (30 March 2015), para. 372.

[283] See, *Cortec Mining Kenya Limited, Cortec (Pty) Limited and Stirling Capital Limited v. Republic of Kenya*, ICSID Case No. ARB/15/29, Award (22 October 2018), para. 345 ff.

[284] Abel (2022), p. 177.

[285] *Mamidoil Jetoil Greek Petroleum Products Societe Anonyme S.A. v. Republic of Albania*, ICSID Case No. ARB/11/24, Award (30 March 2015), para. 378.

[286] *Komstroy (formerly Energoalians) v. Republic of Moldova*, UNCITRAL, Award (23 October 2013), para. 261; *ECE Projektmanagement International GmbH and Kommanditgesellschaft PANTA Achtundsechzigste Grundstücksgesellschaft mbH & Co v. Czech Republic*, PCA Case No. 2010-5, Award (19 September 2013), para. 3.170; *HOCHTIEF Aktiengesellschaft v. Argentine Republic*, ICSID Case No. ARB/07/31, Decision on Liability (29 December 2014), para. 199; *Krederi Ltd. v. Ukraine*, ICSID Case No. ARB/14/17, Excerpts of Award (2 July 2018),

For example, non-compliance with domestic exchange control laws may be characterized as an inadvertent and technical breach not fundamental enough to deprive a tribunal of jurisdiction.[287]

In *Kim v. Uzbekistan*,[288] the tribunal developed a three-step test for case-by-case application in determining an unprotected investment on the grounds of illegality. That is:

(i) the significance of the obligation with which the investor is alleged to not comply;[289]

(ii) the seriousness of the investor's conduct;[290]

(iii) whether the combination of the investor's conduct and the law involved results in a compromise of a significant interest of the host State to such an extent that the harshness of the sanction of placing the investment outside of the protections of the BIT is a proportionate consequence for the violation examined.[291]

Accordingly, a future MIC may also apply this three step-test to determine whether the proper and proportionate consequence for non-compliance with domestic law in the making of an investment is the forfeiture of MIC jurisdiction due to lack of a protected investment under the applicable IIA.

Furthermore, as discussed earlier, arbitral tribunals widely acknowledged that an investor may forfeit treaty protection and consequently the host state's consent to arbitration only if the illegality occurred when the investment was made, not thereafter.[292] However, such temporal restriction may not apply where the domestic law violation equally constitutes a breach of international public policy.[293] The rationale behind this overlook of temporal restriction is that international adjudicatory bodies are not composed to entertain claims in violation of international public policy in line with the principles of good faith and *nemo auditur propiam turpitudinem allegans*,[294] meaning 'nobody is heard recounting his own turpitude'.[295] Therefore, if non-compliance with a domestic law can be linked to a violation of a transnational policy that applies to an investment, whether before or

---

para. 348; *Mamidoil Jetoil Greek Petroleum Products Societe Anonyme S.A. v. Republic of Albania*, ICSID Case No. ARB/11/24, Award (30 March 2015), para. 483.

[287] *Peter A. Allard v. Government of Barbados*, PCA Case No. 2012-06, Award on Jurisdiction (13 June 2014), para. 94.

[288] *Vladislav Kim and others v. Republic of Uzbekistan*, ICSID Case No. ARB/13/6, Decision on Jurisdiction (8 March 2017).

[289] *Ibid.*, para. 406.

[290] *Ibid.*, para. 407.

[291] *Ibid.*, para. 408.

[292] *See*, (fn. 261).

[293] *Bank Melli Iran and Bank Saderat Iran v. Kingdom of Bahrain*, PCA Case No. 2017-25, Final Award (09 November 2021), para. 365.

[294] *Ibid.*

[295] Oxford Reference (2011).

after its establishment, such as the prohibition of fraud, forgery, or corruption, these unlawful activities might result in the lack of a protected investment under the relevant IIA, barring the assumption of jurisdiction, regardless of when the illegality occurred.

4.3.3.1.2 Causality Resulting in a Lost or Diminished Entitlement to Compensation

Once the jurisdiction of an investment tribunal is successfully established, generally the next chapter of the proceedings is the 'merits phase' focusing on the alleged breach of the respondent state's international obligations to the claimant-investor. Majorly, these obligations are derived from investment treaties,[296] however, contractual[297] or domestic law[298] commitments can also be a source of substantive claims in ISDS proceedings.

Importantly, in every ISDS claim, regardless of its substantive origin, the ultimate objective of a claimant-investor is not the assumption of jurisdiction or the attribution of responsibility on the respondent-state for breaching its international obligation. Instead, in most cases, the ultimate aim is the award of monetary damages (compensation). For a tribunal to grant this prayer, the claimant must not only establish a breach of an obligation that is attributable to the host state but also prove that the damages resulting from that breach were **caused** by the unlawful actions of the host state.[299] In other words, a claimant must be able to prove a relationship (i.e., causal link) between the breach and the alleged damage.[300] This is also referred to as the 'but for test'.[301] For example, in the *ELSI*[302] case, the ICJ

---

[296] *MTD Equity Sdn. Bhd. and MTD Chile S.A. v. Republic of Chile*, ICSID Case No. ARB/01/7, Decision on Annulment (21 March 2007), para. 67; *Suez, Sociedad General de Aguas de Barcelona S.A., and InterAgua Servicios Integrales del Agua S.A. v. The Argentine Republic*, ICSID Case No. ARB/03/17, Decision on Liability (30 July 2010), para. 56.

[297] McLachlan et al. (2017), para. 7.166.

[298] See *Interocean Oil Development Company and Interocean Oil Exploration Company v. Federal Republic of Nigeria*, ICSID Case No. ARB/13/20, Award of the Tribunal (6 October 2020), para. 193; *Stans Energy Corp. and Kutisay Mining LLC v. Kyrgyz Republic (II)*, PCA Case No. 2015-32, Award (20 August 2019), para. 9.

[299] *MNSS B.V. and Recupero Credito Acciaio N.V. v. Montenegro*, ICSID Case No. ARB(AF)/12/8, Award (4 May 2016), para. 356.

[300] *Cervin and Rhone v. Costa Rica*, ICSID Case No. ARB/13/2, Award (7 March 2017), para. 699 f; *B3 Croatian Courier v. Croatia*, ICSID Case No. ARB/15/5, Excerpts of Award (5 April 2019), para. 1121; *Deutsche Telekom v. India*, PCA Case No. 2014-10, Final Award (27 May 2020), para. 121.

[301] *El Jaouni v. Lebanon*, ICSID Case No. ARB/15/3, Award (14 January 2021), para. 61 ff; *Muszynianka v. Slovakia*, PCA Case No. 2017-08, Award (7 October 2020), para. 618; *Tethyan Copper v. Pakistan*, ICSID Case No. ARB/12/1, Award (12 July 2019), para. 286.

[302] *Elettronica Sicula SpA (ELSI) Case (United States of America v. Italy)*, Judgement [1989] ICJ Rep 15.

concluded that although the claimant had suffered an unlawful requisition by the host state, the primary cause of the claimant's loss was its own mismanagement sending it into an inevitable insolvency irrespective of the host state's unlawful interference.[303]

It is this 'causality test' in the merits phase that offers a second opportunity to establish indirect accountability for irresponsible investor conduct leading to investor losses that are not compensable, as opposed to investor losses caused by a host state's breach of an international obligation that is compensable. ISDS tribunals often approach this **'causality test'** guided by the commentaries on the ILC Draft Articles on Responsibility of States for Internationally Wrongful Acts ('ILC Draft Articles'),[304] according to which a state is only responsible for compensating those damages **'caused by'** the state's internationally wrongful act.[305]

For example, following this understanding and the *ELSI* case reasoning, the tribunal in *Biwater (BGT) v. Tanzania*[306] affirmed that for BGT to succeed in its claim for compensation against Tanzania, it must prove that:

> [...] the value of its investment was diminished or eliminated, and that the actions BGT complains of were the actual and proximate cause of such diminution in, or elimination of, value.[307]

Applying this rule, even though the tribunal determined that certain Tanzanian measures breached BGT's expropriation[308] and FET[309] guarantees under the UK-Tanzania BIT (1994), it declined to award any compensation to BGT. This was because the tribunal found that the actual cause for the claimant's losses stemmed from its own irresponsible conduct, which had set the investment on a path of destruction before any of the respondent's treaty violations occurred.[310] According to the tribunal, BGT's factual misconduct included *inter alia* a poorly prepared bid which made the investment project non-commercially viable from inception, and numerous mismanagements which made it impossible to generate profit or meet its contractual obligations.[311] Consequently, the investment was heading for an inevitable doom caused by an accumulation of BGT's own errors. By the time the treaty breaches occurred, BGT was found to be of no economic

---

[303] *Ibid.*, paras. 100-101.

[304] Draft Articles on Responsibility of States for Internationally Wrongful Acts, with commentaries (2001).

[305] *SolEs Badajoz GmbH v. Kingdom of Spain*, ICSID Case No. ARB/15/38, Award (31 July 2019), para. 477f; *Pey Casado v. Chile (I)*, ICSID Case No. ARB/98/2, Award (13 September 2016), para. 205; *Copper Mesa v. Ecuador*, PCA Case No. 2012-02, Award (15 March 2016), para. 6.87.

[306] *Biwater Gauff (Tanzania) Ltd. v. United Republic of Tanzania*, ICSID Case No. ARB/05/22, Award (24 July 2008).

[307] *Ibid.*, para. 787.

[308] *Ibid.*, para. 519.

[309] *Ibid.*, para. 624 ff.

[310] *Ibid.*, para. 798.

[311] *Ibid.*, para. 789.

value, the loss of which could have attracted compensation if caused by the state's treaty breaches. For the tribunal, none of Tanzania's BIT violations caused any loss of economic value to BGT nor broke the chain of causation that already existed beforehand.[312]

Notably, given the acknowledged irresponsible conduct of BGT as recognised by the tribunal, and the significant negative impact this had on the general population of Dar es Salaam, one could argue that such misconduct should have been sufficient to dismiss the substantive claims without finding Tanzania in breach of the treaty. Thus, the tribunal's decision underscores the fact that the merit phase of ISDS proceedings primarily centers around states' accountability to their treaty obligations, irrespective of an investor's conduct. This fact is pertinent since most IIAs impose treaty obligations solely on states, without corresponding duties on investors.

However, the one-sided nature of IIAs does not equate to an insurance policy against every investor loss experienced in the host state. With the application of the causality test, a host state will only be liable to compensate for investment losses resulting from its own unlawful actions. Conversely, for investment losses **caused** by the investor's own irresponsible acts, accountability for such losses will automatically fall where the fault lies. With this form of indirect accountability, investors will be mindful not to engage in conduct that could jeopardise their interest in achieving the ultimate goal of an ISDS claim, which is often the award of monetary compensation.

Further on causality, an investor's misconduct may not be the sole cause but rather a partial cause of the losses it has incurred. In such instances, indirect investor accountability can also take the form of a **diminished entitlement to compensation** for contributory fault. This follows the CIL understanding that a state's responsibility to pay reparation is due for injuries caused and nothing more.[313] ISDS tribunals have applied this rule to reduce the compensation due to an investor for an unlawful state action by taking into account the investor's contributory fault for the loss suffered.[314] The doctrine of contributory fault thus provides another internationally recognised rule that a future MIC may apply to ensure that investors are not absolved from taking responsibility for their misconduct which contributed to the loss suffered in the host state.

Significantly, as opposed to the current decentralised arbitral system, the MIC could offer greater certainty in the application of contributory fault doctrine in

---

[312] *Ibid.* para. 798.

[313] Article 39 (commentary, para. 2), ILC Draft Articles.

[314] *Occidental Petroleum Corporation and Occidental Exploration and Production Company v. Republic of Ecuador*, ICSID Case No. ARB/06/11, Award (5 October 2012), para. 678; *Casinos Austria International GmbH and Casinos Austria Aktiengesellschaft v. Argentine Republic*, ICSID Case No. ARB/14/32, Dissenting Opinion (5 November 2021), para. 442; *Copper Mesa Mining Corporation v. Republic of Ecuador*, PCA Case No. 2012-2, Award (15 March 2016), para. 6.95; *Quiborax S.A. and Non Metallic Minerals S.A. v. Plurinational State of Bolivia*, ICSID Case No. ARB/06/2, Award (16 September 2015), para. 330; *Yukos Universal Limited (Isle of Man) v. Russia*, PCA Case No. 2005-04/AA227, Final Award (18 July 2014), para. 1633.

securing accountability for investor misconduct that undermines a host state's sustainable development policies. Existing jurisprudence suggests that arbitral tribunals approach this topic quite narrowly and are reluctant to reduce awarded damages based on contributory fault,[315] even when an investor has acted detrimentally to the sustainable development interests of the host state.

For example, as held in the dissent of Phillip Sands in *Bear Creek Mining v Peru*,[316] the claimant-investor, in that case, had failed to effectively carry out necessary consultations and observe rights owed to the indigenous communities affected by its investment project, as provided under the ILO Convention 169 (Indigenous and Tribal Peoples Convention).[317] This failure had crystallised into public protests, causing social unrest and the eventual intervention by the state to preserve public order, which led to the treaty violations and losses to the investor.[318] For the dissenting arbitrator, this fault of the claimant contributed to its losses which had to be taken into account in the awarded damages.[319] However, the majority decision disagreed with this view for some notable reasons. First, on the basis that the ILO Convention only imposes obligations on states and not on investors, and in any case does not foresee an obligation of result.[320] Second, that the claimant enjoyed continuous approval and support for its project from the state, thus it could be taken that it had fulfilled all legal requirements for its investment, including under the ILO Convention.[321] Additionally, the fact that the indigenous communities are not parties to the arbitration made their objection to the investment irrelevant to the determination of the dispute.[322]

The majority decision demonstrates how uncertain it is in the current ISDS system to ensure investor accountability for acts that undermine the object and purpose of international conventions relating to sustainable development, especially when the host state has also failed to proactively safeguard such interest for its local populace directly affected by an investment. However, with an MIC primarily designed to protect investments that are sustainable, the court will be inherently incentivised to consider investor conduct that falls short of internationally recognised standards on sustainable development, especially when such misconduct crystallises into a treaty violation by the host state. In assessing the entitled compensation in such instances, compensation may be reduced for the contributory fault

---

[315] Jarrett et al. (2023), p. 267.

[316] *Bear Creek Mining Corporation v. Republic of Peru*, ICSID Case No. ARB/14/21, Partial Dissenting Opinion of Professor Philippe Sands QC (30 November 2017).

[317] *Ibid.*, paras. 7 ff.

[318] *Ibid.*, paras. 13 ff.

[319] *Ibid.*, paras 4, 39.

[320] *Bear Creek Mining Corporation v. Republic of Peru*, ICSID Case No. ARB/14/21, Award (30 November 2017), para. 664.

[321] *Ibid.*, para. 666.

[322] *Ibid.*

that resulted in harm not only to the investor but also to the sustainable development interest of the host state.

For greater certainty on this point, the MIC statute may incorporate a provision similar to that in Article 23 of the Netherlands Model Investment Agreement (MIA), which states:

> [...] a Tribunal, in deciding on the amount of compensation, is expected to take into account noncompliance by the investor with its commitments under the UN Guiding Principles on Business and Human Rights, and the OECD Guidelines for Multinational Enterprises.[323]

The above provision offers a model for an MIC to indirectly ensure accountability for investor conduct that violates recognised international standards on sustainable development, regardless of their losses due to a host state's treaty violation.

Overall, the prospect of being held **accountable for cause** leading to lost or diminished entitlement to compensation would incentivise investors to diligently engage in responsible investment decisions and reduce the likelihood of disputes arising in the first place.

4.3.3.1.3   Counterclaim by the Host State

A counterclaim is another indirect method through which an investor may be called to account for its unlawful actions in the host state. While there is no universal definition for the term, in ISDS, it basically involves claims initiated by the respondent-state in response to an investor's claim against the state. For instance, in response to an investor claim, the respondent-state may counterclaim that the investor has also violated a duty owed to the respondent-state entitling the state to damages. Otherwise, a respondent-state may also counterclaim as a defense strategy to offset potential damages they might owe to the investor.[324]

Various international courts and tribunals have asserted their authority to entertain counterclaims as an extension of their inherent authority, even in cases where their founding instruments are silent on this matter.[325] The right to submit a counterclaim is a procedural guarantee in the majority of arbitration rules used in ISDS proceedings, including the ICSID,[326] UNCITRAL,[327] and ICC rules.[328] However, the power of ISDS tribunals to entertain counterclaims is limited by two critical considerations worth noting: *first*, the restrictive scope of the ISDS clause in the relevant IIA, and *second*, the applicable law or legal basis for determining the merits

---

[323] Article 23, Netherlands Model Investment Agreement (2019).

[324] *Gardabani Holdings B.V. and Silk Road Holdings B.V. v. Georgia*, ICSID Case No. ARB/17/29, Award (27 October 2022), paras. 432, 735 f; *Oxus Gold plc v. Republic of Uzbekistan*, UNCITRAL, Final Award (17 December 2015), para. 960, 965 f.

[325] Waibel and Rylatt (2014), p. 1.

[326] Article 46, ICSID Convention (1965); Rule 48, ICSID Arbitration Rules (2022).

[327] Article 21(3) and (4) UNCITRAL Arbitration Rules (2021).

[328] Articles 5(5) and (6) ICC Arbitration Rules (2021).

of the counterclaim.[329] For the former, jurisdiction over a counterclaim may be declined if the ISDS clause is interpreted as covering only claims from investors against the host state, but not vice versa.[330] As for the latter, jurisdiction will also fail if the respondent state cannot establish a legal basis for its counterclaim under the applicable law.[331] Significantly, investment treaties as applicable law in most ISDS cases foresee no substantive obligation on investors that could form the legal basis for a counterclaim. Also, for the same reason, rules and principles of international law as may be applicable may not provide the necessary legal basis for a state's counterclaim against an investor. Overall, due to the inherently asymmetric nature of the current ISDS regime, satisfying the conditions for a successful counterclaim is a herculean task with limited success recorded in jurisprudence.[332]

The need to address the obstacles impeding the use of counterclaims in ISDS has been recognised as an important reform consideration necessary to correct the imbalance in the existing ISDS system.[333] Fundamentally, this requires the reform of both the substantive and procedural guarantees currently in force in the vast majority of IIAs. For the former, this entails a clarification of the legal basis upon which a counterclaim may be based, while the latter requires a reform of the ISDS clauses to unequivocally permit counterclaims. Notably, recommendations on these two issues have been heard in UNCITRAL Working Group III,[334] however, a resolution on this matter is inevitably stalled for now since the working group's mandate is limited to procedural considerations.[335]

Regardless of this fact, the MIC under consideration can be designed in a manner that enhances the ability of its members to submit counterclaims. To achieve this, the MIC Statute may consider adopting a clarifying provision already proposed in UNCITRAL Working Group III on this subject, which states:[336]

---

[329] EI-IILCC Study Group on ISDS Reform (2022), p. 52.

[330] *Oxus Gold plc v. Republic of Uzbekistan*, UNCITRAL, Final Award (17 December 2015), para. 948; *Iberdrola Energia S.A. v. Republic of Guatemala II*, PCA Case No. 2017-41, Final Award (24 August 2020), para. 390; *Karkey Karadeniz Elektrik Uretim A.S. v. Islamic Republic of Pakistan*, ICSID Case No. ARB/13/1, Award (22 August 2017), para. 1013; *Spyridon Roussalis v. Romania*, ICSID Case No. ARB/06/1, Award (1 December 2011), para. 869; *Rusoro Mining Ltd. v. Bolivarian Republic of Venezuela*, ICSID Case No. ARB(AF)/12/5, Award (22 August 2016), para. 627 ff.

[331] *Limited Liability Company Amto v. Ukraine*, SCC Case No. 080/2005, Final Award (26 March 2008), para. 118.

[332] Shao (2021), p. 159; Scherer et al. (2021), p. 414.

[333] UNCITRAL, *Possible Reform of Investor-State Dispute Settlement (ISDS) – Multiple proceedings and counterclaims*: Note by the Secretariat of 22/1/2020, A/CN.9/WG.III/WP.193, para. 33.

[334] *Ibid.*, para. 39 ff.

[335] *Ibid.*, para. 42.

[336] See, UNCITRAL, *Possible Reform of Investor-State Dispute Settlement (ISDS) – Draft provisions on procedural and cross-cutting issues*: Note by the Secretariat of 26/7/2023, A/CN.9/WG. III/WP.231, draft Provision 11.

1. When a claim is submitted for resolution pursuant to Draft Provisions 3 or 4, the respondent may make a counterclaim:

   (a) Arising directly out of the subject matter of the claim;
   (b) In connection with the factual and legal basis of the claim; or
   (c) That the claimant has breached its obligations under the Agreement, domestic law, an investment contract or any other instrument binding on the claimant.

2. For the avoidance of doubt, the consent of the respondent to the submission of a claim by the claimant is subject to the condition that the claimant consents to any submission of a counterclaim referred to in paragraph 1.

By adopting the above draft provision, an MIC statute will provide clarity on the two major considerations critical for hearing a counterclaim in ISDS, i.e., the parties' consent and the legal basis for bringing the counterclaim. Particularly, paragraph 2 of the above draft would eliminate any ambiguity regarding the investor's consent to a counterclaim, while paragraph 1 addresses the legal basis upon which a counterclaim may be sought.

Notably, paragraph 1 (lit a-b) of the above draft reveals an adoption of the ICSID condition for bringing a counterclaim.[337] However, the introduction of 'lit c' with the word 'or' suggests a counterclaim may be submitted on a legal basis not connected to the factual and legal basis of the investor claim. Essentially, an investor obligation under the IIA, contract, domestic law, or any other international instrument applicable to the claimant could independently provide the legal basis for a counterclaim against the claimant investor.[338]

It is noteworthy that a growing number of IIAs now include explicit provisions on investor obligations that provide the legal basis for a counterclaim, including the AfCFTA with a whole dedicated chapter.[339] Beyond Africa, the incorporation of investor obligations in IIAs is also gaining gradual recognition in capital-exporting countries that have once declined such inclusion. For example, Article 16 of the Canada Model BIT 2021 provides that:

> [...] investors and their investments shall comply with domestic laws and regulations of the host State, including laws and regulations on human rights, the rights of Indigenous peoples, gender equality, environmental protection and labour.[340]

Also, Article 18 of the Belgium-Luxembourg Model BIT includes an express provision on corporate social responsibility which mandates that:

---

[337] See, Article 46, ICSID Convention (1965); *Urbaser S.A. and Consorcio de Aguas Bilbao Bizkaia, Bilbao Biskaia Ur Partzuergoa v. The Argentine Republic*, ICSID Case No. ARB/07/26, Award (8 December 2016), para. 1151.

[338] UNCITRAL, *Possible Reform of Investor-State Dispute Settlement (ISDS) – Annotations to the draft provisions on procedural and cross-cutting issues*: Note by the Secretariat of 31/7/2023, A/CN.9/WG.III/WP.232, para. 28.

[339] See, Chapter 5, AfCFTA.

[340] Article 16(1), Canada Model FIPA (2021).

Investors of one Contracting Party in the Territory of the other Contracting Party shall abide by its national laws, regulations, administrative guidelines and policies and act in accordance with internationally accepted standards applicable to foreign investors to which the Contracting Parties are a party. Investors and their investments should strive to make the maximum feasible contributions to the sustainable development of the Host State and local community through socially responsible practices.[341]

Also, Article 7 of the Netherlands MIA mandates that:

Investors and their investments shall comply with domestic laws and regulations of the host state, including laws and regulations on human rights, environmental protection and labor laws.[342]

Importantly, even when an IIA is silent on investor obligations, there remains an implicit duty for investors to conduct their activities in accordance with the laws of the host state.[343] This creates the possibility of a counterclaim based on the violation of domestic laws applicable to the investor-claimant. Furthermore, as discussed earlier, investors are not absolutely immune from assuming responsibilities under international law (Sect. 3.1.3). It is recognised that foreign investors bear both rights and duties under international law.[344] Therefore, established international standards and instruments on investor behaviour, especially those to which the respondent MIC member and the claimant investor's home state are parties, could serve as a legal basis for a counterclaim before an MIC.

With the right design and implementation, the procedural guarantee of counterclaims within an MIC represents another promising avenue for achieving greater investor accountability within the international ISDS framework. This would ensure that investors are not shielded from responsibility in an MIC when their actions negatively impact the host state's interests. Consequently, investors are incentivised to act responsibly in compliance with domestic and international laws, especially those relating to sustainable development standards recognised by the MIC members. This improvement will ultimately contribute to correcting the power imbalance between the host state and investors, which has been a major deficiency and criticism of the traditional ISDS system, not only from an African perspective.

4.3.3.2 Direct Accountability for Investor Misconduct Through State-Investor Dispute Settlement ('SIDS') Claims

Unlike the preceding discussions on indirect methods of ensuring investor accountability, an alternative approach exists where host states can directly pursue

---

[341] Article 18(1) Belgium-Luxembourg Economic Union Model BIT (2019).

[342] Article 7(1), Netherlands Model Investment Agreement (2019).

[343] Diel-Gligor and Hennecke (2015), p. 566.

[344] Kryvoi (2012), p. 234 f; UNGA, *Report of the Special Representative of the Secretary-General on the issue of human rights and transnational corporations and other business enterprises, John Ruggie** of 19/2/2007, UN DOC. A/HRC/4/35, para. 33 ff.

accountability for wrongful conduct by investors without waiting for the impugned investor to file a claim first.[345] In other words, it is procedurally possible for the international investment law system to accommodate both ISDS and state-investor dispute settlement ('SIDS') claims.

It is worth noting that, while direct actions by states against investors are not established in treaty-based disputes, this does not hold true for contract-based disputes.[346] When a state enters into an investment contract directly with an investor, unless otherwise agreed, both parties, the contracting state and the investor, typically have equal rights to invoke the contract's dispute resolution clause, which often involves arbitration. Such arbitration could proceed *ad hoc* or through an institution, including ICSID.[347] In fact, the founding fathers of the ICSID system had conceived a Centre that:

> [. . .] permits the institution of proceedings by host States as well as by investors and the Executive Directors have constantly had in mind that the provisions of the Convention should be equally adapted to the requirements of both cases.[348]

The adaptation of the ICSID system to administer both ISDS and SIDS proceedings is deductible from Article 36 of the ICSID Convention, which provides that: *[a]ny Contracting State or any national of a Contracting State wishing to institute arbitration proceedings [. . .]*. Read together with Article 25 of the ICSID Convention, the commentary to this provision confirms that the ICSID system is designed to accommodate both ISDS and SIDS claims.[349] Although the majority of ICSID claims had proceeded at the instance of investors, there are few instances where states have directly initiated claims to seek accountability against investors who violated their obligation to the host states'.[350] Even the 'constituent subdivisions' of host states are not excluded from this right of direct action,[351] provided the conditions of Article 25(1) and (3) of the ICSID Convention are satisfied.[352] Notably, the SIDS examples in the ICSID record have been limited to contract-based disputes. However, this does not imply that treaty-based SIDS are excluded. The only barrier to such proceedings is the lack of investors' consent.[353]

Most IIAs in force today contemplate only the submission of ISDS claims. However, there are a few IIAs with broadly worded ISDS clauses that could be

---

[345] See in this regard, Jarrett et al. (2023), p. 268 ff.

[346] *Ibid.*, p. 268.

[347] *Ibid.*

[348] ICSID (1965), para. 13.

[349] Escobar (2019), p. 271, paras. 4.07–4.09; Schreuer et al. (2009), p. 458.

[350] See, *Republic of Peru v. Caravelí Cotaruse Transmisora de Energía S.A.C.*, ICSID Case No. ARB/13/24; *Gabon v. Société Serete S.A.*, ICSID Case No. ARB/76/1.

[351] See for example, *Government of the Province of East Kalimantan v. PT Kaltim Prima Coal and others*, ICSID Case No. ARB/07/3.

[352] Schreuer et al. (2009), p. 458.

[353] Jarrett et al. (2023), p. 270.

interpreted as allowing 'either' of the disputing parties to submit a claim.[354] For example, Article VI(3) of the US-Lithuania BIT (1998) provides:

(a) Provided that the national or company concerned has not submitted the dispute for resolution under paragraph 2 (a) or (b) and that six months have elapsed from the date on which the dispute arose, the national or company concerned may choose to consent in writing to the submission of the dispute for settlement by binding arbitration [...]

(b) Once the national or company concerned has so consented, either Party to the dispute may initiate arbitration in accordance with the choice so specified in the consent.

An identical provision is also contained in Article VII of the US-Argentina BIT (1991).[355] Similarly, Article X(3) of the Spain-Argentina BIT (1992) provides that:

The dispute may be submitted to an international arbitral tribunal in any of the following circumstances:

(a) At the request of either party to the dispute, when no decision has been reached on the substance 18 months after the judicial proceeding provided for in paragraph 2 of this article began [...].

(b) When both parties to the dispute have so agreed.

In *Urbaser v. Argentina*,[356] the above provision in the Spain-Argentina BIT was up for interpretation. Although contested within the context of the tribunal's jurisdiction over the respondent's counterclaim, the tribunal's decision confirmed that the BIT's arbitration clause may be invoked by either party. According to the tribunal:

> This view is confirmed in Article X(3), stating that in certain circumstances the dispute may be submitted to an international arbitral tribunal "at the request of either party to the dispute." It results clearly from these provisions that either the investor or the host State can be a party submitting a dispute in connection with an investment to arbitration.[357]

Notably, while the *Urbaser* tribunal confirmed that the Spain-Argentina BIT allowed arbitration submissions by *either party*, it is important to stress that this alone does not constitute the consent of both parties to arbitration, which must still be derived. In the *Urbaser* case, the moment the claimant submitted its claim against Argentina under Article X of the BIT, its consent to arbitrate disputes arising between the parties was deemed granted, not excluding the counterclaim brought by the respondent.[358]

Conversely, if Argentina had initiated a direct claim against Urbaser, the latter's consent may not be deemed readily available, as the investor had not previously

---

[354] Schwebel (2008), p. 5; Jarrett et al. (2023), p. 270; Laborde (2010), p. 108.

[355] Article VII(3)(a) and (b), US-Argentina BIT, entered into force 20 October 1994.

[356] *Urbaser S.A. and Consorcio de Aguas Bilbao Bizkaia, Bilbao Biskaia Ur Partzuergoa v. The Argentine Republic*, ICSID Case No. ARB/07/26, Award (8 December 2016).

[357] *Ibid.*, para. 1143.

[358] *Ibid.*, para. 1145 ff.

initiated a claim that could serve as its acceptance of the relevant IIA's dispute resolution clause. Therefore, if a treaty permits a SIDS claim but an investor fails to provide its consent to such a procedure, and no default rule applies in case of such a disagreement, the SIDS clause becomes ineffective. It is noteworthy that the Spain-Argentina BIT provides for either ICSID or *ad hoc* arbitration as the default forum, whichever applies if the disputing parties cannot agree on a forum for an arbitral proceeding requested by either party. However, this treaty represents only an exception among the thousands of IIAs in existence that restrict the submission of claims to only one party, namely the investor.

Nevertheless, given the increasing clamour for a much more balanced ISDS system, and the rapid growth in the inclusion of investor obligations in modern IIAs, the possibility for states to directly enforce treaty-based obligations against investors in an international forum with broader enforcement scope compared to domestic court litigation may become a more attractive option. To be ready for such a potential future, the MIC can be designed like the current ICSID system with certainty that it can handle both ISDS and SIDS claims arising from IIAs, provided that the relevant IIA confers the court with such jurisdiction and the consent of the disputing parties are given.

For states interested in exploring the possibility of treaty-based SIDS before an MIC, existing IIAs could be amended, or new ones contracted, explicitly providing, for example, that:

> Disputes stemming from investments under the treaty may be submitted to the MIC at the request of either party to the dispute.

To eliminate any uncertainty regarding an investor's consent to SIDS claims before an MIC, it is possible to precondition the admission of foreign investment upon the investor's consent to direct claims by the host state.[359] Such precondition to admission may be implemented under a domestic legislation applicable to all foreign investments or targeted at specific sectors most sensitive to the host state's national interest. Notably, this approach has its limitations because it is conceived as a precondition for the admission of investments. This means it would not be applicable to investments that were already admitted before such a law requiring consent to SIDs. However, it may still apply to investments subject to license renewal. When a term expires, an investor's application for renewal may be contingent on their consent to direct claims from the state before an MIC.

Another possibility is to derive investors' consent to SIDS claims before an MIC through a standing offer made by home states in IIAs on behalf of their investors. This may cover both pre-existing and future investors protected under the contracted IIA by the home state. There is scholarly support for the view that individuals may assume treaty obligations created on their behalf by their home states.[360] This point is confirmed by examples of new-generation IIAs fully contracted by states,

---

[359] Laborde (2010), p. 111.
[360] Jarrett et al. (2023), p. 272.

incorporating investor obligations that directly bind nationals of the respective contracting parties. Therefore, if states can contract binding substantive obligations on their nationals in IIAs, arguably, they can likewise contract binding procedural obligations on their nationals in IIAs, including consent to SIDS claims.

Importantly, in addition to ensuring the investor's consent to SIDS claims, the state must also establish the legal basis for such a claim, namely the applicable law governing the obligation breached by the investor. This could be the IIA, domestic law or other international instruments, including recognised international standards on investor behaviour applicable to the disputing parties. The earlier discussion on the legal basis for counterclaims applies *mutatis mutandis* to direct claims by host states (Sect. 4.3.3.1.3).

In current reality, SIDS claims for holding investors accountable for misconduct in host states are unpopular, if not nonexistent, particularly in treaty-based disputes. However, the foregoing discussion has shown that it is procedurally possible to envision an MIC where both investors and states are treated as equals, with the possibility for both sides to initiate direct actions against each other. The MIC only needs to be designed as open to both ISDS and SIDS claims. Whatever form the dispute it adjudicates takes will ultimately depend on the consent of the disputing parties and the powers conferred upon the court under the applicable IIA.

By ensuring openness to investor accountability through the indirect and direct approaches so far discussed, an MIC can strike a fairer equilibrium between the protection of investors and states interests under the international investment law regime.

4.3.4 Addressing the Concern of Third Party Interest Protection

The protection of third-party interests is another critical aspect of ensuring that ISDS through an MIC is conducted not only in a fair and just manner but also fundamentally in an all-inclusive manner. As discussed in Chap. 3 (Sect. 3.2.3), one major contributor to the backlash against traditional ISDS arises from the need for better **'openness'** and **'accessibility'** of the process to the public.[361] Currently, there are two mediums through which this concern is addressed. *Firstly*, through **transparency provisions** that offer openness of the process to the public by the publication of arbitration-related documents,[362] and allowing public hearings.[363] *Secondly*, through

---

[361] See, Douglas (2015), p. 112.

[362] See for example, Article 2 and 3, UNCITRAL Rules on Transparency 2013; See also, Rule 62-65, ICSID Arbitration Rules 2022.

[363] See for example Article 6, UNCITRAL Rules on Transparency 2013.

provisions on **third-party participation** that guarantee a limited form of access as an *amicus curiae* to interested third parties.[364]

Significantly, under the ICSID procedure, where the majority of ISDS claims are raised, its procedural rules on transparency remain inadequate as they are subject to parties' consent.[365] This makes it uncertain whether arbitration-related documents or hearings will be available to the public, particularly to those interested third parties whose rights may be at stake in an ISDS process.[366] Although the UNCITRAL Rules on Transparency do not require parties' consent for public hearings or the publication of arbitration-related documents, its application is not yet widespread given that only a few states have signed, and even fewer have ratified the Mauritius Convention.[367] Furthermore, the restriction of third-party participation to *amicus curiae* submissions and the challenges that impede such interventions by NDPs (Sect. 3. 2.3) make it doubtful whether either the ICSID or UNCITRAL procedural framework guarantees adequate protection for third party interest.[368]

The question then is how can an MIC do better. Undoubtedly, the UNCITRAL Rules on Transparency offer greater certainty regarding transparency and third-party participation in ISDS (Sect. 3.2.3). Hence, to secure the protection of third-party interests within an MIC, it is pragmatic to integrate the UNCITRAL Rules on Transparency into the court's statute,[369] as has already been done in recent IIAs,[370] including the now troubled ECT.[371] As earlier stated, the UNCITRAL transparency rules guarantee public hearings[372] and the publication of arbitration-related documents,[373] which are fundamental to ensure that the public, including third parties with a vested interest, can access crucial information pertaining to their affected interest in ISDS.

---

[364] See for example, Article 4 and 5, UNCITRAL Rules on Transparency 2013; See also, Rule 67, ICSID Arbitration Rules 2022.

[365] See generally, Rule 62-64, ICSID Arbitration Rules 2022.

[366] See, Coleman et al. (2019), p. 4 f, (illustrating how the rights or interests of third parties may be at stake in ISDS).

[367] *UNCITRAL*, Status: United Nations Convention on Transparency in Treaty-based Investor-State Arbitration (New York, 2014), https://uncitral.un.org/en/texts/arbitration/conventions.

[368] Coleman et al. (2019), p. 6 f.

[369] Bungenberg and Renisch (2020), p. 137; UNCITRAL, *Submission from the European Union and its Member States* of 24/1/2019, A/CN.9/WG.III/WP.159/Add.1, para. 28.

[370] For examples of new generation IIAs incorporating the UNCITRAL Rules on Transparency see, Article 11, Hungary-Kyrgyzstan BIT, entered into force 10 April 2022; Article 20(12), Côte d'Ivoire-Portugal BIT, signed 13 June 2019; Article 12(15), Lithuania-Turkey BIT, signed 28 August 2018; Article 8.36 CETA, signed 30 October 2016; Article 36, Canada Model FIPA (2021); Article 19(O), Belgium-Luxembourg Economic Union Model BIT (2019); Article 20(11), Netherlands Model Investment Agreement (2019).

[371] Article 26(6), Agreement in Principle on the Modernisation of the Energy Charter Treaty, 24 June 2022, https://www.bilaterals.org/IMG/pdf/reformed_ect_text.pdf; See also, ECT Secretariat (2022), p. 5 (point on dispute settlement).

[372] See. Article 6. UNCITRAL Rules on Transparency 2013.

[373] See. Article 2 and 3, UNCITRAL Rules on Transparency 2013.

Although regarding third-party participation, it might be more beneficial to adopt a 'modified version' of Article 4 of the UNCITRAL Rules on Transparency to ensure the meaningful involvement of third parties whose rights or interests may be directly at stake in disputes before an MIC. Similar to the ICSID Rules,[374] Article 4 of the UNCITRAL Rules on Transparency grants a tribunal the discretion to allow *amicus curiae* submissions from third parties with a significant interest in the proceedings,[375] provided such submissions address matters within the scope of the dispute.[376] However, history has shown that third-parties may have a significant interest at stake in ISDS that does not necessarily fall within the scope of the dispute brought before a tribunal. A typical example are NDP submissions involving human rights interests, which have been rejected for falling outside the scope of the tribunal's adjudicative mandate.[377] Recognising that the current system provides very little opportunity for interested third parties to participate in ISDS proceedings, it has been emphasised in UNCITRAL Working Group III that a reform is desirable to allow, for example, third party interests related to environmental or human rights protection to be considered in investment tribunals.[378]

Accordingly, an MIC should strive to achieve this improvement by not limiting the subject matter of an *amicus* submission to only those within the scope of the dispute submitted to it. For example, to enhance the protection of third party interest in an MIC, a modification of Article 4 of the UNCITRAL Rules on Transparency might read:

> After consultation with the disputing parties, the arbitral tribunal may allow a person that is neither a disputing party, nor a non-disputing Party to the treaty ("third person(s)"), to file a written submission with the arbitral tribunal regarding a matter within the scope of the dispute, which includes the third person(s) rights or interest under the applicable IIA, domestic law, or any other international instrument binding on the disputing parties, affected by the proceedings.

The underlined text reflects the modification required under the current UNCITRAL transparency rules to encompass amicus submission on third party rights or interests not connected to the disputing parties' claims before the tribunal. As seen in the *Pezold v. Zimbabwe*[379] case, there is no guarantee that the disputing parties will consider a third party's interest as a disputed issue, which disqualifies it from being

---

[374] Rule 67(2), ICSID Arbitration Rules 2022.

[375] See. Article 4(3)(a), UNCITRAL Rules on Transparency 2013.

[376] See. Article 4(1), UNCITRAL Rules on Transparency 2013.

[377] See, *Bernhard von Pezold and Others v. Republic of Zimbabwe*, ICSID Case No. ARB/10/15, Procedural Order No. 2 (26 June 2012), para. 59; *Eco Oro Minerals Corp. v. Republic of Colombia*, ICSID Case No. ARB/16/41, Procedural Order No. 6 Decision on Non-Disputing Parties Application (18 February 2019), para. 28; *Angel Samuel Seda and others v. Republic of Colombia*, ICSID Case No. ARB/19/6, Procedural Order No. 7 (1 December 2021), para. 42.

[378] UNCITRAL, *Report of Working Group III (Investor-State Dispute Settlement Reform)* of 9/4/2019, A/CN.9/970, para. 31.

[379] *Bernhard von Pezold and Others v. Republic of Zimbabwe*, ICSID Case No. ARB/10/15, Procedural Order No. 2 (26 June 2012).

considered an *amicus*.[380] This underscores the importance of the above-mentioned modification.

By explicitly linking the possibility to submit an amicus brief to the impacted third-party rights or interest under the laws applicable to the disputing parties, this ensures that the *amicus* is not making a legal submission outside the jurisdiction of the court to consider. In short, the fact that the disputing parties did not raise the issue is the compelling reason why the court should accept the *amicus* for providing a perspective under the applicable laws to the dispute, assisting the tribunal in reaching a just and equitable outcome of the case. This will be consistent with the express provision in the UNCITRAL Rules on Transparency requiring the amicus curiae to provide *'a perspective, particular knowledge or insight that is different from that of the disputing parties'*.[381]

Considering the increasing inclusion of investor obligations in IIAs, especially those related to human rights, labour, and environmental protection standards, the host citizens who are the intended beneficiaries of the investor obligations under IIAs should have a role in ISDS proceedings whenever their IIA-related interests are endangered. Even without explicit inclusion in the IIA, the interests of third parties in human rights, labour, environmental protection, or other sustainable development objectives under national or international law instruments applicable to the parties may be at stake in ISDS. Under the modified draft provision above, such third-party interests would also qualify for *amicus curiae* consideration, whether or not the disputing parties challenge these interests in their pleadings. As confirmed by the *Methanex v. USA*[382] tribunal, there are disputes whereby the substantive issues at stake go 'far beyond' those raised by the disputing parties, and supporting an *amicus* participation in such instance is crucial for the transparency and fairness of the process.[383] Accordingly, not limiting amicus participation to the substantive issues raised by the disputing parties will ensure an MIC that fosters not only transparency and fairness but, most importantly, inclusive justice.

Significantly, as further acknowledged in UNCITRAL Working Group III, the legitimacy of ISDS also depends on the ability of affected communities, individuals, including public interest organisations, to participate in ISDS proceedings beyond making submissions as third parties.[384] In this regard, arguments have been made to allow affected individuals or communities to initiate claims directly against investors.[385]

---

[380] *Ibid.*, para. 59.

[381] Article 4(3)(b), UNCITRAL Rules on Transparency 2013.

[382] *Methanex Corporation v. United States of America*, UNCITRAL, Decision of the Tribunal on Petitions from Third Persons to Intervene as 'amici curiae', (15 January 2001).

[383] *Ibid.*, para. 49.

[384] UNCITRAL, *Report of Working Group III (Investor-State Dispute Settlement Reform)* of 9/4/ 2019, A/CN.9/970, para. 31

[385] Laryea (2018), p. 2866 ff; Jarrett et al. (2023), p. 275 ff.

Although acknowledged that such reform has several drawbacks that could discourage FDI, including: (1) the risk of increased claims against foreign investors; (2) an increased cost of doing business; (3) delays in projects due to investors being entangled in individual claims; (4) and, in any case, the inability of affected individuals to afford international proceedings. Nevertheless, it is worth emphasising that besides the cost factor, none of the other mentioned downsides are absent in local litigation, which foreign investors are already exposed to.[386] Additionally, even though the cost of international proceedings, such as arbitration, is undisputedly expensive, local litigation that could span for several years, up to the apex court of the host state, does not necessarily come cheap. This supports the argument that cost alone is not a sufficient justification to deny individuals access to claims before international investment tribunals.[387] Access is particularly critical in cases when an investor can take advantage of the lack of an effective domestic remedy to blatantly abuse the rights of individuals (natural or legal persons) in its host state.

While there is no place for direct claims by individuals in the current system, with the right political will, it is procedurally possible to design an MIC that is open to direct claims by individuals. Just like the SIDS approach discussed above, having an MIC that is open to direct claims from its members' citizens against foreign investors does not mean that the court automatically has jurisdiction over such disputes. This option will only be available to MIC members who are open to providing such access to their citizens under their respective IIAs. Most importantly, the jurisdiction of the MIC to entertain such proceedings would ultimately depend on the unequivocal consent of the disputing parties. One possible means of obtaining such consent, as already highlighted in academic scholarship, is through state delegation.

Essentially, in a similar manner under international law permitting states to assign their authority to private investors to enforce the legal obligations owed by states as outlined in IIAs, states may also choose to delegate their rights to enforce legal obligations owed by foreign investors to their private citizens.[388] Notably, this idea assumes the earlier discussion that a direct action (i.e., SIDS) by the state is possible under the applicable IIA (Sect. 4.3.3.2). Based on such possibility, the right to claim may be delegated to any private citizen having a direct or immediate interest in enforcing the investor obligation, and any decision by the MIC will be binding on the state with res-judicata effect as if the state had directly participated in the proceedings. This option may be particularly welcomed by states that, for certain political or economic reasons, are not interested in prosecuting a claim against an investor but would not mind delegating such a right to a citizen interested in prosecuting the claim.

One possible model that has been proposed for states interested in the delegation of claims to interested citizens is an IIA provision stating that:

---

[386] Laryea (2018), p. 2867.

[387] *Ibid.*

[388] Jarrett et al. (2023), p. 276.

> The jurisdiction of the tribunal shall extend to any legal dispute arising directly out of an investment, between a State and a national of another State. The State may designate any constituent subdivision or agency, public or private body, or natural or moral person to bring a dispute or claim on behalf of the State and the conditions of this delegation[. . .].[389]

If the designated tribunal under the above model provision is an MIC, the court would therefore have jurisdiction over a delegated SIDS claim to a private third party. For the avoidance of doubt, a similar provision may be adopted under the MIC Statute stating that:

> When provided for under the applicable IIA to a dispute, a State as a disputing party may designate any constituent subdivision or agency, public or private body, or natural or legal person to bring a dispute or claim on behalf of the State to the MIC, and the conditions of this delegation.

Significantly, there will be a need to clarify the exact conditions for a state-delegated claim to private citizens, its withdrawal, its binding nature, and the enforcement of awards resulting from such delegation to interested third parties, among other considerations. Achieving such reform will require a rather radical transformation of the current system, which is not an easy task and is quite unlikely under present realities.

Additionally, independent of a state delegation of claims to its private citizens, there are other suggestions on how an international investment tribunal can entertain a direct action from host state citizens who have suffered injury due to an investor's violation of its domestic or international obligations in the host state.[390] Similar to the earlier submission (Sect. 4.3.3.2), the host state through an investment authorisation regime applicable to all or specific investments in its territory, may authorise an investment under the condition that the investor consents to direct actions from its citizens before an international forum.[391] Alternatively, such consents may also be provided in contractual clauses between the host state and investor or granted after the dispute arises in a submission agreement directly between the investor and the affected host citizen.[392]

The designated international forum in the instrument of consent in any of the aforementioned options could be an MIC. The instrument of consent could also specify the legal basis for such direct claims by the host's nationals, which may involve seeking remedies for injuries arising from the investor's violation of its domestic or international legal obligations in the host state. For greater certainty that the MIC may entertain such claims, it would be necessary to also clarify under the court's statute that the MIC's jurisdiction may extend to direct actions from its member states citizens against investors from another contracting member, provided consent to such actions are unequivocally given in an instrument of consent.

---

[389] Jarrett et al. (2023), p. 277 ff.

[390] Laryea (2018), p. 2866 ff.

[391] Jarrett et al. (2023), p. 277 f.

[392] *Ibid.*; Laryea, (2018), pp. 2869 ff.

Whether through delegation or direct recourse, the possibility of host state citizens taking action against foreign investors in an MIC or any other international forum would necessitate a significant reform of both the procedural and substantive laws currently in place for the protection of foreign investment. This represents a radical shift in policy that is currently hardly foreseeable. Nevertheless, for states and non-state actors open to the prospect of such a future, this discussion aims to highlight the possibilities of maintaining an MIC that remains open for delegated state claims to interested third parties or direct actions by host nationals against investors, provided that the disputing parties consent to such procedures, thereby advancing the protection of private third party interest in an MIC beyond what exists under the traditional ISDS regime.

4.3.5 Addressing the MIC's Impact on the Development of Local Judicial Systems in ISDS

As previously discussed, developments within the African continent indicate a preference for a return to the CIL exhaustion of local remedies rule in ISDS.[393] According to UNCTAD's data, at the time this study was concluded, only 90 out of the 2592 mapped treaties on UNCTAD's database require initial recourse to local remedies.[394] This confirms that the vast majority of IIAs under which ISDS claims are brought are silent on the subject of local remedies. In the absence of explicit inclusion within an IIA, it is unlikely that a future MIC will handle recourse to local remedies any differently from investment arbitration tribunals, ruling that it lacks general applicability.[395]

However, it is crucial to ensure that the development of local judicial competence in investment dispute resolution is not hampered due to direct recourse to an MIC. Essentially, there is a need to ensure that an MIC only exists as a court of last resort to potential claimants, regardless of whether this is an investor—the conventional claimants, or the host state or its private citizens as potential claimants in an MIC as earlier discussed.

Notably, the need to enhance recourse to local remedies is already acknowledged as a reform worth contemplating in UNCITRAL Working Group III,[396] as a means of fostering the development of local judicial systems in investment dispute

---

[393] See, (fn. 132, 133).

[394] See, UNCTAD Mapping of IIA Content, https://investmentpolicy.unctad.org/international-investment-agreements/iia-mapping.

[395] *PL Holdings S.A.R.L. v. Republic of Poland*, SCC Case No V2014/163, Partial Award (28 June 2017), para. 441; *Gavrilovic and Gavrilovic d.o.o. v. Republic of Croatia*, ICSID Case No. ARB/12/39, Award (26 July 2018), para. 889.

[396] UNCITRAL, *Report of Working Group III (Investor-State Dispute Settlement Reform)* of 9/4/2019, A/CN.9/970, para. 30.

resolution. In July 2023, the UNCITRAL Secretariat published a set of draft provisions for potential inclusion in existing and future IIAs,[397] which included a draft provision on 'recourse to local remedies'. Draft provision six provides:[398]

No claim may be submitted for resolution pursuant to Draft Provisions 3 or 4 unless:

(a) the investor had first initiated a dispute resolution proceeding before a court or competent authority of a Contracting Party with respect to the measure alleged to constitute a breach of the Agreement; and
(b) the investor obtained a final decision from a court of last resort of that Contracting Party or [period of time] have elapsed from the date the proceeding in subparagraph (a) was initiated.

Notably, this draft provision is not novel as it is formulated after existing models in IIAs that require the exhaustion of local remedies or local litigation within a stipulated timeframe before initiating international proceedings.

Whether the above Draft Provision 6 will find widespread expression in future IIAs and existing ones through treaty amendment is unknown. At present, this is an unpredictable future, as the sentiments that led to the adoption of the current ISDS system, permitting the bypass of domestic remedies, persist. These include the desire to depoliticize investment disputes and the perceived inadequacies of domestic courts.[399] These factors also diminish the likelihood of Draft Provision 6 being adopted directly in a future MIC Statute. The lack of unified interest would likely hinder any future attempt to mandate a general requirement of first recourse to local remedies before access to a multilateral forum like the MIC may be granted.

While opinions on the necessity of local remedies before international proceedings may differ, there is no contention that any chosen reform, such as the creation of an MIC, should strengthen rather than weaken the development of local judicial systems in the resolution of investment disputes. Consequently, the following discussion outlines three practical approaches for designing an MIC that promotes the development of local judicial systems in handling investment disputes, rather than undermining it. It is also important to clarify that while the recommendations discussed below are focused on private investors as claimants before the MIC, the same considerations regarding recourse to local remedies would apply in the unconventional case of having a state or its private citizens as claimants before an MIC.

---

[397] UNCITRAL, *Possible Reform of Investor-State Dispute Settlement (ISDS) – Draft provisions on procedural and cross-cutting issues*: Note by the Secretariat of 26/7/2023, A/CN.9/WG.III/WP.231, para. 3.

[398] *Ibid.*, Draft Provision 6.

[399] See in this regard, Kaufmann-Kohler and Potestà (2020), para. 20 ff.

4.3.5.1 Encouraging (Effectively) Initial Recourse to Local Remedies

While it might be a far-reaching endeavour to attain multilateral consensus on an MIC jurisdiction generally conditioned upon initial recourse to local remedies, the situation could be different if the objective is to establish an MIC that effectively encourages, without mandating, the settlement of investment disputes through local remedies. Such encouragement could be achieved through a treaty provision similar to Article 11(2) of the Republic of Korea-Republic of Uzbekistan BIT (2019), which states that:

> The investor and the Contracting Party in whose territory the investments are made shall endeavour to settle the dispute by consultations and negotiations in good faith, and at the same time, by local remedies of the Contracting Party [. . .].[400]

This BIT provision may be replicated in an MIC statute. Although the term 'endeavour' does not imply a mandatory duty, it does encourage the disputing parties to explore other options for dispute settlement, including local remedies. Importantly, for such a treaty provision to have **effective meaning**, it should not be unjustly disregarded at the whims of a party without any form of accountability. Notice that the duty to endeavour local remedies as foreseen in the BIT example above is incumbent upon both parties. Therefore, for instance, if a host state makes a good faith endeavour to seek a dispute resolution through local proceedings, but the investor, **without just cause**, ignores the local proceedings for direct recourse to the MIC, the MIC may consider this behavior when determining the allocation of costs for the proceedings.

Generally, the existing rules on the cost of proceedings in ISDS grant the tribunal discretion to decide the allocation of costs.[401] Ideally, this rule would also apply within an MIC. Hence, without mandating recourse to local remedies, allocation of cost may be a way of taking into account a party's blatant disregard of available local remedies, except the disputing parties mutually agree to such bypass. Thus, even when victorious, the MIC may order a party to bear the costs of proceedings that might not have been incurred if available local remedies had not been unjustly disregarded. This would incentivize potential MIC claimants to carefully count the cost before unjustly disregarding reasonably available local remedies. This consideration may apply to all or part of the issues in dispute that could have been reasonably resolved at the local level. The ELR futility exception[402] may offer guidance to the MIC in this regard to determine whether a party had unjustly

---

[400] Article 11(2), Republic of Korea-Republic of Uzbekistan BIT, entered into force 5 April 2023.

[401] See, Rule 28, ICSID Arbitration Rules (2022); Article 42, UNCITRAL Arbitration Rules (2021); Article 42, PCA Arbitration Rules (2012); Article 38(3 - 6), ICC Arbitration Rules (2021).

[402] Article 15(a), International Law Commission, Draft Articles on Diplomatic Protection (2006); Mollengarden (2019), p. 408; *Swissbourgh Diamond Mines (Pty) Limited and others v. Lesotho*, PCA Case No. 2013-29, Judgment of the Singapore Court of Appeal (27 November 2018), para. 211.

neglected the duty to endeavour settlement through local remedies, as encouraged in the MIC Statute.

4.3.5.2   Adopting Article 26 ICSID Convention Approach

In addition to effectively encouraging initial recourse to local remedies, consent to dispute settlement before an MIC may be mandatorily subject to the ELR rule. For this purpose, a provision similar to Article 26 of the ICSID Convention may be incorporated into the MIC Statute, which states that: *A Contracting State may require the exhaustion of local administrative or judicial remedies as a condition of its consent to arbitration under this Convention.*[403] For clarity, this provision could be adapted to include local litigation within a stipulated timeframe. For example, an MIC adaptation of Article 26 of the ICSID Convention could be:

> A Contracting State may require the exhaustion of local administrative or judicial remedies, or recourse to such local remedies within a stipulated timeframe as a condition of its consent to the jurisdiction of the MIC under this Statute.

By so doing, future IIAs that adopt the recent UNCITRAL Draft provision on recourse to local remedies[404] or any existing IIA that foresees recourse to local remedies in one form or the other would encompass a mandatory consent require-ment to MIC jurisdiction that must be enforced by the court.

Furthermore, in such cases, it is ideal to explicitly confirm the application of the CIL futility exception for the necessary balance. This entails, on one hand, preserv-ing the host state's interest in having the first shot at redressing any wrongdoing before international proceedings can be initiated,[405] while, on the other hand, rejecting the local remedies rule when doing so would be futile due to unreasonable delay or unavailability of an effective remedy.[406]

4.3.5.3   Adopting a Preliminary Ruling Procedure

Another possibility that may be worth considering in the relationship of an MIC with domestic judicial systems is the adoption of a procedure similar to the EU's

---

[403] Article 26, ICSID Convention (1965).

[404] See (fn. 397, 398).

[405] Brauch (2017), p. 2; Adler (1990), p. 641; Mollengarden (2019), p. 405.

[406] See, on the futility exception, *Lion Mexico Consolidated L.P. v. United Mexican States*, ICSID Case No. ARB(AF)/15/2, Award (20 September 2021), para. 561 f; *Swissbourgh Diamond Mines (Pty) Limited and others v. Lesotho*, PCA Case No. 2013-29, Judgment of the Singapore Court of Appeal (27 November 2018), para. 211; *Philip Morris Sarl (Switzerland) & others v. Uruguay*, ICSID Case No. ARB/10/7, Award (8 July 2016), para. 503; *Yukos Universal Limited (Isle of Man) v. The Russian Federation*, PCA Case No. 2005-04/AA227, Final Award (18 July 2014), para. 1425; *ST-AD GmbH v. Republic of Bulgaria*, UNCITRAL, PCA Case No. 2011-06, Award on Jurisdiction (18 July 2013), para. 365.

preliminary ruling procedure which allows the court of an EU member state under certain circumstances to request the interpretation of an EU law question from the Court of Justice of the European Union.[407] A similar idea has already been presented in UNCITRAL Working Group III,[408] which is also applicable within an MIC.

Although the EU law procedure in Article 267 of the TFEU contemplates a bottom-up procedure, wherein a domestic court refers an EU law question to a regional court (CJEU), the preliminary ruling procedure proposed for the MIC in this thesis contemplates a top-down approach. Meaning, by adopting a preliminary ruling procedure, an MIC is designed to cooperate with local courts by referring unsettled questions of local law to a designated local forum for a preliminary ruling. Such designated local forums may be communicated by the respective MIC members in their instrument of ratification.

Since the resolution of investment disputes by international tribunals is not always independent of domestic law considerations, this approach will ensure that the task of interpreting **unsettled domestic law questions** remains the primary responsibility of the host state. As emphasised, only unsettled domestic law questions should qualify for referral, as clear legal provisions need no interpretation following the *acte clair* doctrine.[409] Upon referral, and for procedural efficiency, only the determination of an issue connected to the domestic law question referred may be suspended until the designated local court for the preliminary ruling returns with an answer. Further, there should be a stipulated time limit within which the local court is expected to provide a response. After this period, the MIC can turn to traditional sources for guidance on matters related to domestic law, such as seeking expert witness on an unclear domestic law question.

In the event of a timely response, unlike the EU preliminary ruling binding upon the referring court,[410] the MIC Statute may treat a local court's preliminary ruling on a domestic law question as a matter of fact that may be discountenanced if derived from a procedure that offends a sense of judicial propriety under acceptable international standards. Arbitral jurisprudence confirms that, in general, a high degree of deference is accorded to local courts' interpretation of domestic law save the procedure fails to meet the standards of judicial propriety accepted under international norms.[411] The same principle may be applied by the MIC to a preliminary ruling derived from the courts of its member states.

---

[407] See Article 267, Treaty on the Functioning of the European Union ('TFEU').

[408] See, UNCITRAL, *Possible Reform of Investor-State Dispute Settlement (ISDS): Consistency and Related Matters*: Note by the Secretariat of 28/8/2018, A/CN.9/WG.III/WP.150, para. 46, ('Under this option, arbitral tribunals should be allowed to refer any question concerning the application and interpretation of a legal matter to a specific body').

[409] European Parliament (2017), p. 5.

[410] *Ibid.*, p. 10.

[411] See, *Bosh International, Inc. and B&P, LTD Foreign Investments Enterprise v. Ukraine*, ICSID Case No. ARB/08/11, Award (25 October 2012), para. 280; *Jan de Nul N.V. and Dredging International N.V. v. Arab Republic of Egypt*, ICSID Case No. ARB/04/13, Award (6 November 2008), para. 206; *Krederi Ltd. v. Ukraine*, ICSID Case No. ARB/14/17, Excerpts of Award (2 July 2018), para. 589.

By entrusting this role to local courts, the relationship between the MIC and the judicial systems of its member states will be further strengthened. This ensures that domestic courts remain actively involved in the interpretation of their laws applicable to foreign investments, particularly those that the MIC deems unsettled from the evidence before it and require clarification. Rather than rely on experts or arguments from opposing parties, the MIC can simply refer puzzling questions of domestic law to the domestic body constitutionally designated to interpret the law, with a presumption of impartiality and independence. However, the MIC would reserve the authority to decline deference to a domestic court's preliminary ruling in case of juridical impropriety.

By encouraging initial recourse to local remedies as described earlier; adopting Article 26 ICSID Convention approach; and cooperating with domestic courts through a preliminary ruling procedure, this would signify the MIC's support for the strengthening and development of local courts, increasing its legitimacy and likelihood of acceptability among African states.

4.3.6 Promoting ADR

Similar to the preceding discussions on recourse to local remedies, the relevance of ADR mechanisms as a limitation to direct access to international tribunals depends on the wording of the ISDS clause in the relevant IIA. Consequently, the underutilisation of ADR in the history of ISDS can mainly be attributed to the lack of clarity regarding its mandatory or non-mandatory nature as incorporated in IIAs.

However, in what now appears as a general interest, developments in UNCITRAL Working Group III have revealed that increased resolution of investment disputes through ADR mechanisms has become a crucial issue deemed worth addressing by multiple states beyond Africa.[412] Given the widespread support for this reform, the Working Group III requested the UNCITRAL Secretariat to develop for its consideration, draft provisions aimed at strengthening the use of ADR in ISDS, particularly through '**mediation**'.[413] This has since resulted in a 'draft provision on mediation'[414] and 'draft UNCITRAL guidelines on investment mediation'.[415] Both final drafts were officially adopted during the 56th session of UNCITRAL in Vienna in July 2023, respectively as—the '**UNCITRAL Model**

---

[412] UNCITRAL, *Possible Reform of Investor-State Dispute Settlement (ISDS): Dispute Prevention and Mitigation - Means of Alternative Dispute Resolution*: Note by the Secretariat of 15/1/2020, A/CN.9/WG.III/WP.190, para. 29 ff.

[413] UNCITRAL, *Possible Reform of Investor-State Dispute Settlement (ISDS): Draft Provisions on Mediation*: Note by the Secretariat of 13/7/2022, A/CN.9/WG.III/WP.217, para. 1.

[414] UNCITRAL, *Draft Provisions on Mediation*: Note by the Secretariat of 25/4/2023, A/CN.9/1150.

[415] UNCITRAL, *Draft UNCITRAL Guidelines on Investment Mediation*: Note by the Secretariat of 21/4/2023, A/CN.9/1151.

Provisions on Mediation', and the 'UNCITRAL Guidelines on Mediation for International Investment Disputes'.[416]

The 'UNCITRAL Model Provisions on Mediation' is designed as a model provision that can be incorporated into investment treaties or a potential multilateral instrument on ISDS reform.[417] For states that adopt the model provisions, this will clarify:

- the availability of mediation as a means for settling investment dispute;[418]
- the information required in an invitation to mediate;[419]
- the mediation's relationship with other ISDS proceedings like arbitration;[420]
- the settlement agreements compliance with the Singapore Convention.[421]

For further clarity, the draft UNCITRAL Guidelines on Investment Mediation' was adopted to clarify, *inter alia*, the factors to be taken into account when determining the suitability of mediation to resolve investment disputes,[422] how consent to mediate may be derived,[423] the timing and duration for mediation,[424] including possible applicable mediation rules.[425] Notably, this guideline is not a binding instrument, it is only a source of reference for guidance on the topics it addresses in relation to mediating investment disputes.[426]

While the above-mentioned drafts aimed at strengthening mediation in ISDS have been officially adopted independently of the MIC proposal, their implementation can still be effectively integrated into the framework of a future MIC. This integration would be highly beneficial, as the model provisions and guidelines on mediation would be applicable to all disputes submitted to the MIC, potentially having a broader impact due to the MIC's multilateral status. As opined by the EU and its member states regarding the importance of promoting mediation in ISDS, an MIC could address the various procedural, logistical, and other requirements necessary to

---

[416]UNIS (2023).

[417]UNCITRAL, *Draft Provisions on Mediation*: Note by the Secretariat of 25/4/2023, A/CN.9/1150, p. 2.

[418]UNCITRAL, *Draft Provisions on Mediation*: Note by the Secretariat of 25/4/2023, A/CN.9/1150, draft provision 1, (defines mediation, 'irrespective of the expression used' as a process whereby parties attempt an amicable settlement of their dispute with the assistance of a third party(s)).

[419]*Ibid.*, (draft provision 2).

[420]*Ibid.*, (draft provision 3).

[421]*Ibid.*, (draft provision 5).

[422]UNCITRAL, *Draft UNCITRAL Guidelines on Investment Mediation*: Note by the Secretariat of 21/4/2023, A/CN.9/1151, paras. 3–4.

[423]*Ibid.*, paras. 5–7.

[424]*Ibid.*, paras. 8–10.

[425]*Ibid.*, para. 11.

[426]*Ibid.*, para. 1.

facilitate mediation, aligning with its overall mandate to resolve investment disputes.[427]

By adopting the model provision and guideline on mediation, the availability of ADR becomes integrated into the institutional framework of the MIC with a degree of certainty regarding *inter alia*, the encouragement to consider mediation;[428] the form an invitation to mediate should take (in writing);[429] content of the invitation;[430] time frame for the other party to communicate acceptance (30 days) and assumed rejection if acceptance is not communicated in 60 days;[431] upon acceptance, non-initiation or continuation of any other proceedings (e.g. in the MIC or elsewhere) until the mediation is terminated, etc.

Importantly, if the UNCITRAL Model Provisions on mediation are implemented through an MIC, it becomes crucial to address how any inconsistencies between its provisions and ADR provisions in the member states' IIAs will be resolved. For example, the UNCITRAL model adopts a voluntary approach to mediation, encouraging parties to consider mediation but not making it mandatory.[432] However, specific African IIAs include a mandatory mediation requirement.[433] Should an IIA with a mandatory ADR provision be invoked, it is essential to consider such a mandatory ADR provision as a condition for the concerned member state's consent to MIC jurisdiction in that specific case.

Furthermore, another adaptation through which an MIC could enhance the use of ADR in ISDS is to include as part of the job responsibilities of MIC judges, the duty to encourage disputing parties to engage in mediation. This role aligns perfectly with the flexibility that disputing parties have to agree on mediation at any time, even after the commencement of adjudicatory proceedings.[434] MIC judges could leverage this flexibility to encourage disputing parties to explore mediation whenever there is a possibility for an amicable outcome.

---

[427] *UNCITRAL*, Submissions of the European Union and its Member States on: Mediation and other forms of alternative dispute, p. 9, https://uncitral.un.org/sites/uncitral.un.org.

[428] UNCITRAL, *Draft Provisions on Mediation*: Note by the Secretariat of 25/4/2023, A/CN.9/ 1150, draft provision 1(21).

[429] *Ibid.*, draft provision 1(4).

[430] *Ibid.*, draft provision 2.

[431] *Ibid.*, draft provision 1(5).

[432] *Ibid.*, draft provision 1(2), ('The parties **should consider** mediation to settle an international investment dispute amicably').

[433] Article 46(1), AfCFTA Investment Protocol, ('In the event of a dispute [. . .] the investor and the Host State **shall initially seek** to resolve amicably the dispute through [. . .] mediation [. . .]'); Article 26(1), Nigeria-Morocco BIT, signed 3 December 2016, (although this provision does not explicitly mention mediation, it involves a third party facilitating mandatory consultation and negotiation, making it fall within the definition of mediation as per draft provision 1 of the UNCITRAL Model Provisions on Mediation).

[434] UNCITRAL, *Draft Provisions on Mediation*: Note by the Secretariat of 25/4/2023, A/CN.9/ 1150, draft provision 1(3), ('The parties may agree to engage in mediation at any time, including after the commencement of any other dispute resolution proceeding').

For instance, after the exchange of pleadings, the strengths and weaknesses of each party's case become clearer. This clarity can expose *part or all* of the dispute that is better suited for resolution through an amicable process. In this context, the MIC can play an important role by encouraging the disputants to pursue ADR when the pleadings at any stage indicate the potential for a mutually beneficial outcome. An example of such a tribunal duty can be found in the 2021 ICC Arbitration rules, which state that the ICC arbitral tribunals should:

> encourag[e] the parties to consider settlement of all or part of the dispute either by negotiation or through any form of amicable dispute resolution methods such as, for example, mediation under the ICC Mediation Rules;[435]

A similar provision to this ICC Arbitration Rule may be incorporated into the procedural rules of the MIC. It is important to emphasise that whether by encouraging or mandating the resolution of investment disputes through ADR processes, there is no obligation on parties to agree to a settlement. However, by attempting to do so, this places the MIC in the position it is ideally meant to be, that is—a court of last resort where disputants can be assured of justice after exhausting all other avenues for remedy.

Overall, incorporating investment mediation within the framework of an MIC presents a viable option for resolving investment disputes in a manner that promotes cooperative co-existence, aligning with the African continent's cultural and historical approaches to dispute resolution. Hence, by harnessing the benefits of mediation, an MIC can attract the participation of African states by offering a dispute resolution mechanism that not only promotes adversarial outcomes but also seeks mutually beneficial outcomes for all parties involved in ISDS, whenever possible.

4.4 Interim Conclusion

This chapter has focused on six critical factors essential for garnering African states' support for an MIC. In rounding up this chapter, it is important to stress that the consideration of these six factors does not imply the non-significance of the other issues and topics being debated in UNCITRAL Working Group III. African states are actively engaging with their international counterparts to shape the future of ISDS, considering all reform elements and topics before UNCITRAL Working Group III beyond what is discussed in this chapter.[436] The focus on the aforementioned six considerations is based on their significant popularity as a desirable reform, as evinced by ISDS reform policies emerging from Africa. As such, highlighting these specific aspects aims to draw attention to their importance and

---

[435] Appendix IV(h) lit (i), Case Management Techniques, ICC Arbitration Rules, 2021.

[436] For other reform elements and topical considerations being debated, See generally, *UNCITRAL*, ISDS Reform Elements, https://uncitral.un.org/en/working_groups/3/investor-state.

the need to engage in a comprehensive and inclusive dialogue on these critical areas in the constitution of an MIC.

For an MIC to be accepted as a legitimate forum for ISDS in Africa, this chapter has underscored the importance of striking the right balance between the protection of foreign investments and preserving the member states' autonomy to pursue their national interests within the context of sustainable development. While the recommendations made in this thesis for achieving this balance would involve substantive law reforms, importantly, substantive law reform within an MIC framework would not be inconsistent with Articles 39 and 40 of the VCLT, as discussed earlier (Sect. 4.3.1). Utilising the MIC framework for substantive law reform as canvassed in this thesis is especially advantageous given the numerous IIAs among prospective MIC members that could be collectively reformed under this multilateral system.

Beginning with the GNTI proposal in this thesis, the ambiguity in old-generation IIAs regarding the regulatory space states have reserved for themselves, without violating their treaty obligations, could be clarified. Additionally, the GNTI clarification of frequently invoked IIA guarantees would help address the issue of divisive interpretations to which older-generation IIA guarantees are susceptible, owing to their vaguely worded nature. Overall, the GNTI would help facilitate judicial outcomes in line with the current investment protection policy of the MIC members, particularly when interacting with old-generation IIAs.

Secondly, without compromising the priority for correct interpretation per case pursuant to Articles 31–33 of the VCLT, this chapter underscores the importance of pursuing consistency in an MIC through the formal recognition of the civil law *jurisprudence constante* doctrine in the MIC's judicial practice. This doctrine should be applied through a rigorous dialogue with past decisions, considering how they fit with a present case, in order to determine whether deference to a consistent line of precedents on a related issue is warranted or whether a different outcome is justified to ensure a decision that sits within the boundaries of Articles 31–33 of the VCLT.

Thirdly, this chapter advocates for an MIC that holds investors accountable for their actions, encouraging responsible and sustainable investment practices, even if such goals were not explicitly outlined in the relevant IIA. Recognising that addressing the issue of investor accountability primarily requires substantive law reform, this chapter identifies existing procedures that could be explored to indirectly or directly guarantee investor accountability within an MIC. Thereby, ensuring a fairly balanced system for the protection of both private and sovereign interests in the court.

Fourthly, this chapter underscores the need for an MIC that is inclusive and protective of third party interest in ISDS. To achieve this, drawing on existing rules and practices, this chapter discusses how transparency and third-party participation can be more effectively secured within an MIC, going beyond mere participation as *amicus curiae*.

Fifthly, recognising the importance of local courts in investment dispute resolution, this chapter highlights the African states desire for an MIC that does not impede but enhances the growth and development of local courts in ISDS. To address this crucial interest, this chapter proposes means through which an MIC can promote the development of domestic judicial systems by: 'effectively encouraging the use of local remedies'; and, enforcing such recourse when required. Additionally, it explores the possibility of referring unsettled domestic law questions for preliminary rulings by domestic courts, further ensuring a progressive relationship between the MIC and domestic judicial systems.

Finally, the *sixth* consideration discussed in this chapter emphasised the need for an MIC to promote the use of ADR in the resolution of investment disputes. To achieve this desirable goal, it is recommended that the MIC adopt existing rules and guidelines in practice on the promotion of amicable dispute settlement through ADR methods. The chapter also highlights the potential for MIC judges to play a more active role in encouraging parties toward mutual settlement whenever this is possible.

By giving adequate consideration to these interests, based on the recommendations proposed in this chapter, an MIC has the potential to establish itself as a legitimate and viable forum for ISDS in Africa, ultimately contributing to the sustainable development of its members by ensuring the protection of foreign investment, while also upholding the rights and interests of its participating states and their citizens.

Other Documents

ECT Secretariat (2022) Decision of The Energy Charter Conference of 24/6/2022, CCDEC 2022

European Commission (2010) Towards a Comprehensive European International Investment Policy, COM(2010) 343 final

European Commission (2017) Impact Assessment: Multilateral reform of investment dispute resolution, SWD(2017) 302 final

European Council, Negotiating Directives for a Convention Establishing a Multilateral Court for the Settlement of Investment Disputes, 12981/17 ADD 1

Joint Interpretative Instrument on the CETA, OJ L 11/3, 14/1/2017

NAFTA Free Trade Commission (2001) Notes of interpretation of certain Chapter 11 provisions. https://files.pca-cpa.org/pcadocs/bi-c/2.%20Canad.

UNCITRAL, Draft Provisions on Mediation: Note by the Secretariat of 25/4/2023, A/CN.9/1150

UNCITRAL, Possible Reform of Investor-State Dispute Settlement (ISDS) – Draft provisions on procedural and cross-cutting issues: Note by the Secretariat of 26/7/2023, A/CN.9/WG.III/WP.231

UNCITRAL, Possible Reform of Investor-State Dispute Settlement (ISDS): Consistency and Related Matters: Note by the Secretariat of 28/8/2018, A/CN.9/WG.III/WP.150

UNCITRAL, Possible Reform of Investor-State Dispute Settlement (ISDS): Dispute Prevention and Mitigation - Means of Alternative Dispute Resolution: Note by the Secretariat of 15/1/2020, A/CN.9/WG.III/WP.190

UNCITRAL, Possible Reform of Investor-State Dispute Settlement (ISDS): Draft Provisions on Mediation: Note by the Secretariat of 13/7/2022, A/CN.9/WG.III/WP.217

UNCITRAL, Possible Reform of Investor-State Dispute Settlement (ISDS) – Multiple proceedings and counterclaims: Note by the Secretariat of 22/1/2020, A/CN.9/WG.III/WP.193

UNCITRAL, Possible Reform of Investor-State Dispute Settlement (ISDS) – Annotations to the draft provisions on procedural and cross-cutting issues: Note by the Secretariat of 31/7/2023, A/CN.9/WG.III/WP.232

UNCITRAL, Report of Working Group III (Investor-State Dispute Settlement Reform) of 9/4/2019, A/CN.9/970

UNCITRAL, Report of Working Group III (Investor-State Dispute Settlement Reform) of 26/2/2018, A/CN.9/930/Add.1/Rev.1

UNCITRAL, Standing Multilateral Mechanism: Selection and Appointment of ISDS Tribunal Members and Related Matters: Note by the Secretariat of 8/12/2021, A/CN.9/WG.III/WP.213

UNCITRAL, Standing Multilateral Mechanism: Selection and Appointment of ISDS Tribunal Members and Related Matters – Initial Draft: Comments of the EU and its Member States. https://uncitral.un.org/sites/uncitral.un.org.

UNCITRAL, Submission from the European Union and its Member States of 24/1/2019, A/CN.9/WG.III/WP.159/Add.1

UNCITRAL, Submission from the Government of South Africa of 17/7/2019, A/CN.9/WG.III/WP.176

UNCITRAL, Submissions of the European Union and its Member States on: Mediation and other forms of Alternative Dispute. https://uncitral.un.org/sites/uncitral.un.org.

UNGA RES/70/1 Transforming Our World: The 2030 Agenda for Sustainable Development of 25/9/2015, UN DOC. A/RES/70/1

UNGA RES/76/300 The Human Right to A Clean, Healthy and Sustainable Environment of 28/7/2022, UN DOC. A/RES/76/300

UNGA, Report of the Special Representative of the Secretary-General on the issue of human rights and transnational corporations and other business enterprises, John Ruggie* of 19/2/2007, UN DOC. A/HRC/4/35

UNIS (2023) UNCITRAL Concludes 56th Session in Vienna, UNIS/L/346. https://unis.unvienna.org/unis/en/pressrels/2023/unisl346.html.

References

Abel P (2022) International investor obligations: towards individual international responsibility for the public interest in international investment law. Nomos, Baden-Baden

Abimbola O (2020) The Regulatory Chill, Africa is a Country. https://africasacountry.com/2020/11/the-regulatory-chill

Adekemi A (2021) Effecting consistency in investor-state dispute settlement through the introduction of precedent in a multilateral investment court. ZEuS 24(4):663–682

Adler MH (1990) The exhaustion of the local remedies rule after the international decision in ELSI. ICLQ 39(3):641–653

Ahmad S, Liebman B, Wickramarachi H (2022) Disentangling the effects of investor-state dispute settlement provisions on foreign direct investment, U.S. International Trade Commission, November 2022. https://www.usitc.gov/publications/332/

Akinkugbe OD (2021) Africanization and the reform of international investment law. CWRJIL 53: 7–34

Bjorklund AK (2007) Private rights and public international law: why competition among international economic tribunals is not working. HLJ 59(2):241–308

Bjorklund AK (2008) Investment treaty arbitral decisions as jurisprudence constante. In: Picker C, Bunn I, Arner D (eds) international economic law: the state and future of the discipline. Oxford University Press, Oxford, pp 265–280

Born G (2021) international commercial arbitration, 3rd edn. Kluwer Law International, Alphen aan den Rijn

Brauch MD (2017) Exhaustion of Local Remedies in International Investment Law (IISD). https://www.iisd.org/system/files

Bungenberg M, Reinisch A (2020) From bilateral arbitral tribunals and investment courts to a multilateral investment court: options regarding the institutionalization of investor-state dispute settlement, 2nd edn. Springer, Berlin

Bungenberg M, Reinisch A (2021) Draft Statute of the multilateral investment court. Nomos, Baden-Baden

Busse M, Königer J, Nunnenkamp (2010) FDI promotion through bilateral investment treaties: more than a bit? RWE 146:147–177

Butler N, Subedi S (2017) The future of international investment regulation: towards a world investment organisation? NILR 64:43–72

Cate I (2013) The costs of consistency: precedent in investment treaty arbitration. CJTL 51:418–478

CCSI, OHCHR (2018) Impacts of the International Investment Regime on Access to Justice. https://www.ohchr.org/sites/default/.

Chaudhuri A (2020) Systemic integration: resolving the dichotomy of competing obligations in international investment law. https://aria.law.columbia.edu/s

Chen RC (2019) Precedent and dialogue in investment treaty arbitration. HILJ 60(1):47–94

Chidede T (2019) The right to regulate in Africa's international investment law regime. ORIL 20: 437–468

Cleeve EA, Debrah Y, Yiheyis Z (2015) Human capital and FDI inflows: an assessment of the African case. WD 74:1–14

Client Earth (2019) Investor-State Dispute Settlement Must Go To Protect Our Environment, Client Earth Communications. https://www.clientearth.org/latest/latest-updates

Coleman J, Johnson L, Güven B, Cotula L, Berger T (2019) Third-party rights in investor-state dispute settlement: options for reform (CCSI). https://scholarship.law.columbia.edu/sustainable_investment_staffpubs/150/

Colen L, Maertens M, Swinnen J (2013) Foreign direct investment as an engine for economic growth and human development: a review of the arguments and emperical evidence. In: De Schutter O, Swinnen J, Wouters J (eds) Foreign direct investment and human development: the law and economics of international investment agreements. Routledge, New York, pp 70–115

Danish T, Uribe D (2022) The proposed standing multilateral mechanism and its potential relationship with the existing universe of investor – state dispute settlement. https://www.econstor.eu/handle/10419/270387

Diel-Gligor K (2017) Towards consistency in international investment jurisprudence: a preliminary ruling system for ICSID arbitration. Brill, Leiden

Diel-Gligor K, Hennecke R (2015) Investment in accordance with the law. In: Bungenberg M, Griebel J, Hobe S, Reinisch A (eds) International investment law: a handbook. Nomos, Baden-Baden, pp 566–576

Dolzer R, Schreuer C (2008) Principles of international investment law, 1st edn. Oxford University Press, Oxford

Douglas M (2015) The importance of transparency for legitimising investor-state dispute settlement: an Australian perspective. HS XIX:111–121

Dumberry P (2022) Article 8.10 CETA. In: Bungenberg M, Reinisch A (eds) CETA investment law: article by article commentary. Baden-Baden, Nomos, pp 256–276

EI-IILCC Study Group on ISDS Reform (2022) Reform of investor-state dispute settlement – current state of play at UNCITRAL. ZEuS 01:15–74

El-Kady H, De Gama M (2019) The reform of the international investment regime: an African perspective. ICSID Rev. FILJ 34(2):482–495

Escobar AA (2019) Arbitration. In: Fouret J, Gerbay R, Alvares GM, Parchajev D (eds) The ICSID convention, regulations and rules: a practical commentary. Elgar, Cheltenham, pp 271–750

European Commission (2015) Consultation on Investment Protection in EU-US Trade Talks. https://ec.europa.eu/commission/presscorner

European Commission Press (2015) Commission Proposes New Investment Court System for TTIP and other EU Trade and Investment Negotiations. https://ec.europa.eu/commission/presscorner/detail/en/

European Parliament (2016) Suspension of the TTIP Negotiations, July 2016, https://www.europarl.europa.eu/doceo. Accessed 24 June 2024

European Parliament (2017) Briefing: Preliminary Reference Procedure. https://www.europarl.europa.eu

Fan K (2018) Rebalancing the asymmetric nature of international investment agreements?, Kluwer Arbitration Blog. https://arbitrationblog.kluwerarbitration

Fon V, Parisi F (2006) Judicial precedents in civil law systems: a dynamic analysis. IRLE 26(4):519–535

Grande E (1999) Alternative dispute resolution, Africa, and the structure of law and power: the horn in context. JAL 43(1):63–70

Harten GV (2010) Five justifications for investment treaties: a critical discussion. TLD 2:19–58

ICSID (1965) Report of the executive directors. ICSID, Washington DC

ICSID (2006) History of the ICSID convention – Vol. II(1). ICSID Publication, Washington DC

IIED Briefing (2019) Reforming investor-state dispute settlement: what about third-party rights?. https://www.iied.org/sites/default/files/pdfs/migrate/17638IIED.pdf

Jarrett M, Puig S, Ratner S (2021) New options for investor accountability in ISDS, EJIL Talk. https://www.ejiltalk.org/new-options-for-investor-accountability-in-isds/

Jarrett M, Puig S, Ratner S (2023) Towards greater investor accountability: indirect actions, direct actions by states and direct actions by individuals. JIDS 14(2):259–280

Kaufmann-Kohler G, Potestà M (2020) Investor-state dispute settlement and national courts: current framework and reform options. Springer, Cham

Kelsey J, Mohamadieh K (2021) UNCITRAL Fiddles While Countries Burn, Third World Network. https://library.fes.de/pdf-files/bueros/genf/18297.pdf

Kern JS, Assefa GB (2020) Investor obligations: Africa leads the way. Kluwer Arbitration Blog. https://arbitrationblog.kluwerarbitration.com/2

Kriebaum U (2022) Article 8.12 CETA. In: Bungenberg M, Reinisch A (eds) CETA investment law: article by article commentary. Baden-Baden, Nomos, pp 297–336

Kryvoi Y (2012) Counterclaims in investor-state arbitration. MJIL 21(2):216–252

Kurtz J (2016) The WTO and international investment law: converging systems. Cambridge University Press, Cambridge

Laborde G (2010) The case for host state claims in investment arbitration. JIDS 1(1):97–122

Lamprou N, Iluezi-Ogbaudu E (2023) The AfCFTA investment protocol – a potential game changer for the African continent?. https://www.linklaters.com/en/insights/blogs/

Langford M, Potestà M, Kaufmann-Kohler G, Behn D (2020) UNCITRAL and investment arbitration reform: matching concerns and solutions: an introduction. JWIT 21:167–187

Laryea E (2018) Making investment arbitration work for all: addressing the deficits in access to remedy for wronged host state citizens through investment arbitration. BCLR 59(8):2845–2876

Laryea E, Fabusuy O (2019) African countries and international investment law: right to regulate or appropriate regulation or both? ARAS 40(2):27–54

Mbengue MM (2019) Africa's voice in the formation, shaping and redesign of international investment law. ICSID Rev. FILJ 34(2):455–481

Mbengue MM, Schacherer S (2017) The 'Africanization' of international investment law: the Pan-African investment code and the reform of the international investment regime. JWIT 18: 414–448

McLachlan C, Shore L, Weiniger M (2017) International investment arbitration: substantive principles, 2nd edn. Oxford University Press, Oxford

Menon T, Issac G (2018) Developing country opposition to an investment court: could state-state dispute settlement be an alternative?, Kluwer Arbitration Blog. https://arbitrationblog.kluwerarbitration.com

Mollengarden Z (2019) The utility of futility: local remedies rules in international investment law. VJIL 58(2):403–460

Ofodile UE (2014) Africa and the system of investor-state dispute settlement: to reject or not to reject? TDM 11(1):1–32

Oxford Reference (2011). https://www.oxfordreference.com/display/

Papazoglou S (2019) The good, the bad and the ugly 'of ISDS reforms: rebalancing the system? KCL Blog. https://blogs.kcl.ac.uk/kslr/files/2019/10/Stephanie-P-.pdf

Pasipanodya T, Olmedo JG (2021) 21st Century Investment Protection: Africa's Innovations In Investment Law Reform, IBA Legalbrief Africa. https://www.ibanet.org/africas-innovations-in-investment-law-reform#_edn16

Pathirana DL, Gathii JT (2022) Termination, amendment, modernization and reform of investment treaties: which way forward? In: Shirlow E, Gore KN (eds) The Vienna Convention on the law of treaties in investor-state disputes: history, evolution and future. Kluwer Law International, Alphen aan den Rijn, pp 271–304

Perrone NM, Vásquez IA (2023) Bridging the gap between investor rights and obligations: how academics can contribute to a fairer international law on foreign investment (IISD). https://www.iisd.org/itn/en/2023/07/01

Peterson LE, Gray K (2003) International human rights in bilateral investment treaties and in investment treaty arbitration, (IISD). https://www.escr-net.org/sites/default/files/Luke_Peterson___IHR_in_bilateral.pdf

Reinisch A (2017) Article 8.7 CETA. In: Bungenberg M, Reinisch A (eds) CETA investment law: article by article commentary. Baden-Baden, Nomos, pp 216–230

Reinisch A, Schreuer C (2020) International protection of investments: the substantive standards. Cambridge University Press, Cambridge

Republic of South Africa (2009) Bilateral Investment Treaty Policy Framework – Government Position Paper, Department of Trade and Industry. https://static.pmg.org.za/docs/090626trade-bi-lateralpolicy.pdf

Saei J (2017) Amicus curious: structure and play in investment arbitration. TLT 8(3):247–295

Salacuse J, Sullivan NP (2005) Do BITs really work: an evaluation of bilateral investment treaties and their grand bargain. HILJ 46:67–130

Schacherer S (2019) The CETA investment chapter and sustainable development: interpretative issues. In: Mbengue MM, Schacherer S (eds) Foreign investment under the comprehensive economic and trade agreement (CETA). Springer, Berlin, pp 207–238

Schefer KN (2020) International investment law: text, cases and materials, 3rd edn. Elgar, Cheltenham

Scherer M, Bruce S, Reschke J (2021) Environmental counterclaims in investment treaty arbitration. ICSID Rev. FILJ 36(2):413–440

Schill S (2011) System-building in investment treaty arbitration and lawmaking. GLJ 12(5): 1083–1110

Schill S (2015) Reforming Investor-State Dispute Settlement (ISDS): Conceptual Framework and Options for the Way Forward (E15Initiative). https://dare.uva.nl/search?identifier=ccd751bd-b2b4-4b19-84eb-0f335ed02289

Schreuer C (2011) Interaction of international tribunals and domestic courts in investment law. In: Rovine A (ed) Contemporary issues in international arbitration and mediation: the fordham papers (2010). Brill, Leiden, pp 71–94

Schreuer C, Malintoppi L, Reinisch A, Sinclair A (2009) The ICSID convention: a commentary, 2nd edn. Cambridge University Press, Cambridge

Schrijver N (2008) The evolution of sustainable development in international law: inception, meaning and status. Brill, Leiden

Schwebel S (2008) A BIT about ICSID. ICSID Rev. FILJ 23(1):1–9

Shao X (2021) Environmental and human rights counterclaims in international investment arbitration: at the crossroads of domestic and international law. JIEL 24(1):157–179

Stifter L (2022) Article 8.32 CETA. In: Bungenberg M, Reinisch A (eds) CETA investment law: article by article commentary. Baden-Baden, Nomos, pp 739–756

Tarawali N (2019) Towards or away from investment treaty arbitration in Africa? EMRJ 9:1–5

Titi C (2014) The right to regulate in international investment law. Nomos, Baden-Baden

Titi C (2015) International investment law and the European Union: towards a new generation of international investment agreements. EJIL 26:639–661

Titi C (2022) The right to regulate in international investment law (revisited). ICLRC 18:11–97

UNCTAD (2023) Investment Flows to Africa. https://unctad.org/news/investment-flows-africa-dropped-45-billion-2022

United Nations OHCHR (2011) Guiding Principles on Business and Human Rights. https://www.ohchr.org/sites/default

Villiger ME (2009) Commentary on the 1969 Vienna Convention on the law of treaties. Brill, Leiden

von der Decken K (2018) Article 39. In: Dörr O, Schmalenbach K (eds) Vienna convention on the law of treaties: a commentary. Springer, Berlin, pp 757–766

Waibel M, Rylatt JW (2014) Counterclaims in international law. https://papers.ssrn.com/sol3/papers.cfm?abstract_id=2511847

Chapter 5
Overview and Final Conclusions

Since the peak of decolonisation in Africa during the second half of the twentieth century, African states have had to enter the international investment community as players in order to compete for FDIs necessary for economic expansion within their respective nations. This development also meant that African states had to adopt the foreign investment protection regime designed by their former colonizers to safeguard the interests of their nationals whose capital African states sought to attract within their borders. This investment protection regime is grounded in multiple IIAs encompassing various substantive standards of investment protection, along with an ISDS mechanism through investment arbitration adopted to enforce compliance.

This thesis began by introducing three of the substantive guarantees that are most frequently invoked against African states in traditional ISDS ($\rightarrow$ Chap. 2), followed by an examination of the African dissatisfaction with the old-generation IIA guarantees as enforced by the traditional ISDS system ($\rightarrow$ Chap. 3). Over time, as African states gained experience, skills, and expertise in international investment law, they came to realise the inequities inherent in the web of IIA guarantees they had become entangled in. This dissatisfaction was further underscored by the interpretations given to these IIA guarantees by arbitral tribunals, which confirmed their one-sided and imbalanced nature, much to the displeasure of African states.

However, while this thesis primarily focused on African dissatisfaction with outdated investment protection guarantees as applied by arbitral tribunals, this discontent is not unique to African states. As highlighted in this thesis, similar concerns have spurred the call for investment law reforms not only in Africa but also in various nations across the globe. Significantly, in Europe—particularly among EU member states with whom the majority of extra-African IIAs are contracted, there has been a pivotal shift in investment protection policy, as evidenced by the CETA. Notably, the Côte d'Ivoire-Portugal BIT[1] and the Cabo

---

[1] Côte d'Ivoire-Portugal BIT (2019), signed 13 June 2019.

A. O. Adekemi, *Attracting African States Participation in a Multilateral Investment Court*, EYIEL Monographs - Studies in European and International Economic Law 39, https://doi.org/10.1007/978-3-031-73861-6_5

Verde-Hungary BIT,[2] both contracted in 2019, also reflect the new investment protection policy emerging between African and EU nations. However, hundreds of extra-African IIAs with EU states and beyond remain in force under the old regime. This raises concerns about the potential perpetuation of inequities present in old-generation IIAs within an MIC if the gaps in these old agreements are not addressed. Hence, without substantive law reform, the current proposal for an MIC could entrench several major flaws of the traditional ISDS system,[3] making it unappealing to African states.

To address this challenge, this thesis argues that even though the MIC is primarily a procedural reform proposal under consideration, this does not preclude the examination of substantive law concerns critical to the adjudicative effectiveness of an MIC. Underlying the crucial considerations necessary to attract African states' participation in an MIC is the need to ensure a court that protects foreign investments while also safeguarding the sustainable development interest of the host states' within the three SD pillars i.e., economic, social development, and environmental protection. To achieve this crucial balance, this thesis canvasses the following recommendations.

Regarding the concerns associated with the gaps in old-generation IIA guarantees, this thesis demonstrates how the innovative adoption of a GNTI within the MIC's framework could play a pivotal role in preventing unintended treaty interpretations. This is particularly crucial for older IIAs, not drafted with the same level of precision and foresight as more recent IIAs. Recent developments in Africa, Europe, and other regions of the world indicate a convergence in the investment protection policies being adopted in recent IIAs that show better precision in language to avoid the unintended gaps in old-generation IIAs, that have been a subject of criticism over time. This factor can be leveraged to design a GNTI that clarifies a significant number of the substantive law issues often at stake in ISDS, including establishing clarity regarding a state's right to regulate, what constitutes an expropriation, FET, FPS, or a breach of the MFN standard. These are often contested issues in ISDS susceptible to divisive outcomes due to their imprecisely worded inclusion in old-generation IIAs. That way, the fears about how an MIC will interact with old-generation IIAs without manifesting its flaws, particularly those inconsistent with the current investment protection policies of its members, would be substantially mitigated. Importantly, this approach of addressing substantive law reform through the MIC system would not be inconsistent with the relevant international law rules on treaty reform under Articles 39 and 40 of the VCLT ($\rightarrow$ Sect. 4. 3.1).

As further underscored in this thesis, while the accuracy (correctness) of decisions to the applicable law per case takes priority over consistency with past decisions, the MIC must crucially consider the relevance of its past decision to current cases with similar or identical interpretative issues. The concept of

---

[2] Cabo Verde-Hungary BIT (2019), signed 28 March 2019.
[3] Kelsey and Mohamadieh (2021), p. 23 f.

'*jurisprudence constante*' provides a valuable guide to the MIC in this regard. When a consistent line of past decisions aligns with a current case, it is justifiable to follow the established jurisprudence for the sake of consistency. However, when the fit is not present, the MIC's primary duty to interpret the relevant IIA consistently with Articles 31–33 of the VCLT must prevail. Either conclusion can only be justifiably reached after the court engages in a rigorous dialogue between a present dispute and related precedents, to determine the applicability of the latter to the former. This process ensures that the MIC's decisions not only adhere to the rule of law but also contribute to the advancement of sustainable development by addressing the unique challenges and complexities of each case in a fair and equitable manner.

Furthermore, this thesis proposes certain procedural strategies that are not entirely strange to the traditional ISDS system, which could be adopted in an MIC to guarantee investor accountability. For example, a form of indirect accountability is already established in practice which can be adapted within the procedural framework of an MIC ($\rightarrow$ Sect. 4.3.3.1). This adaptation aims to establish an MIC that not only safeguards covered investors against harm stemming from unlawful host state conducts, but equally guarantees the protection of host states against harm to their sustainable development interest stemming from unlawful investor conducts. Precisely, drawing from existing procedural models, this thesis proposes how indirect investor accountability could be ensured in an MIC through the forfeiture of jurisdictional protection ($\rightarrow$ Sect. 4.3.3.1.1), loss or reduction in entitled compensation ($\rightarrow$ Sect. 4.3.3.1.2), or damages in counterclaims by the host state ($\rightarrow$ Sect. 4.3.3.1.3).

Further on investor accountability, this thesis posits that an MIC could be open to the possibility of direct claims from a host state against an investor for injuries suffered due to the latter's breach of duty to the host state. Both the ICSID and UNCITRAL framework that commonly governs ISDS procedures today confirm that nations worldwide are not inherently opposed to the possibility of SIDS procedure,[4] provided that both the claimant-state and the respondent-investor consent. While consent to such a procedure is uncommon, this does not mean it is impossible. As demonstrated in this thesis, there are ways through which consent to a SIDS procedure may be obtained ($\rightarrow$ Sect. 4.3.3.2), and the MIC can simply stay accessible to such states and investors consensually open to SIDS claims before an MIC.

Additionally, there is a general acknowledgment in UNCITRAL Working Group III of the need to enhance the protection of third party interests in ISDS, especially those related to environmental or human rights interests.[5] While adopting the UNCITRAL Transparency Rules into the framework of an MIC may represent a

---

[4] ICSID (1965), para. 13; Escobar (2019), p. 271, paras. 4.07–4.09; Schreuer et al. (2009), p. 458; See also, Article 1, UNCITRAL Arbitration Rules (2021), (the clause detailing the scope of application foresees no *ratione personae* restrictions as to the identity of claimants or respondents in a dispute referred to arbitration under the UNCITRAL Arbitration Rules).

[5] UNCITRAL, *Report of Working Group III (Investor-State Dispute Settlement Reform)* of 9/4/2019, A/CN.9/970, para. 31.

progressive step in this regard, this thesis argues for a modified adoption of the *amicus curiae* rules (→ Sect. 4.3.4), which are currently deemed inadequate.[6]

Moreover, besides participation as *amicus curiae*, this thesis also expounds on the clamour for the protection of third party interest in investment disputes beyond mere participation as *amicus curiae*.[7] Significantly, the same rationale that justified permitting SIDS procedure within an MIC, can also justify leaving an MIC open to direct claims by host state's nationals against foreign investors, under the principle of 'parties consent'. Provided consent to such claims are given, the MIC could adjudicate claims from host-country citizens resulting from an investor's breach of obligations within the host state, causing harm to the affected host national. Support can already be found for such procedures in the academia,[8] with proposals on how consent to such claims may be derived and the source of investor obligation that may give rise to a host national's claim against an investor.

Admissibility of such proceedings in an MIC would significantly boost the protection of third parties, particularly host state citizens whose interests are often at risk of loss to an investor's economic interest, with no guarantee that the host government would aid their protection. Although this would represent a radical departure from the traditional investment protection regime, it is not impossible for states to reach an agreement on an MIC that could adjudicate claims submitted by host state nationals, provided that jurisdiction, as always, is subject to the clear and unequivocal consent of the disputing parties (i.e., host citizens and investors).

Furthermore, there is a consensus among states that an MIC should not diminish the authority of local courts in the field of investment protection. This assertion is validated by another common interest shown by states in UNCITRAL Working Group III, recognising 'recourse to local remedies' as an important reform agenda worth considering.[9] So far, the UNCITRAL Secretariat has presented a draft proposal on this subject for potential inclusion in future IIAs, which is currently being considered in UNCITRAL Working Group III.[10] Since there is a shared interest that access to an international tribunal should not undermine but rather promote the development of local judicial authorities in investment dispute settlement, this study recommended three strategies through which an MIC can foster that goal.

Precisely, in addition to mandating the use of local remedies as prescribed in the IIAs invoked within its purview, the MIC can effectively encourage recourse to local remedies in other instances by making appropriate cost allocation decisions when a claimant unjustly disregards available local remedies for direct recourse to the MIC.

---

[6]Coleman et al. (2019), p. 6 f; *Ibid.*, para. 53.

[7]UNCITRAL, *Submission from the Government of South Africa* of 17/7/2019, A/CN.9/WG.III/ WP.176, para. 52.

[8]Laryea (2018), p. 2866 ff; Jarrett et al. (2023), p. 275 ff.

[9]UNCITRAL, *Report of Working Group III (Investor-State Dispute Settlement Reform)* of 9/4/ 2019, A/CN.9/970, para. 30.

[10]UNCITRAL, *Possible Reform of Investor-State Dispute Settlement (ISDS) – Draft provisions on procedural and cross-cutting issues*: Note by the Secretariat of 26/7/2023, A/CN.9/WG.III/ WP.231, (see Draft Provision 6).

Also, drawing from the EU's preliminary ruling procedure, albeit in an inverse manner, this thesis suggests that an MIC could potentially cooperate closely with local judicial authorities in fulfilling its adjudicative mandate. This is done by referring unsettled domestic law questions for preliminary ruling to designated domestic courts, which is then differed to by the MIC, save the domestic ruling is tainted in judicial impropriety. By this approach, the MIC can further contribute to the broader goal of sustainable development in its member states through the enhancement of local judicial capacity in investment dispute resolution.

Lastly, on the recommendations proffered in this thesis on designing an MIC that could attract African states' participation, developments in UNCITRAL Working Group III also confirm that there is widespread support for promoting the use of ADR in ISDS. This consensus has already led to the successful adoption of a 'model provision on mediation' and 'guidelines on mediation in international investment disputes', by the assembly of states in UNCITRAL.[11] This factor suggests that establishing an MIC that inherently promotes ADR should not be difficult to achieve with widespread consensus. As demonstrated in this study, while an MIC should be duty-bound to enforce the ADR requirements as prescribed in the IIAs under its consideration, the integration of the recently adopted UNCITRAL mediation rules and guidelines into the MIC framework would also promote the use of ADR even in disputes under IIAs that are silent on the use of ADR. Moreover, this thesis also underscores the significant role that MIC judges could play in taking proactive steps to encourage disputing parties to pursue mutually agreeable settlements whenever such opportunities arise, whether before or after the commencement of adjudicatory proceedings.

In conclusion, while the ultimate decision to join an MIC remains the prerogative of African nations, the recommendations put forth in this thesis represent a constructive and promising pathway towards encouraging their participation in a future MIC. By addressing the specific considerations and concerns of African states through the recommendations presented, there is a chance to finally create an investment dispute resolution system that is more inclusive and balanced in the protection of all interests commonly at stake in an investor-state relationship.

Other Documents

UNCITRAL, Possible Reform of Investor-State Dispute Settlement (ISDS) – Draft provisions on procedural and cross-cutting issues: Note by the Secretariat of 26/7/2023, A/CN.9/WG.III/WP.231

UNCITRAL, Report of Working Group III (Investor-State Dispute Settlement Reform) of 9/4/2019, A/CN.9/970

---

[11] UNIS (2023).

UNCITRAL, Submission from the Government of South Africa of 17/7/2019, A/CN.9/WG.III/WP.176

UNCITRAL, Submissions from the Government of Morocco of 11/2/2020, A/CN.9/WG.III/WP.161

UNIS (2023) UNCITRAL Concludes 56th Session in Vienna, UNIS/L/346. https://unis.unvienna.org/unis/en/pressrels/2023/unisl346.html.

References

Coleman J, Johnson L, Güven B, Cotula L, Berger T (2019) Third-Party Rights in Investor-State Dispute Settlement: Options for Reform (CCSI). https://scholarship.law.columbia.edu

Escobar AA (2019) Arbitration. In: Fouret J, Gerbay R, Alvares GM, Parchajev D (eds) The ICSID convention, regulations and rules: a practical commentary. Elgar, Cheltenham, pp 271–750

ICSID (1965) Report of the executive directors. ICSID, Washington DC

Jarrett M, Puig S, Ratner S (2023) Towards greater investor accountability: indirect actions, direct actions by states and direct actions by individuals. JIDS 14(2):259–280

Kelsey J, Mohamadieh K (2021) UNCITRAL Fiddles While Countries Burn, Third World Network. https://library.fes.de/pdf-files/bueros/genf/18297.pdf

Laryea E (2018) Making investment arbitration work for all: addressing the deficits in access to remedy for wronged host state citizens through investment arbitration. BCLR 59(8):2845–2876

Schreuer C, Malintoppi L, Reinisch A, Sinclair A (2009) The ICSID convention: a commentary, 2nd edn. Cambridge University Press, Cambridge

Printed by Printforce, the Netherlands